MORE PAGES FROM GOD'S CASE-BOOK

By the same author:

Pages from God's Case-book
Character studies of Pharaoh,
Nebuchadnezzar, Saul and Joseph

More Pages from God's Case-book

by

JOHN HERCUS

LONDON
INTER-VARSITY FELLOWSHIP
39 BEDFORD SQUARE WC1

© The Inter-Varsity Fellowship

First Edition   February 1965
Reprinted   January 1966

Printed in Great Britain by
BILLING & SONS LTD.
GUILDFORD AND LONDON

CONTENTS

CHAPTER ONE

DIAGNOSIS SERIOUS

Most of us make quite a considerable effort to keep reasonably well adjusted to our society. We like to be distinctive enough, individual enough, to rate; and self-restrained enough, well-mannered enough, not to be a nuisance. All people are not normal, of course. Some are far too pushing; prickly, uncomfortable to brush against. Others are just human mice, hidden away in a personality recess out of which it is a tiresome effort to have to drag them. Extroverted, introverted; over-aggressive, lacking aggressiveness, we say.

But we are normal people. This is just the thing about us that gives us the right to call ourselves normal. *We* know when we are shoving too hard and try seriously to control ourselves. We know when we are letting the side down and try to rally ourselves to put our backs into things.

And because we are normal, reasonably conscientious and concerned with these very important personal relationships in society, I am not going to over-bother myself (or you) in this book with the rugged individualist or the introspective mystic and all the other odd-bods. Let us hand them over to the psycho-therapists or the head-shrinkers or the tranquillizers and press on in consideration of our own reasonably successful attempt to live The Well-adjusted Life.

And yet, while I insist that I am in fact quite well adjusted in my society, I must now admit that I have become involved in a very great and disturbing problem which is striking right at the roots of all my social relationships. Indeed, it may in some measure even prove to be a threat to my very life. And before you have a chance to start whispering behind your hand or shaking your head because you are sure of You Know What, I must hurry in and tell you it is a problem a number of other ordinary people share with me, and it's not being a secret tippler or a drug addict or keeping a mistress or being a homosexual or even just being afraid of crawlies. No,

7

nothing like that at all. Nothing as petty or uninteresting as that.

And it's nothing to do with being a doctor. That is, not just with being a doctor. It does concern my doctoring, but only because I happen to be one. If I were a panel beater or a research scholar it would concern panel beating or research. But because in medical practice I do really like helping my patients and like trying to understand at least a little of the vast expanse of knowledge that is pouring into our professional world, just as the great majority of my medical colleagues do, then the problem has a lot to do with being a doctor.

So that if you do in fact share my problem it will not be because you are a professional colleague, any more than it will be because you are not a professional colleague. If you come to realize that you have this same concern it will only be because, as a good everyday example of an average man, your social setting has been shaken by the same disturbance in your particular way of life that I have felt in my medical way of life.

And finally, before I tell you what the trouble is, and how it has arisen, may I clear up a few little matters which may otherwise embarrass me as I write or you as you read? These are essentially the matter of our mutual attitude to each other and the matter of your attitude to the topic about which this book is written.

From the little bit you have read so far it probably strikes you rather strongly that this could turn out to be one of those cloying exposés in which a writer tries to make his reader a sort of soul-mate, opening up all those deep recesses that you quite sensibly think should be reserved for poetry or psycho-analysis. Let me assure you it will not prove so in this case. It is written about my problem but not about me.

So that if you feel inclined to shake your head disdainfully or sneer contemptuously, then you just shake or sneer away as merrily as you like. Troubled and all as I am, it is not your shoulder I am seeking to weep on; and I am certainly not foolish or conceited enough to be proffering you mine.

And as for the matter of your attitude to the topic about which this book is written, I trust you will take up the attitude that is really your own. If you are young and inexperienced you will probably feel all hot and cold. Matters involving death – and this whole book will never allow us to go more than one step from the disturbance of death – should rightly give you that hot and cold, shivery feeling, unless you are very skilled and trained in detachment.

But equally, and on the other hand, if you are just such a skilled and trained reader, you may find that the abstract of truth you will then be able to discover may well have for you a correspondingly greater authority and compulsion. A great deal of my own reading is done like this and I do know quite a bit about what I am saying here.

You see, I read medical journals, which are full of accounts of people facing death (in some form or other), and I rarely get an all-upset-inside feeling for the people I read about. I get concerned about the sicknesses. More still about the treatments. But not about the people. If they were patients of mine I should be concerned. Really concerned. If they were close friends, much more concerned. If my family, I think more concerned than I could bear. But not about a case in a journal. If I read about Y.Z., aged 50, occupation statistician, number 16 in a series of 27 cases of *meningioma-en-plaque,* I should be very interested in his sickness. But about the man himself, Mr. Y.Z., I should feel just as detached as I should expect him, as a statistician, to feel about J.H., aged 50, occupation medical practitioner, just one of a number of rather ordinary people involved in a situation in which they face most serious social disturbances.

Now, I feel that all this preamble is of some importance. For I am going to ask you to consider what I think to be the most serious disturbance in all human relationships, try to understand it, and then seek a solution that will satisfy both the emotional impact it may make on life and the intellectual requirements of logical argument.

And this great disturbing problem is simply that of being a Christian.

Now, please. Please! Don't just toss the book aside and feel that you have been robbed. If you think this is not a problem, then you have indeed been robbed, but not by me! And if you think this is just too, too funny for words, and just a stupid joke, then you toddle back to your children's comic strips where you belong.

And if you think this is just my idea of cooking up a subject to write a book about in the manner of the charlatan world of tongue-in-the-cheek twentieth-century advertising, then you may think anything you like about me and I couldn't care less. But you will be wrong. Quite wrong. Because this is not a problem I thought up, it is a problem in which I am caught up. It is not an announcement I am making, it is an announcement I have heard.

It is an announcement made by none other than Jesus Christ Himself. And it is not a tentative suggestion of His, it is a terse incisive thrust. Just listen – 'If the world hates you, it hated me first, as you know well. If you belonged to the world, the world would love its own; but because you do not belong to the world, because I have chosen you out of the world, for that reason the world hates you. . . . As they persecuted me, they will persecute you. . . . It is on my account that they will treat you thus.'

The Well-adjusted Life, did we call it? That is the reasonable objective of all ordinary citizens, *we* said. Hatred, not-belonging, division, persecution, *Jesus* said. That is the life of His followers, He insists.

And this is not a single statement from one of the Gospel records. You might think that the statement I have just quoted is rather coloured by St. John's spiritualizing of everything – and it is from John's Gospel, true enough.

But listen to this – from Matthew's Gospel this time : 'Be on your guard, for men will hand you over to their courts, they will flog you. . . . Brother will betray brother to death, and the father his child; children will turn against their parents and send them to their death. All will hate you for your allegiance to me. . . . You must not think that I have come to bring peace to the earth; I have not come to bring peace, but a sword; I have come to set a man against his father . . . a young wife against her mother-in-law; and a man will find his enemies under his own roof.'

Luke, the doctor, records Jesus' words in this form : 'Even your parents and brothers, your relations and friends, will betray you. Some of you will be put to death; and you will be hated by all for your allegiance to me.'

In fact, if you read your Gospels through, looking for that sort of statement, you may be as disturbed as I have been to see how clearly, how repeatedly, how dramatically Jesus says this over and over again. He insisted that if anyone became one of His followers, then he was in for the same sort of treatment that Jesus Himself was going to get. And He got a cross! That's what His society thought of Him. That's what Jesus finished up with in terms of The Well-adjusted Life!

Now perhaps you are beginning to understand why I said this is a big problem. Not just one of the petty sordid messes, like adultery, neurosis, perversion and the human like. This is war, murder, social violence; this is blazing hatred ripping society to pieces. This is not meanly skulking; this is savagely rampant.

Now also, you can understand the simple honesty of St. John's statement in one of his Epistles: 'My brothers, do not be surprised if the world hates you.' Surprised! I think St. John would have been as surprised as St. Paul or any other of the original disciples if they had not been hated.

No, I didn't invent this idea. . . . I am still reeling from the impact of it as I read and re-read the New Testament. I see those disciples and their immediate successors in conflict and turmoil and strife that never once lets up. St. Paul seems to have been in bonds more often than in freedom. As I read St. Peter's grand First Epistle I confess to being profoundly moved in simply trying to imagine all the knocks and hurts that make a fiercely aggressive man like that come to the point of being able to write calmly, 'My dear friends, do not be bewildered by the fiery ordeal that is upon you, as though it were something extraordinary. It gives you a share in Christ's sufferings, and that is cause for joy.'

For it is always the same. Always back to that cross, to the Master who Himself 'learned obedience in the school of suffering'. To look in the New Testament for the example of peaceful co-existence is to look in the wrong book. In the matter of how to be liked by everyone, Jesus is right at the very bottom of the class.

What a devastating directness was His, as He swung round on the civil and ecclesiastical leaders of His time, seemingly the most eminently proper and worthy-looking group in His whole country, and burst out: 'Alas for you, lawyers and Pharisees, hypocrites! You are like tombs covered with white-wash; they look well from outside, but inside they are full of dead men's bones. . . . So it is with you : outside you look like honest men, but inside you are brim-full of hypocrisy and crime. . . . You snakes, you vipers' brood, how can you escape being condemned to hell?'

'Gentle Jesus, meek and mild', did you sing in your Sunday School days? Is that the way to describe a living tornado? But watch Him again, listen again. He is in the Temple, this time sitting down in the teacher's place, the place where any one of these ecclesiastics may well be seen any other day. Suddenly, in through the door bursts a group of these very men, the doctors of law and the Pharisees, whom He has so bitterly attacked. And in their midst they have a woman they had caught in the very act of adultery. See on their faces that peculiar look of elation and concern that you sometimes observe in men caught up in the excitement of malice. Their spokesman burst out, 'In the Law Moses laid down that such women are to be stoned. What do you say about it?' You watch as their astute little trap is sprung. If He says that they ought to be condemned to hell, what then of this wretched woman? If He criticizes them for slight uncharitableness or the like, how about this? Now see what thundering and condemnation He will come out with. And we watch spellbound as His challenge, His presence, His finger writing on the ground, slowly and insistently drive them out. Only Jesus and the woman are left. 'Has no one condemned you?' He asks. 'No one, sir.' 'No more do I.'

Did I call it a difficulty of social relationships? A disturbing problem? I am sorry I was so mealy-mouthed. I apologize for being so politely diplomatic. But you will please remember that I did at least insist that if you thought it a trifle, then you have no serious place in our attention at all. If you feel yourself coolly objective and intellectually detached, then at least you remember that I suggested it should be the sort of detachment that the doctor shows in his reading of cancer and death. It is the calculated detachment that is evoked by understanding well the magnitude and seriousness of the condition.

Yes, this is big. This is too big altogether, and we will try and keep it big enough to keep it real. If you are one of Jesus' followers, as I claim to be myself, then you and I are wrapped up in this right up to the neck. And if you are not one of Jesus' followers, then you are in it even more still, because He insists that you do in fact hate Him and will show it by hating me and His other followers like me.

I asked the publisher to leave a bit of a space there because I think that the time has come to draw a rather deep breath. I do this often when talking to patients. I have made my investigations, asked my questions, arrived at some answers, understood some of my patient's fears – and stop to talk it out. I usually move my chair back a few inches, put down my pen, give my bifocals a bit of a polish, *etc., etc.* You know the idea, don't you? Then you do just that now. Throw another log on the fire, take another sip of coffee, or port, or whatever you may be drinking. If you are reading in bed, now's your chance to have a wriggle, shake the pins and needles out of your left arm.

Well, then. Back to our problem. And may I please do what I do so often in my ordinary practice? Let me start again, approaching the subject from a new slant. . . .

If you got hold of a Bible for the very first time in your whole life – and I mean the whole Bible, not just a snippet from here or there, and please, oh please not one in some ancient language our ancestors used to use – then I think two completely dominant general ideas would stand out. The first is the never-changing idea that the God of the Bible is the one single Author of every conceivable thing in all existence. This is said in a hundred different ways. It is thundered, whispered; declared, implied; assumed, argued; and then illustrated in all the language man is capable of using. This is surely the first great truth the Bible is declaring.

And if it says this so categorically about God, then it says something equally emphatic about man. It says all mankind is split into two camps, and into two camps only : those who are God's people and those who are not. It separates them into those who are His friends and those who are His enemies; those whom He has chosen and those whom He has rejected.

And remember well – nowhere in the Bible is this devastating division made more clearly and insistently than in the Gospels. If, as I suggested a minute ago, anyone taught you to sing about 'Gentle Jesus, meek and mild, Look upon a little child' and did not at the same time teach you this, then in Jesus' own words, 'It would be better for him to be thrown into the sea with a millstone round his neck.' You couldn't imagine a more tragic 'cause of stumbling' than just this. For all the time and everywhere He moved through His country, Jesus was in fact doing just this – either drawing some men into His company, with words of the warmest invitation and most gracious encouragement; or else setting them against Himself with bitterest hatred on their part and unrelenting sternness on His.

Don't ever be the least bit surprised when people tell you they like the Bible to remain a choice museum piece in Latin or Elizabethan English! Yes, it's a brutally direct and uncompromising book, no matter what part of it you read. (And notice also what a rock-like fortress its truths are to those who have set out to follow the clear, straight path of light they have seen shining from it!)

For that is really what it finally comes back to every time we look at this problem. White, black. Love, hate. Friends, foes. For, against. In, out. It's like a lot of modern electronic gear, only ever on or off. Nothing in between. No neutral. No no man's land. I sometimes think it's rather like marriage – you are either single or married. Being engaged doesn't really do anything to this matrimonial estate – you either get married or you don't get married. And the girl who wears an engagement ring for the rest of her life and still 'thinks' about getting married is just as unmarried as the one who for some reason or other has never even received a proposal.

That's the trouble with the Bible. That's the trouble with God. He sees right inside in one glance. We can deceive other people, often easily enough. We can deceive ourselves even, with practice. But Him, never. To God, a man is only ever seen as white – dazzlingly, spotlessly white; or black – horribly, hellishly black.

How altogether different this is from our nice Well-adjusted Life programme. We smile rather deprecatingly, often almost patronizingly, at those rare and rather embarrassing times when for a sudden moment we see in the life of a neighbour something that is in fact the dazzling white flash of sheer truth or honour or purity; and how tolerantly we pass off as mere foibles or eccentricities those disturbing things that we see in our friends and neighbours when they are caught out in some manifestation of simple pride or greed or malice. Oh no. That searing flash of white we see much more happily as a nice pale grey; and that ominous glimpse into the blackness of the Pit we describe as being just a rather darker grey. No pure white. No jet black. Just shades of grey.

And yet all this smooth greyness that we see enveloping our nice friends and neighbours, and which we hope so much that they can see about us, is not seen by God at all. In His judgment it is non-existent. It is only a chimera of the fatuous hope we build about ourselves and the people we like. And far more disturbing still, God can at times see through what we think to be a dirty grey cloud of social unpleasantness and declare the inner person utterly white and spotless. People don't really find the Christian gospel dull, however much they pretend to! The fact is that Christ's company is liable to lead a man into such terribly exciting truth that the stubborn human littleness in him shies off at its merest mention. You had better wait! Don't risk going to church until Mother's Day, or Remembrance Day, or Christmas Day, when you can count on the services being so sentimental and sloppy that none of this searing beam will penetrate the emotional fog.

(And I confess that this rather puzzles me: that even at Easter, when you would think that it might be really dangerous for the non-disciple to turn up at church, oddly enough it's usually pretty safe. The simple-minded Christians very rarely seem to be able to distinguish between the back-to-life story of Lazarus or Jairus' daughter or cardiac massage or the like, and the on-through-death wonder of the risen Lord, the one and only resurrection story in all history. Think of the bombshell St. Paul dropped on the members of the Court of Areopagus in Athens, with his account of the resurrection. And then try and wonder just how it can happen that Tom, Dick and Harry can turn up in church on Easter Day and not get jolted clean out of their pews by the impact of the Christian faith. But it happens and it happens. And what with Easter eggs and Easter bunnies and here in Sydney our Royal Easter Show, there is getting even less risk still of being disturbed on Easter Day. I agree that Easter is not yet as pagan as Christmas, but that is about all you can say!)

I think you can see why I asked for that space again. I am just a bit out of breath, as it were. When I think of Christ tearing spiritual strips off the great pundits and Pooh-Bahs of His time; and see His velvet-soft touch as He encounters that poor condemned woman – as I see this so much and so often in all the sacred volume – I feel almost desperate for some guide to lead me through the pleasant greyness of our smug, contented Western world. Some finger to point into my own life (and yours, too, if you so desire) and indicate just what God is doing.

Never mind about the neighbours – they are sure to see some sort of grey in any case. But how to find the pure white, how to avoid the awful black : that is the one entirely sensible search of life. Will God be good, be gracious enough, to show us this? Can we learn from His Word just what key unlocks this treasure-chest of heaven, just what key locks fast the dungeon-pit of hell? What a simpleton a man must be to channel all his attention into science or medicine or business or anything else at all if he has not first and foremost learned this supreme truth. Has God got this answer for us?

This, then, is the objective in my mind as I write this book. If I have anything helpful to give you, then this is it. . . .

If you want a clear, simple, terse description of what it feels like to be in the army, then go and ask a private soldier in the front line. He'll tell you. If he's an Aussie he'll tell you in one-syllable four-letter words! But don't ask him for a description of how the war is going on in its world-wide front. He won't be able to see further than his dug-out or his cook-house or his sanitation. To assess the war as a whole you need to find someone who is detached enough to see it in its full sweep. To the digger in the fox-hole right on the enemy lines it's a matter of a lousy so-and-so of a sergeant cook who hashes up the bully beef and pinches all the butter ration and generally makes the hell of war more hellish. But to the C.-in-C. it's a story of sunk transport ships and directing supplies to a new offensive on the northern flank and holding back reinforcements for the eastern front and generally measuring it by countries, continents and hemispheres.

And I am like that. I am just a very commonplace footslogger in the spiritual battle of life, and how can I possibly look into the vast complexity of a huge twentieth-century Western city and measure accurately and wisely the pressures and tensions as I feel them and live within them? Is there perhaps some way I can get outside all this, and just for once look in from some place of detachment and objectivity and get the answer clearly?

Don't bother to answer me, please. I know the answer before I ask. I know it can't be done, and I don't really need you to tell me. Mere isolation in some monastic order is worse than useless. Getting elected to innumerable committees and boards and 'Having one's finger on the pulse', as we say so brightly, is even more useless still – that is just a step in the direction of ulcers and strained home relationships.

No; common soldiers just don't get this view of the war. It must be done some other way altogether, if it is to be done at all.

Now you may say that the whole idea is in fact wrong, and to pursue it is just crazy. You may be quite sure that what Jesus said about Himself and His disciples nineteen hundred years ago is quite irrelevant to our world. You may insist that at face value either Jesus was hopelessly wrong in His forecast; or I am absurdly wrong in thinking that He meant anything – or knew anything – about followers in centuries later than His own.

How, then, to proceed?

That is my problem, and to attempt to sort it out I am going to do what I have often found most helpful. I am going to ask you to look at some other societies altogether and actually watch this process at work. That is essentially my job of course: analysing, investigating, interpreting. A doctor spends his whole life doing just that, asking very personal and intimate questions without embarrassment, expecting always to be given his answers, hoping always to make the diagnosis, to prescribe the cure.

Now this is not the fallacy of arguing from the particular to the general. Rather, this is the most helpful of all clinical tutoring methods : learning the mild form of the disease from a study of the severe. This is using the dramatic findings of the gross, extreme case of hypertension to help interpret the barely perceptible signs and symptoms of the man whose blood-pressure is just that little bit elevated. This is the essential validity of the deduction whereby the radiologist diagnoses active tuberculosis from an X-ray in which only the tiniest possible shadow appears. This is the concept of natural history in disease : the great hydatid cyst that fills nearly a quarter of the cranial cavity was known to have been once but a tiny single scolex.

Oh no. There is no problem in the method. The problem is to find the suitable examples to study. They must be 'Big' enough, clear enough, to paint the sharp-etched clinical picture by which the pale grey-white contrast of ordinary people like you and me (like me, at any rate) can be understood. The cases will need to be so strongly delineated, their experience so dramatic, the whole issue so obvious in all its outworking, that the basic search will be immediately and clearly rewarded.

And further still, the cases must be recorded so reliably and so honestly that we need have no fear of being misled as we have studied them. This is of the greatest possible importance, surely. For the whole vastly important matter of The Well-adjusted Life is at stake.

Now I suppose I could learn something of this from historians – but would I not need to know even more certainly the attitude and personal position, in this spiritual sense, of each historian himself? Again, could the archaeologists give us these answers? Perhaps they could, if I were trained enough and experienced enough to be able to piece together the complex of information they are collating – and I'm not. What, then, of biographers? Lots of biographies have been written as if they could give us these answers to our spiritual questions. But while I can (and occasionally do) read such books, I have to make constant adjustments to account for the personal slant of the biographer himself. And, not knowing the authors either, I never feel too sure just how much adjustment even is needed. All too often, if we look very carefully and critically at the man as he must have been as husband and father and citizen, rather than at the man as told in the story, we find that the biographer has allowed distortions to develop that make the story useless in this didactic sense. Think of the many 'Lives' where the real man in the story is overlaid with such an aura of piety and sanctimony that any hope of really seeing God's grace at work is utterly destroyed.

So, to avoid these problems of ordinary literature, to escape the inevitable pro or con bias in a human mind, I am going to ask you to come with me in a study of some accounts written by none other than God Himself.

In His Word God has preserved many, many records of the spiritual encounter and adventure of men. Remember, the Bible is not written as being *just* historical any more than it is written as if it were *not* historical. The Bible is the one single material source of knowledge which God, in His utterly sovereign will and providence, has given to man as the unchallengeable fount of spiritual truth. For some reason which is as illogical as it is just human, many scholars and theologians find this a most baffling and unpalatable truth. But I am not going to ask you to stop here to argue this issue – we don't want to lose too much sight of the main purpose of this book, if you please – so come with me while I tell you just what is in my mind.

Firstly, I am going to ask you to join me as we study a society which is openly and unashamedly and bitterly opposed to God. A society described in terms of its encounter with God and His people, yet a society which is only ever seen in terms of ruthless malice and rapacity and lust. Now make no mistake, there were other qualities in this nation, to be sure The archaeologists have discovered plenty. But God does not confuse us, as He writes about them, by including these other facets. Here, in His Word, is the only clear account I know of in which we may see all the enveloping grey veneer stripped clean away from a people until only the deadly black heart remains. And let me say this – this is no story for the squeamish and lily-livered. If you faint at the sight of blood then you might as well stop reading right away. For this is to be a God's-eye glimpse into the very soul of the most fearsome of all ancient fighting people – the Assyrians. Assyrians and bloodshed of the most fearsome manner simply go together. And we shall get so close to them that we shall see the very whites of their eyes, as it were. We can feel the hot breath of the Assyrians on our faces, we get so near, so horribly near to them. And as we do this, as we see the enemy close up, full-face, eye-to-eye, we may well recognize some of the things in our world for what they really are – Assyrian! Don't be surprised if you can begin to detect the reek of Assyria in some of our Big Business. Don't be too disillusioned, as you read tomorrow's newspaper, if you find occasional little bits of party politics that could only ever have been learned from Shalmanezer and Sennacherib. And let me admit that I often feel that many of our Sydney taxi-drivers must surely have got their first driving licences in Nineveh!

I remember vividly an experience in my student days in medical school. A man had come to the out-patients' department with a huge necrotic malignant ulcer on one temple. It had eaten through the skin and muscle and was now slough-ing out the bone, about an inch and a half in diameter, and a horrible death from infection and meningitis the inevitable and imminent prospect – and all he had come for was a new pair of spectacles!

Now the second story which I am asking you to look at is just like that. We will be studying a society that is literally rotting to its death with spiritual apathy and petty sordid preoccupation with personal gain – and altogether un-concerned with a mounting weight of divine judgment that finally fell and swept its people to tragic and pitiful destruc-tion. We shall see no TV, central heating, jet flights or man in space. But we will see spiritual facets and attitudes that belong so equally to mid-twentieth-century Sydney, London or New York that I feel I can hardly dare to look, such tragedy it is. And, like the man in the out-patients' depart-ment, all the time within immediate grasp of life and safety and survival. For we shall be seeing Jerusalem through the eyes of Jeremiah, as the little city was finally engulfed by the overwhelming might of all-conquering Babylon. And I can assure you of this – I have myself learned more about my patients and their needs from this study than I have learned in any dozen medical journals that I have last read. Jeremiah and his insight into the doomed city of Jerusalem has given me more understanding and sympathy with the people I meet every working day in my life in Sydney than I think I had in all my life before.

I have a particular and quite personal reason for wanting to add the next, third story. This has to do with my life as a doctor. In a mirror-image sort of way it probably has just as much to do with you, if you are not a doctor, because you are very liable to be or to become a patient!

This is how it comes about.

Most of my working life-time is spent in association with people in trouble. Much of the time it is not serious trouble, and just occasionally there may be the one who says he has no trouble – just wants a check-up. But all too frequently it is real trouble, and I am the one who has to explain the trouble. You don't have to be a doctor to appreciate that this is often very difficult. I know of a few colleagues who can assume a sphinx-like mask and just make bald statements of truth quite cold-bloodedly. I know of a few others who just don't say anything at all. I must confess that the only thing I envy in these non-talkers is the fact that at least they are never mis-quoted! But that is not doctoring. A doctor is supposed to be a teacher – patients come to us for instruction as much as anything, and what we teach may play more final a part in the course and significance of the illness than any other thera-peutic aid we may employ.

Now you can probably begin to see what I am coming to. If Jesus was right in His statements about His disciples in their world, then it must be true at this very level. If being one of His disciples and not being one constitutes the greatest single conflict in all human relationships, then it has a very down-to-earth reality in a doctor's consulting-room. This is a meeting-ground of need on one side and an intention to help that need on the other; but if I am to be a disciple of Christ then I am utterly committed to Truth (isn't that one of His noblest names?) as far as I can know truth. And perhaps even more significantly still, it becomes an essential part of my discipleship to understand, if I can, how to reconcile my limited understanding of the technical truths I learn in my medical world with the revelation of the nature and mind of God as I see Him in Christ. What answer can I give to the

man with a brain tumour when he asks with frightened eyes
and trembling lips, 'Doctor, just what does this mean?' What
answer can you suggest for the sob-shaken mother whose
child is going to die as she cries out, 'Doctor, why did this
happen to my darling little Rosemary?'

Now let me say very clearly that if you don't like questions
like that and don't like having to answer them any more than
you hope you don't ever have to ask them, then I should
advise you not to set out to practise medicine. If you like the
medical sciences, but not like this, then all right – get yourself
a job in a research department and work on experimental
animals. They ask exceedingly few questions! You might
perhaps allow yourself to move somewhat closer still and join
that ever-growing number of medical graduates who practise
in institutional medicine, that caricature of doctoring in
which the patient may cease to be a person and just become
a case. The Consultants will study the X-rays and path.
reports and discuss all the history with the Registrars; the
Registrars make sure the House Surgeons have understood
the nature and the seriousness of the case; the House Surgeons
have checked with Sister about diet, pre-op. prep., post-op.
nursing and so on. But the teaching, the instruction, the
answering of all the questions, the explanation of the after-
effects, what about the job, the care of the children, all these
matters that are as relevant as the diathermy cutting-point –
who cares for all these? All too often in the big institution
like this it is simply left to the nurses to do it. The pretty little
twenty-year-old who is shaving and prepping the man for his
operation, for his descent into the valley of the shadow of
death – as often as not it is she, and she alone, who stops to
help him in this way.

But this is not the theme I may pursue here. If this were a
medical journal then it would be very much worth pursuing;
and far greater minds and abler pens than mine are beginning,
lately, to pursue it with great seriousness and concern. For the
institution to become the last word instead of being the last
resort may be excellent technology and high-class science; but
it makes for very difficult doctoring. And it is this personal
relationship in the practice of medicine that calls for all the
faith and understanding that the disciple of Jesus can muster,
for the Master Himself showed this as no man has ever been

able to equal. The simple directness that Jesus combined with such unfailing kindness is the pattern for all men for all time; and in the issues of life and death, of pain and suffering, we will most surely need the instruction of God Himself.

This, then, is the reason for the third story. And it is because I myself learned so very much from it, that I am now writing about it. It is a story of slavery, of mud and slush, of heartbreak and loneliness almost without parallel; and a story of integrity and courage and obedience to truth such as has never to my knowledge been equalled.

It is the story of Ezekiel.

Need I tell you that I would not presume to write about these case records just because of a background of medicine? Oh no, a thousand times no! Rather, because of many years now in the company of the Great Physician, and a singularly rich privilege of close fellowship with many men of faith who are scholars, pastors, thinkers, teachers. Long years, now. And through many of these years the endless and always exciting contact with every conceivable sort of person in the ordinary run of an ordinary-enough doctor's life. This is the only validity a book like this could ever claim.

This, then, is why I hope to have the pleasure of introducing you to Isaiah, Jeremiah and (particularly) Ezekiel.

I trust you will be neither surprised nor embarrassed at the directness of some of the things I may do, or at the unusualness of some of the things I may say. If God's Word is to speak in the day-to-day affairs of life, then His voice must be real. Experientially real. In the jargon of philosophy, it must have an existentialism at least equal to this morning's coffee and this afternoon's surgery. So that if need be I shall breakfast with Ezekiel, discuss war with Sennacherib, chat in the Temple with Isaiah, even invite Jeremiah to visit us in twentieth-century Sydney. And time and time again I shall make fleeting trips to the Galilee and Jerusalem of Jesus' day, trying to be as certain as ever can be that I am not listening to any old voice of history, but rather to *the* Voice of History.

CHAPTER TWO

MALIGNANT DISEASE

DURING my second year in high school my parents came from New Zealand to live in Australia.

New Zealand, as you know, is much, much more British than Britain. And so, of course, the only history I had ever learned was British history. In fact I had the quite distinct impression that history consisted of British history which was taught in school, and the history of the world which was taught in the Bible. We heard an occasional reference to Abel Tasman and Captain Cook, and a certain oblique account of some active disagreement we had had with the Maoris about settling in New Zealand; but of course that was not really history. I knew the French were in history, because Britain had fought against them for so long; and the Russians came into history early last century in a shabby Crimean encounter; and India had become a part of history perhaps a hundred years earlier still, but that was all. Since the Aztecs and the ancient Chinese and the like weren't in British history, and weren't in the Bible either, they just weren't in history at all.

You may imagine, then, my genuine dismay when I came to live in Sydney and found that part of our history time-table was given over to Australian history. I listened politely during the single lesson per week which this Australian history was accorded, and my dismay hardened into a cold and bitter contempt. It wasn't history at all! In New Zealand the Maoris had at least provided a couple of Maori wars; but in Australia there wasn't even a single war of any kind. It seemed as though the whites cleared out the blacks simply by finding ways to cross the Blue Mountains and graze their sheep on the other side. In fact the only single bit of excitement in the whole miserable affair lay in the stories of a few bush-rangers, and they weren't even crack shots! Not one of them would have even been noticed by Zane Grey or Clarence Mulford. I felt the entire subject had a distinctly unsavoury aroma of sheer disloyalty, and I wasn't going to budge from the Union Jack and British history.

So you may further imagine my delight when I found that in the Intermediate Examination at the end of third year the history paper was set in two parts, and it was possible to obtain a B pass on the British history alone. Australian history was only necessary for an A. Thus relieved and liberated, I stuck nobly to the Treaty of Utrecht and the Wars of the Roses and the like; and duly gained my B. Which was all the encouragement I really needed the following year to drop history altogether and take for Matriculation the alternative and altogether near-to-my-heart subject of mechanics (applied mathematics). How exciting to exchange Green and his tiresome history for Newton and his laws of motion.

Now I can already hear some of you beginning to mumble. Just what on earth has all this drivelling anecdote to do with the subject in hand? What's the point of this preamble?

Let me explain. I am planning in this chapter to take you on a sort of conducted tour of a very specially chosen page in history, and I feel you should at least have some warning as to the background of your guide! If you react to history as I (and indeed most of the maths-science types at school with me) reacted, then you'll at least realize that you share my very warm sympathy. Or, if you feel yourself to be a cultural soul-mate to Green or Warner and Martin, then you'll sensibly recognize that you are now in the company of a fool rushing in.

For the part of history into which we shall be delving concerns an episode in the story of the Assyrians, and any single page at all in their history is enough to make you catch your breath.

The time is just a little more than 700 years BC and the Assyrians were doing what they were always doing – fighting. That doesn't mean that they didn't do anything else. Far from it. They could do a lot of things besides fighting, and, what is more, they did them all extremely well. They built splendid cities, they kept great libraries, they produced glorious works of art, they made scholarship really great – but all this against the unceasing thunder and shout of battle. They fought as probably no race has ever fought before or since. They just loved killing. They gloated in destruction. An

Assyrian king returning from a campaign would spend the winter evenings writing up his records, like this: 'Their corpses I piled in heaps; their young men and maidens I burned in the fire; their governor I flayed and his skin I spread upon the walls of the city; the city I destroyed, I laid waste, I burnt with fire.'

Assyria was the greatest nation in the world, and that was her greatness. The young princes were conditioned to it from their play-pens. No sissy games like rugby or grid-iron for an Assyrian princeling. No, sir! His sport was to track out into the desert and loose a live lion and there engage it in single-handed combat! And if he learned to risk spilling his own blood like that, how it excited him to shed someone else's blood!

Battle was their very life, fighting their greatest skill. They developed great inventions for assault and siege, they evolved wonderful skills of strategy and deployment, and always they killed. Torture, pain, cruelty they loved, and always because it led to death. Taking captive hostages from one conquered city, they would tie them in naked strings with ropes round their necks, or with iron bits forced into their mouths, and lead them to the gates of the next town to be attacked. And there, before the terrified gaze of the citizens peering over the walls, these miserable wretches would be hoisted up as human pennants on great Assyrian stakes thrust through the midriff. And as the victims writhed in their death throes the Assyrian spokesman would bellow his demand for surrender, warning the fear-stricken onlookers of an equal or worse fate if they dared resist. And always the busy clerks in army records recording it all in detail. Among the thousands and thousands of clay tablets that we have discovered, all with their cuneiform inscriptions, there are enough war records like this to tell in detail every cruel bit of devilry.

You may now understand just why I warned you that if you meet the Assyrians you need a stout heart and a strong stomach for blood!

These, then, are the masters of their world, and this is the pattern of their mastery. As they conquered an area, they would uproot every single citizen, and those they left alive they would transplant to some new locality altogether. All racial and tribal ties would be utterly disrupted, while displaced peoples from other parts would be moved in in their stead, so that any chance of their captives grouping up in insurrection would be well-nigh impossible.

This, then, is Assyria.

And the year is about 701 BC.

And the place is the tiny city-state of Jerusalem, a few square miles of fairly rugged hinterland and the tiny fortress of the city itself which would nowhere nearly fill a single suburb in any modern city. And this time it is Jerusalem that the Assyrian maw is planning to swallow up.

Now I feel that I must ask you to wait a moment before we see this balloon go up, while we try and understand the background of it all. To do this I suggest we step back some three hundred years to the time of David. For it was David, with his genius and his ruthlessness and his charm, who united the Jewish people for the first time since their days under Moses, and set them up as a nation and a Power-To-Be-Reckoned-With. In an almost magical ten years he emerged from his hidey-hole obscurity in the very heart of the Philistine country to a place on the throne of a united Jewish nation and to mastery over every surrounding foreign people. With a brilliance and energy that seems to have remained undiminished until his very last years, David finally handed the throne to his son Solomon as a going concern of the highest possible order.

And what Solomon may have lacked in fire and battle he more than made up in shrewd judgment and romance. For he married princesses from every imaginable surrounding race, but in the process tied up trade treaties with all the countries in his known world! And if you think the princesses got a raw deal in this so-mercenary romanticism, then you simply don't know your Solomon! When Solomon made love to a girl she just felt like a million dollars! You read all the love stories on the bookshelves and toss in the poets and the paperbacks – and then see them for the paste they are when you put them alongside the sparkling gem of the Song of Solomon. And *she* was only a slavegirl! Mendel and his genes were never proved so right as with the son of David and Bathsheba – not to mention great-grandfather Ahitophel.

But I dare not stop to talk about Solomon. Solomon, with so much gold that he simply made it into huge shields which he stuck up all over the country in a peculiar mixture of shrewd morale build-up and blatant self-advertising. Solomon, with his vast slave labour force and huge public works programme that bled his people so white that only his genius allowed him to get away with it. Solomon, with his hundreds of wives and more hundreds of concubines. Yes, Solomon, with what seems to be perhaps the greatest problem of all – only one son.

And what a disaster of a son! If Solomon the father had collected all the Mendelian dominants, then poor Rehoboam the son seems to have been endowed with all the recessives. And when Rehoboam took over the throne from Solomon, his meagre IQ of 90-ish and his immature personality blew the last remaining fuse – the whole kingdom split clean down the middle, with ten tribes going off under Jeroboam, and only Judah remaining under Rehoboam with his capital in Jerusalem.

For exactly two hundred years, then, this was to be the story. The ten northern tribes, now known as Israel, with a capital finally settled in Samaria; and as king anyone who was strong enough to grab the throne and hang on to it. And Judah (plus tiny Benjamin) in the south with a king who was always a direct descendant of David and Solomon. Two hundred years of almost continual feud and bloodshed and rivalry. The Judahites always boasting that Jerusalem was the only real royal city, that there alone was the one and only Temple built by the great Solomon himself. The Israelites always contemptuous of their southern brethren's puniness and their stuffy religious ties.

And all through these two hundred years could be felt the nagging pulse of mutual danger from Egypt and Philistia to the south and west and the Arabs and Syrians to the east and north.

And even above all this the ever-swelling crescendo of the battle-cry of the mounting Assyrian menace away up in the north-east. Until finally it was the Assyrian avalanche that burst in. For many centuries Assyria had been slowly growing bigger, stronger and tougher, and it was in about 725 BC that the attack came. The mighty Assyrian flood swiftly swept the whole of the northern tribes of Israel to total and irrecoverable destruction. In 722 BC Samaria, the city built by Omri and Ahab, and perhaps the greatest single piece of building ever constructed by the Jewish people, was burnt out and captured by Sargon II. This last remaining Israelite fortress was taken and the ten tribes of Israel ceased their earthly existence for ever. Great Assyria was moving, and moving in the manner of men whom no-one could stop. And Judah came next!

On the throne of Jerusalem when that final destruction of Israel took place, and watching it with tight lips and pounding pulse from a distance of less than thirty miles, was the young Jewish prince, Hezekiah. We are going to take a rather close look at Hezekiah, because it is he who will be on the direct receiving-end of the Assyrian attack when it comes later.

Hezekiah took over the kingdom in his mid-twenties on the death of his father Ahaz. And if ever it was true that to know something of the father is to help understand the son then it is true of these two. Ahaz seems to have been a king of but little generalship, yet with just enough far-sighted canniness to be able to see clearly the significance of the huge straws blowing in the political and military winds of his time. He had been badly caught out in a local anti-Assyria *entente* that had built up between Syria and Israel to his north and (perhaps) Edom to his east. These little states wanted to form a bloc in the path of Tiglath-pileser III, a terrible fire-eating Assyrian general who had usurped the throne at Nineveh and who was then campaigning down in their direction. Ahaz wanted none of this – he was of the diplomatic stomach of Leopold of Belgium in 1940, who viewed the Hitler–Leopold situation much as Ahaz had viewed his situation twenty-seven centuries earlier. And finally when his little neighbours pressed him almost to breaking-point, Ahaz screamed to Tiglath-pileser for help, claiming that he was really an Assyrian at heart, that he was sure their ways were best, that their religion was right, that he was more than glad to be counted one of their vassal states; and he supported his plan with a lovely big jingly swag of gold and silver that he had lifted from the Temple in Jerusalem.

And Tiglath-pileser leaped to the bait and marched against the little state of Syria with its capital in Damascus.

Syria went. And Ahaz hurried up to Damascus to swear fealty to the conquering Assyrian king, and to swot up the principles of the Assyrian religion, sending a model of the new altar at Damascus down to Jerusalem for immediate copying. And only to find that he had not used a sprat to catch a mackerel, but rather that he himself was the sprat caught ever so tightly in the jaws of the Assyrian Leviathan!

For back to Jerusalem he came, to pay endless and hard-to-find tribute to his greedy masters, and to make desperate attempts to play the game of Assyrian religion, even to the extent of offering some of his sons in blood sacrifice as token of his genuineness.

And watching this, growing up in the black shadow of all this, was his son Hezekiah, coming into manhood, assuming co-regency alongside his fast-failing puppet-king father.

You may readily enough guess what happened. Hezekiah saw clean through the weakness and insincerity and shabbiness of his father, moving into one of the most explosive reactions in all the history of his people. He was probably still in his teens when this sell-out to Assyria had taken place, and all the developing young man and all the growing faith in him turned in utter revolt. I am sure Hezekiah was a timid man by nature, not at all endowed with the tough case-hardened shell of his Assyrian overlords. But if ever you want to see God at work in a man building sheer spiritual courage, then look at Hezekiah. And if God was going to use Hezekiah to humble the proud and arrogant Assyrians, then just as surely, in His endless love and goodness, He will use the heel of the Assyrian jack-boot to shape and strengthen the moral courage in the young king. But this is not Hezekiah's story I am writing, however much I should like to make it his – this is the story of the Assyrians, and I must not let them out of sight for a moment. Remember, if you will, that this is the one single chance we have (as far as I know) to get a clear eye-level full-face close-up of the enemy; and we must not spend too much time and attention on even our best friends.

For Hezekiah had the Assyrians clearly in sight too, you may be sure, and he was not fooled by them or over-impressed by them in the least. He was impressed, of course. Impressed enough to start a never-ending relentless counter-attack from the very first moment he assumed the throne.

In fact his father was barely dead and buried when Hezekiah made his first move.[1] He immediately set about making preparation against the inevitable Assyrian assault.

And you may be quite surprised to find that his very first move in defence preparations, right in the first month of his reign, was to call his people back to God. I have no doubt at all that a great deal of his instruction and advice came from the now late-middle-aged Isaiah, the great prophet who had lived through the evil of Ahaz's reign. And the story leaves us in little doubt also that some of the most reluctant help Hezekiah could muster was from a large section of the priesthood.

Please don't be surprised at this. An upsurge of religion in the affairs of men may very easily show the absence of faith. As C. S. Lewis once reminded the debonair readers of *Punch,* 'Men who have gods worship those gods; it is the spectators who describe this as religion! . . . The moment a man seriously accepts a deity his interest in religion is at an end. He's got something else to think about.'

Ahaz had had plenty of religion. The whole country was choked up so full of religion during his reign that it took someone of the stature of Isaiah to raise a voice for God at all. Religion was even more popular then than now; and faith – that rare, precious jewel in the tale of history, in which a mere man, a mere creature, claims a place in the sovereign will of God – faith was in very, very short supply.

But the Levites came round, and the reluctant priests came round, and the Temple services were re-established. And more interesting still, Hezekiah sent out a bunch of couriers to let the Hebrews in the surrounding cities know what he was doing. And he got just the result you might expect – a loud,

---

[1] I always wonder whether it was at Hezekiah's direction, rather than with his mere sanction, that Ahaz was not buried in the royal burial-ground. I admit I am guessing, but my guess is that it was indeed Hezekiah who saw to it that 'they buried him in the city, in Jerusalem, for they did not bring him into the tombs of the kings'. Let us not forget that God may well choose, in His sovereign will, 'to set a man against his father'; and while you and I might think this is pettiness on Hezekiah's part, let us remember that the only judgments we dare give are judgments on ourselves. And if Hezekiah did in fact insist that Ahaz was not to be buried in the royal tombs, then that is between him and God, not between him and me.

mocking laugh! That was fine for Hezekiah, for it told him what sort of help he could count on in the anti-Assyria campaign. I have no doubt at all that if he had sent out couriers inviting would-be fighters to come up to Jerusalem for a refresher course in assault training, if he had suggested a recruitment for the Royal Pioneer Chariot Division, he would have had plenty of starters. But not for this. No, this was far too unreal to make any real nation-wide impact. Not just this religion and trust in God business. Men don't change. We could tell Hezekiah what to expect, even as Hezekiah has told us just in fact what happened. 'They laughed them to scorn.'

But not everyone. There were then, as now, a few who will rise and take their proper place in the ranks of the children of God. It seems that at times God needs a St. Paul or a John Wesley or a Father Jones, or a Billy Graham, to call such men out of the enemy lines, from the hiding-places they have retreated into. 'A few men of Asher, of Manasseh, and of Zebulun humbled themselves and came to Jerusalem.'

And the Assyrians? Sargon II, the new king, the arrogant conqueror of Samaria, what of him? Did he let this go on? Yes. Assyria is like that. They didn't understand it then any better than they do now. Faith, the real thing, is so far removed from their cocksure world of man-made greatness, that they can never understand it.

Come with me if you will, as I take a quick visit to Nimrud and Nineveh, and get a closer view of what was going on over there at the time. These are the cities of great palaces, where Sargon himself lives. Come and see what stirs. See, if we can, what ticks in the Assyrian mind, as they hear of a great upsurge of faith away down south in Jerusalem.

Here we are, then, standing in the huge decorated entrance foyer in one of the elaborate new public buildings. In imagination I am flipping over the tablets of *The Nineveh Morning Advertiser* of the day. And sure enough, I find what I am looking for. In the lower left-hand corner of tab. 3 is a small-case cuneiform par. referring to the revival movement in Jerusalem. It tells in light-hearted journalese of some small local interest on the part of a few simple-hearted folk in the district. Asked to comment, Sargon II is reported as saying that these are a very non-militant group, and he has, through army intelligence, an accurate on-the-spot dossier on every participant. He knows for certain that not one of them could really manage to mount a war-horse, and the mere thought of Hezekiah handling a chariot was just too too funny for words. The Chancellor of the Exchequer, too, supported his royal master's assessment of the situation by reminding the readers of *The Advertiser* that Judah was a vassal state, and Hezekiah had an excellent name as a good tribute-payer.

Of course the Assyrians didn't understand it, then or now. In a culture where Aggressiveness, Pride and Greed are the Holy Trinity, it is unthinkable that other values can exist. Even the most rank outsider in the city couldn't help recognizing that, in current Assyrian comment, there could be no man who would be foolish enough to risk livelihood, let alone life, for a conviction to seek and obey the will of God.

But Hezekiah was not fooled by this, even if the Assyrians themselves were so fooled. He had spent too many hours in the company of Isaiah to be fooled so easily.

The simple truth is that Sargon was really much too pre-occupied with bigger affairs than the little matter of Hezekiah and his quaint religion. Sargon was far more tied up in suppressing a Damascus–Samaria revolt, in pressing back the Arabs, in holding off the mounting thrust from the now discernible Babylon, in countless small-time rebellions in a score of discontented provinces; and, most of all, in keeping an ever-watchful eye with an ever-ready task force to thunder down upon any hint of Egyptian stirring in the south.

Oh yes, Sargon had his problems all right! Don't ever be so naïve as to think that being a Big Assyrian is all fun and games. Many Christians do make this mistake. Didn't the Psalmist merely voice a common enough misconception in his occasional concern at seeing the wicked flourishing like the green bay-tree; while the poor saint has a very thin time indeed?

Not a bit of it! Sargon packed in about as much trouble and bitterness and hatred and all such man-made 'greatness' as the seventeen years of his reign could conceivably contain. And he certainly was not going to work up a great head of steam over Hezekiah, with his praying and his religion and

B

that sort of stuff. Not that he liked Hezekiah for it, at all. No.
He had Hezekiah on his list, and he was slowly moving him
up the list; but Hezekiah could wait.

Sargon had his spies out everywhere. If the Jerusalem
espionage network had reported just the tiniest jingle of a
spurred boot, just the hint of a rumble of a chariot wheel,
then Sargon would have sprung. But he was so foolish, so
entirely human, that he thought the real strength of Assyria
lay in chariots, horsemen, siege apparatus, assault troops,
mechanization, atomic war-heads, lunar satellite observation
posts and . . . Oh, I'm sorry, Sargon, I had not intended to
disturb you, in your vast empire-building activities; but I seem
to have mixed you up with other foolish men in my own time,
men who are making exactly the same mistake now that you
made then. Thank you for reminding me that your Assyrian
blood still flows in many spiritual veins in the twentieth-
century Western world.

And, Sargon, just one question more, now that we are, as it
were, on speaking terms. Before we leave you in peace, would
you just tell us this – how did you make out at the end? As
you died out there in battle, at Tabal, were you really win-
ning? You know what I mean – not just trampling down a
lot of less skilled, less equipped, less gifted fellow humans
into pitiable pulp, but in the deep satisfaction and serenity
which the inner soul of man cries out for? How did you go
in that, Sargon? Before you answer me, Sargon, I can tell you
this about Hezekiah, the puny little king you left on the
throne in Jerusalem : you can't see him now, and I can't see
him now either, but I do know just a tiny bit of the sheer
wonder of the new appearance of the One he is like. And,
Sargon, if this is the end of the journey for Hezekiah, who
was such a human whipper-snapper alongside your gigantic
stature, can you tell us how you fared?

And across the long centuries I strain my ear to catch the
faintest answer, and somewhere in the eternal silence there
sounds just the tiniest of all voices – I lean forward, hand to
ear, to catch it – '. . . tip of his finger in water, to cool my
tongue . . .'

Sargon, I can't hear you. This is terribly important. Would
you please say that again? There is a fearful noise beginning
to develop here. Would you say it again? And the tumul

around me is mounting higher and even higher, and I think I shall never hear Sargon again, unless it be in some mere cuneiform inscriptions or bas-relief plaque. And I'm about to turn away for ever, when there is a sudden lull in the noise, and I hear, floating in eerie unearthliness, the same voice speaking – listen : '. . . I am in agony in this fire.'

And before I can draw my half-choked breath, before I can mop my sweat-bedewed brow, the whole world shakes with the thunder of battle and I spin around to see whence it comes. And there, at the head of all the might of an even greater and deadlier Assyria, is Sennacherib. The king is dead. Long live the king! King Sennacherib!

And I'm already running, running as I have never run before, running to tell Hezekiah that Sennacherib is now king, and Sennacherib is not like his father Sargon.

Hezekiah, I pant out, as I rush unceremoniously into his private Council Chamber. Hezekiah, Sargon is dead. And Sennacherib is king. Do you know what that means? He won't be long in getting here. And I watch the king's face go white. Hezekiah is far too intelligent to have any silly ideas about Sennacherib. He knows, too, that Sennacherib is as cruel, as ruthless, as bitter – and as powerful – as any man in history may be.

Hezekiah, you have had long years now to get prepared. (I'm getting my breath back and not feeling quite so flustered.) God has been very kind to you, Hezekiah, in giving you so many years' warning. You have always known what it really means, haven't you? You know that you can pay tribute as a vassal-state, you know that you can keep in their good books by being no trouble and by behaving with decency and courtesy. But you know better than to pretend that this can go on indefinitely. These are Assyrians, aren't they, Hezekiah? These are the men who hate you through and through, because they hate God through and through, because they love themselves through and through. Tell me, then, how are your preparations shaping? What are your plans?

Hezekiah looked up with what could quite easily have developed into a smile. The colour was returning to his face, and the faint tremor I had first noticed in his hand was nearly gone, as he took my arm. 'Come and I'll show you,' he said. 'Look over to the east.' We were now on a balustraded look-out on the top of the palace, and much of the tiny city-fortress lay within hailing distance. I turned to the east, gazing over the precipitous fall into the valley of Kedron. The city walls seemed to come soaring out of the very bottom of the brook. 'I've completely rebuilt that wall, and even the Assyrian battering-rams won't breach that.' He paused for the dramatic effect to register properly.

Good for you, Hezekiah. But remember they took Samaria, and they took it without battering down its walls. Do you think you are safer than Samaria was?

Hezekiah looked thoughtful as he answered. He was not a bombast. He was not an Assyrian. 'I've built a second wall, you see. If they did manage to storm the outer wall it would take a lot of dead bodies to fill the gap to reach the second wall. And look at the towers on the walls – I've added them. And the Millo is now as strong and solid as anyone could wish. I think we are safe. I hope so. And I make that my constant prayer.'

H'mmm. What about a siege? How do you think you could stand that? These Assyrians will just camp clean around the whole place and cut you off for years, if need be. Can you stand that, do you think?

'We have been very prosperous and we have been very thrifty.' Something of real pride, and yet something of a noble pride, seemed to light up his face. 'We aren't Ninevites, and we don't live it up high like Assyrians. God has given us wonderful seasons and great trading successes and our people have accepted their wealth as God-given and have given it back in rich measure. We have accumulated vast stores, and can live on here in total isolation for years and years if need be.'

I looked around me and thought fast. One single headland in our beautiful Sydney harbour would contain all of this little city. But it was so steep, so rugged, so densely built up, that I had grave doubts.

Hezekiah, that may be so. But what about water? The rainfall here is very seasonal, and it looks as though it would be very difficult to store it. Rock cisterns abound, of course, but can you make them large enough? You have a lot of people here, and you say you can certainly feed them. But what is food without water? What do you think?

Hezekiah paused a moment before he replied, and I could see that I had hit on something exciting. I couldn't fail to see the adrenergic mechanisms in skin, sweat, pupil, tremor, thickened voice. He almost needed some tranquillizer to allow him to answer coherently!

'Wait till I show you!' he exclaimed.

He took me and rushed me down the stairs into the court-yard. We ran past the guardhouse. (I thought to myself, 'I'll come back later and look at that. That must be the very jail Jeremiah will be in about 100 years from now.' Isn't history fascinating, when it's made up of people!) And off we strode to the southern end of the city, up into the towers in the south-east wall. It was nearly half a mile, and though Hezekiah was some half a head shorter than I he had me quite breathless as I got to the top with him! I can still chase a tennis ball, but motor-cars have ruined me for walking city streets!

'Now,' he said, and his eyes were ablaze. 'Look north into the Kedron valley – you see that little waterhole down there?' I followed his pointing finger, and there was Gihon, a little spring-head near the creek bed high in its course. 'Now look here.' He spun round and pointed down inside the city walls into the very south corner of the strip of fortified city. This was now to our south-west. 'You see that pool of water? That looks like a cistern, a tank, doesn't it?' I nodded. 'And so it is.' He stopped and looked around as though expecting to find someone spying on us. He lowered his voice, and spoke in a conspiratorial half-whisper. 'But the water in it didn't collect from rain. It came from out there in the valley from the Gihon spring. I've got a conduit cut clean through the hillside. Seventeen hundred feet long that channel is. You can walk through it.' He stopped and looked at my torso, and then at my waist-line, and laughed. 'At any rate, I can. And what a job it was! We had to go round rock faults and we followed natural fissures and all sorts of things. But we got the water through. And the Assyrians won't block that up.'

I thought of our surveyors and their theodolites and dumpy-levels and such paraphernalia, of our tungsten-carbide and diamond-tipped modern rock-drilling equipment. More still I thought of our detonators and gelignite, as I took Hezekiah's hand and poured out congratulations befitting such a magnificent piece of construction enterprise. This is worthy of a place in engineering history right alongside the Eiffel Tower, the atomic-powered submarine and the orbiting astronaut.

Hezekiah! I think you have done it. I think even Sennacherib will stop and think twice before attacking. It will be tough going, for sure, but you should make out. Tell me, have you any other plans? Plans for when he does come?

'Oh yes.' Hezekiah had a quick mind, and it was a delight to discuss it all with him. 'I've got a lot of plans which I did not want to start while Sargon was alive. I think he always thought I was pretty harmless, though he hated me perhaps more intently than he hated anyone else on earth. I'm sure he just didn't fear me at all. But Sennacherib is more bitter, I feel. He won't let me alone like that. He'll come, you may be sure. And I'll be ready, you see.' He stopped again and pointed back over into the Kedron valley. 'I've already sent out orders to block up every irrigation canal in that whole valley, when he moves this way. Why should he benefit from our waterways and cultivation? And I have been quietly building up a huge store of hand weapons suited to our defence needs. And our people are already highly organized and utterly loyal in their worship, and it will be simple to group them under well-chosen commanders to defend the city.'

Yes . . . but what about your surrounding kingdom? You have thirty miles of country, nearly, and a lot of little towns and a few bigger cities. Sennacherib will gobble them up in one bite.

'Oh no, he won't. We may lose a lot of the little places, and the people are warned. Remember, Lachish is very strong, and is a very difficult place to capture. . . . But Jerusalem won't fall. Zion is the city of God, and God will help us in our defence.'

I paused a moment before replying. Hezekiah, tell me just this. What does Isaiah think of all these plans for defence?

I could see that this was the really awkward question. I often have to ask patients awkward questions. And anyone who does this a lot becomes quite expert at sensing the momentary hesitation, the change of voice, that indicates sudden tension.

For there was just that subtle difference in tone, that

indefinable nuance, I felt, as he replied. 'You know what
Isaiah is like, don't you? He is a man of great faith and
insight, but he is not always very practical. He is always upset
when I plan any mutual alliance with another outside power.
And I must admit he has been remarkably right in some of
his statements. He certainly tipped me off when we were
planning a revolt against Sargon in conjunction with Egypt
and the little remaining Philistine power. My, that was close.
Isaiah came parading through the city half naked, warning
us that that was what the Egyptians and Philistines would be
like when Sargon got at them – naked and beaten. And he
was so right. Sargon sent his commander-in-chief and he
simply pulverized their stronghold at Ashdod. I was lucky to
get out of that tangle! You just don't know how close a shave
that was.

'But Isaiah can be very difficult. He seems so unreal
at times. I still think Egypt is a power who could give us a
lot of help; and I'm more than interested in the growth of
Babylon under Merodach Baladan. It was hardly more than
a good-sized desert town a few years ago, and I am sure
Assyria is more worried by them than by anyone but Egypt.
I certainly like to be on-side with Babylon, but Isaiah says I
must make no alliances at all. He insists that God will do
everything we need, and all we have to do is to obey Him
and worship Him as He tells us. It is all very difficult at times
– but I cannot say just how glad I am to have Isaiah around.'

And I leave Hezekiah like that, his very practical mind still
rather disturbed by the problem of his desire to serve God and
heed the advice of Isaiah, and the seemingly prudent matters
concerned with survival and politics.

And I am on my way back to Nineveh, to keep my eye on
Sennacherib. And not only on Sennacherib, but also on his
top brass, for it is from a few of these men, backed by a huge
Assyrian task force, that we will learn some of the most valuable lessons God has to teach us.

Try and see, if we may, how it came about.

Sennacherib was northern governor under his father Sargon, when the latter was killed in battle. Now he obviously
knew the northern frontier very well, and knew just how

safely he could leave it. But he also knew that a new immediate menace lay down south in the rapidly expanding form of
the new Babylon. So that his first campaign took him down
there, where he routed the Babylonians and had himself fêted
and acknowledged in the city.

No fool, this Sennacherib. You can see his brilliant, ruthless thinking, still, twenty-six and a half centuries later. What
a blueprint for a Big Business tycoon today. Just study your
competitors carefully and then pick them off one at a time!

And his next campaign was to his west, where he swung
his great assault troops and skimmed down the Mediterranean
coastline in utter and unanswerable mastery. If you look at
the geography of Palestine you can see the strategy of this.
The rugged inaccessible middle, with the precipitous Jordan
gash plunging into the earth sixteen hundred feet below sea
level, is terrible military going for a highly mobile force like
his. Let them wait. Tomorrow is another day. So he by-passed
Hezekiah and his little state and then pounced in from the
coast. Isaiah was right again! There was an Egyptian army
just there, and Hezekiah was certainly tied up with it in
some hush-hush alliance. And Sennacherib simply wiped
them out!

Then he sat there and began to close his pincer-grip on
Hezekiah and his tiny kingdom. For it is now 701 BC. The
great mailed fist of Assyria is poised to come smashing down
on Hezekiah in his little old Jerusalem!

And what a shrewdly calculated blow this was. It was
simply the despatch of a formal demand for tribute money
from Hezekiah. It had a terse insistence, and was for such a
greedy amount, that the arrogant domination it expressed
could not possibly be missed.

And Hezekiah looked over his defences, checked his water
supply, surveyed the ordnance depot, interviewed the com-
missariat heads – and paid the tribute. I think that is why I
like Hezekiah so much. I feel he is still so simply human that
I can understand him, because I am so very much the same.
It's one thing to think and worship and live in a Zion that is
surrounded by the congregation of friend and brother. But
what a different thing to find yourself in a Zion that is right
in the middle of enemy territory.

You know what it is like, don't you? I know I do. Those

times when a group of you have discussed some of the disturbing modern trends in society, in business, in the profession. It's terrible, you say, and I say, just what is going on today. These things ought to stop. If they are wrong then they are wrong and that's all there is to it . . . and then suddenly one day you find yourself in another group altogether. This time you find that you are in a group where you are in fact alone – frighteningly alone. You'll be in this, won't you, Hercus old chap? . . . Just a certificate off work, Doctor. . . . Don't bother about a receipt. . . . You cannot be a spoilsport. . . . Just this once . . . and you haven't time or chance to think, not with Sennacherib's men right alongside you, have you?

'And Hezekiah gave him all the silver that was found in the house of the LORD, and in the treasuries of the king's house. At that time Hezekiah stripped the gold from the doors of the temple of the LORD, and from the door-posts . . . and gave it to the king of Assyria.'

Yes, Hezekiah, we know how you felt when you suddenly trembled with the touch of an Assyrian gauntlet on your jacket. That awful sick feeling a man always gets when the gold and the silver, the real values of life, are suddenly snapped up in one single bite, to disappear into the belching ravening maw of the Assyrians. Don't bother to tell us about it, Hezekiah. We know how you felt. And don't for pity's sake tell Isaiah, will you? He'd never really understand, would he? He's so isolated, so detached, isn't he? God is so often like that, don't you think, Hezekiah? Of course you often think that is what God is really like, don't you, Hezekiah? I do, too, and because we are just men we all think like that. But, Hezekiah, we are wrong. Quite wrong. Terribly and wonderfully wrong. You wouldn't know this, Hezekiah, but God Himself became man once, so that we should never make this mistake ever again. So that we should never for one moment think that God is uninvolved, that He just watches the game from the side-lines. So that we should for ever remember that He is in the thick of the very scrums; that He is the Captain of the team, not just the referee. And yet we do make the mistake that you made, and because you made this mistake we are going to leave you, for you are really teaching us nothing now; we will go down to Lachish with this precious gold and silver and see whether it gets you free of Sennacherib.

And now down at Lachish, just look at what Sennacherib has been doing. First, army detachments were despatched to pick off fortress after fortress in the Judah empire. Sennacherib's records tell us that he took no less than forty-six walled towns and countless villages; and two hundred thousand, one hundred and fifty prisoners. He himself took over the siege and final capture of Lachish, the main south-west bulwark of Hezekiah's kingdom. And Lachish, the redoubtable fortress of Lachish, began to crumble, to totter, to fall.

And Sennacherib was in fact still tied up at Lachish when Hezekiah's tribute money, that Temple silver and gold, arrived. Sennacherib weighed out the three hundred lovely talents of silver, and the thirty beautiful talents of gold. And the whole royal tent shook as he barked out his orders. 'Silver! Gold! If he has this, then he has plenty more like it still. And I'll have the lot. Assyria will never be fobbed off with anything less!'

And I feel for the first time the strength of the devouring blast which Jesus said that any servant of His would feel: 'The world hates you.'

For now the balloon is really up. I think, as I read the story, that I can see enough into the mind of Sennacherib to follow in his thinking what ensued in actual procedure.

He did not himself set out for Jerusalem. He was still concerned in the big Lachish mopping up, where I am sure his main immediate concern lay. Now let me explain this. Assyria was a great aggressive devouring world power, and the greatest, and in fact only real, threat they knew was from any other such great aggressive world power. And they certainly did not think this sort of danger lay in Hezekiah! In spite of his fortifications and conduit and small arms, not even the wildest imagination can conceive of Hezekiah sallying forth in battle array to tear Nineveh to pieces! In fact I always picture in my mind the strategic likeness between Hezekiah, in the reigns of Sargon and Sennacherib, and Switzerland in the two World Wars. In World War II, particularly, Switzerland stood in a most awkward place, and with great nuisance value, right on the German-Italian axis line; she was well armed and very inaccessible, and altogether more trouble for Hitler and Mussolini to take than to leave. But Switzerland in the role of aggressor in such a war is about as unrealistic as the Swiss Navy!

No. Sennacherib was all eyes for Egypt, then under a dynasty of black-skinned Ethiopians, and it was the black Egyptians he was afraid of. He wasn't going to budge from Lachish until this fortress menace was crushed, and crushed for keeps. But that didn't make him any fonder of Hezekiah. Not a bit of it. If nothing else, it was bad for the morale of the army to know that back behind their line of advance, and in some sense straddling their main line of communication, was an unconquered, unyielding city. And Sennacherib was the bitter, invincible tyrant who could not let that sort of thing pass for long.

So that it was the Tartan, the Rab-saris, and the Rab-shakeh that he selected to make the advance on Jerusalem. And we will be wise to understand as clearly as we can just who these three Assyrian envoys were, because we are going to have quite a lot to do with them.

The Tartan was the commander-in-chief. I like that – I think I should have felt a bit hurt if a mere major-general or rear-admiral had got the job. I need not have been anxious, really. This is in fact all God's work, as we shall come to see, and when God finally moves into a human life He will not be answered by some inconsequential voice from the mere fringe of our human experience. I am glad it was the Tartan. And, oh my, you can be very, very certain of this : you don't land a job like that under Sennacherib by being anything less than a rip-roaring fire-eater of a commander-in-chief. He was *the* Tartan.

The Rab-saris is hard to place. The prefix Rab to his office is rather like Lord or Duke, but whence or of what his nobility nobody (so far as I know) is really certain. Perhaps he was sent to make up the numbers. Perhaps he was due for military re-appointment and Sennacherib took this chance to make the shuffle. I don't know, and I haven't been able to find out; and I'm sure that if I were a John Bunyan I could draw a great spiritual truth from the thought of an Assyrian V.I.P. of whom human history has just nothing to say.

But the Rab-shakeh is different. He is the politician. He is the talker. He can speak the Hebrew lingo, and he is the mouthpiece of the envoy and he is as windy a talker as anyone in the whole of our seven Australian Parliaments – and that is certainly saying something! You won't need to ask the kids to turn the TV down so that you can hear the Rab-shakeh, you don't need to line up a P.A. system for him. He can bellow it all out in any language he chooses. He is just the same as every other Rab-shakeh in all the history of man answering God. He thinks that if he bawls loudly enough and often enough, and generally sounds tough enough and big enough, then God will be cowed and silenced. Rab-shakeh, you are merely a poor puny little human, and the Most High God, the One who, in the ages before all ages, planned and designed every tiniest detail of this very journey on which you are about to set out – He will listen patiently and hear you right through, as you say your miserable piece. But, Rab-shakeh, when God answers you He will not speak your language. He will speak His. And His single word will roll into your tiny Assyrian world, that world which to your thirteen-hundred-and-fifty-gramme brain seems so large and grand, and will carry both you and your world into a confusion such as still makes our ears tingle as we hear it thousands of years later. Rab-shakeh, if you could but see yourself as you really are, a creature standing in the presence of the Creator Himself, you could never possibly go through with it. But even with you, Rab-shakeh, God is Love. He will see to it that the full light of truth never reaches your pride-bemisted eyes to sear them from their sockets. He will allow you to shield behind the pomp and greed and malice of Assyria, until in the obscurity of that spiritual smog you will think that your loud voice and mailed fist must really sound impressive and look menacing to God. No, Rab-shakeh, the real truth you will never know; God will never torture you unnecessarily with that.

And finally, Rab-shakeh, first lord of Assyria, political envoy for the great Sennacherib, this is not true of you only, nor true of you just because you are so important. Of course not. It is certainly true of you, to be sure; but it is just as true of every Tom, Dick and Harry (and John Hercus) in all human history; those who have in their much humbler social

setting done just what you did in your ambassadorial role.
This is what it means to be man, to be unregenerate, natural
man, whose aggressive, proud, greedy humanity has just this
very same attitude as your own in its first reaction to the
declared will of God. Rab-shakeh, I can't say this to you,
because it is too late; but I can say it to myself and all the
other little Rab-shakehs like me : that unless the Rab-shakeh
is willing to die, to die to every last trace of rebellious self-will,
then he will go out with you into the eternal shadow of outer
blackness, where there can only ever remain nothing but that
now lost voice and withered hand shouting and shaking in
the ear and face of God.

The Tartan; the Rab-saris; and the Rab-shakeh. These are
the three who will lead the thundering Assyrian task force as
it moves up the mountain-side to Jerusalem, to throw down
the gauntlet of mighty Assyria in the face of Hezekiah and
his puny little city. These are the men Sennacherib has chosen
to bring Hezekiah to his knees.

Come with me and get a good vantage-spot, then, as we
wait outside the gate of Jerusalem to see this drama played
out.

What time of day, say, will the curtain rise on this historic
stage? I think it was ten-thirty a.m., and I'll tell you why I
think it was then.

Obviously the Tartan would be all for daybreak. 'Snap in
on them at the crack of dawn, and scare the living daylights
out of them before they have got the sleep out of their eyes
and when the night watch is more dead than alive after a full
guard duty.'

'What about dusk, just when they are all getting tired and
hungry and tempers are pretty thin?' I imagine this from the
Rab-saris, because I feel it is unfair for him to come all this
way and not say anything at all.

'Ten-thirty in the morning.' There is no mistaking this
voice. If you have heard one Rab-shakeh you have heard them
all. They all speak the same. Bumptious, arrogant, and above
all else, wordy. Talk, talk, talk. Wear 'em down with words!
'I've got to do the talking, and I'm not going to talk to a few
sleepy half-awake night watchmen, any more than I'm going
to compete with the yelling babies and rattling cups and
saucers just at meal-time. I want the best time of the day, and

that is mid-morning when everyone is out and about and the marketing is on the way and I won't miss out on a single listener. . . . Gentlemen, none of this half-awake audience attention for me. I demand the very pick of the times . . . and I must have a coast-to-coast hook-up . . . front page or nothing at all . . . our research indicates that that is the time when almost every TV set in the country is on, and that's the time we want, and that's the time we'll have. . . .'

Oh yes, you can take a Tartan and a Rab-saris in tow, but the Rab-shakehs of the world never change and I guess it was ten-thirty a.m.

Not that the Tartan and the Rab-saris don't count. Far, far from it. Stand the Rab-shakeh on a soap-box out in the middle of Hyde Park, and he's just the common little agitator who helps while away a dull afternoon out in the sun. But stick a big party label on his back or let him wave the Big Business flag and that's quite a different thing. Oh yes, the Tartan and the Rab-saris are important. All-important.

And they rolled up in front of the tightly shut gates of Jerusalem at the head of a mighty detachment of crack Assyrian troops. This was a task force with a deadly enough voice to demand anybody's attention, without any Rab-shakeh tagging along; but it is the Rab-shakeh who really pipes the tune, even if it is the crack of the Tartan's whip which makes every puppet dance.

'Envoy from Sennacherib, God-King of Assyria, demanding audience with Hezekiah!'

The great barking voice of the Rab-shakeh rolled out in the warm mountain morning air as the envoy party with their attendant guards stamped to a sharp, suddenly silent, halt. All the gold braid and exotic caparisoning of the crack invasion division of the world's number one power lay there in dazzling and awesome might. And looking down, looking out, from every possible battlement, tower, loop-hole and vantage-spot, were the ashen faces of every citizen who could find a viewing-place to which he could cling.

There was that moment of dreadful hush, as the Rab-shakeh's voice stopped. A sudden whispering near the gate — and feet running. Not the half-hearted running of the errand boy, but the swift staccato sprint of the messenger to the king. Hezekiah is commanded to appear! Hurry, Hezekiah, they are at the gate, thousands and thousands of them, and it turns our stomachs over to see them right up at the very gates of Jerusalem. Quickly, Hezekiah; you were a simpleton to have paid out that gold and silver – you'd better race down to the gate and try and talk your way out of this! It really looks bad this time. The army of Assyria outside a city is the most terrible sight that has ever been seen in all human history, and now they are here outside your city. Come on, Hezekiah, see what you can do about it.

And we crane our necks to see Hezekiah come out through the gates. To see, if we can, whether he will come in all his military gold braid; or whether he will come in formal diplomatic morning suit with nice grey striped trousers and topper – I wonder just what line he will take.

There is still hanging over the whole scene the taut, emotional atmosphere of a tension in which it seems to require a profound effort even to breathe. The Assyrian guards riding and standing in motionless mastery, the three envoys looking around in an aloof mixture of curiosity and disdain. And always a sea of faces on the wall, scarcely ever a movement, only ever an occasional half-choked whisper.

It seems ageless. Will Hezekiah never come? Nerves can stand only so much – someone will scream in just another moment – or is it a ghastly nightmare and we will blink our eyes and waken to find it all gone?

And then at last the gate creaks, it opens to let the king come out. And it is not Hezekiah at all!

Hezekiah, let me clasp your hand. If I were a Frenchman, Hezekiah, I'd kiss you on both cheeks. Hezekiah, this is the loveliest bit of bluffing, the most incredible act of gamesmanship that the diplomatic world has ever recorded. Hezekiah is not going to talk to a mere envoy – if Sennacherib is not here to talk to him as king to king, then he is not going to talk to a mere envoy, plenipotentiary and all the rest of it notwithstanding.

No, sir! I'll send out an envoy too, and they can parley it at that level.

Hezekiah, you made a lot of mistakes, and I love you for it, and I thank God for telling us about these so very frankly

and openly, because I make so many myself. But this is sheer
genius. This is where every hat should be tossed high in the
air as every voice is strained to absolute bursting-point in
unrestrainable Hurrahs! But, Hezekiah, I'm afraid there is
not in fact a single hat in the air and there is an even more
deadly silence now broken only by the tramp of the three
miserable white-faced, knocking-at-the-knees men you have
sent as your envoy. And just entirely between ourselves,
Hezekiah, and I'm not wanting to be unkind, for I should
never ever have had the nerve to do it if I had been in your
place – but wasn't it really old Isaiah's idea? Didn't he put
you up to it? Didn't he even quiz you a bit about who should
comprise the envoy? Isaiah was never very happy when
Shebnah held the high office of Chief of State, was he? I'm
sure he's still pretty caustic about allowing him to remain on
even as Chief Secretary. But never mind, Hezekiah, you did
it, and you have given us all a real shot in the arm – let the
man of God stand firm and demand that the enemy come out
cleanly and personally and a fig to this envoy business! It's
asking for trouble, but you have never really been deceived
into thinking you weren't already in all the trouble you could
get into, so a thousand thanks and our warmest congratulations, and we'll dash back to watch your envoy as they meet
the Assyrians. This should be worth watching.

Eliakim, then, the Chief of Hezekiah's household, was the
leader of the trio, if leader is really the right word to use. On
one side, and very happy to be a half-pace further back, was
Shebnah, the Chief of State, and a man Isaiah had once ticked
off very soundly for feathering his own nest at public expense.
I think that just at this very moment in time Shebnah would
quite happily have gone back on the labour market in any
humble, ill-paid job you could suggest, rather than be out
here outside the city gates right under the very noses of the
all-devouring Assyrian army. And of Joah, the Recorder, I
have no knowledge at all, except that he was number three.
But I know I am not guessing when I maintain that he was
never asked to scribble notes of any meeting he so utterly
detested as this one. Eliakim, Shebnah and Joah.

The Rab-shakeh stood there for a moment dumbfounded.

He had demanded audience with the king, small-time, two-bit king that he was, and the fellow had had the nerve to send out a diplomatic envoy, ostensibly with the intention of starting a parley and talking him, the Rab-shakeh, the Grand Slam Mouthpiece of Assyria, into changing his mind or out-bargaining him!

I am sure that for the one and only time in his whole political career the Rab-shakeh was momentarily speechless. This was not just insulting, it was completely and incredibly preposterous.

And then the words began. And once begun they could not be stopped.

'Well, what on earth does this Hezekiah of yours mean? Doesn't he know that he is up against the great King – King Sennacherib of Assyria? Does he know just what that means?'

He paused to let the impact of this tremendous backing sink into the minds of the utterly speechless Jews. They were in no position or frame of mind to say boo to a goose, but even if they had been able to reply, able to explain about Hezekiah and God, the Rab-shakeh would never have understood. The very idea that anyone could possibly place the voice of God above the voice of Sennacherib was as unthinkable to the Rab-shakeh of Assyria then as it is today to the Rab-shakeh of Big Business, Politics, Education, Pharmacology or any other of the man-made gods of any part or time of human history.

'Then how on earth can you explain this absurd, fool-hardy attitude you are taking? Surely to goodness you are not dim-witted enough to think you can simply talk your way out of the trouble you are in. Because that is just the most ridiculous thing in the world. When we fight, we fight! Don't you dare try and just talk us out of that!' And I could almost smell the garlic in his breath as he jutted his swarthy mien right up into the bloodless faces of Eliakim and company. I noticed also a sudden, quick lift of his brows as he flashed a sharp glance up at his gallery, the serried faces of the people of the city, who were peering down in silent terror, hearing every single word he uttered.

'Yes,' he bellowed out, warming up nicely now that he knew he had the full attention of a good house. 'Don't you

let your Hezekiah forget that Assyria means war, and neither
you nor your king will just come and talk us out of it. And
look here, you fools have been trying to make a deal with
Egypt, and don't think for a moment we don't know all
about it. Egypt! Ha! We've got wind of every move as fast
as you have made it. And do you want to know what sort of
help you can expect from Egypt? I'll tell you what Egypt is
like – it's like using a splintered reed for a staff – it will just
pierce the hand of the stupid fellow who leans on it! That's
what we think of Pharaoh of Egypt!' And he dropped his
voice to a dramatic hiss as he almost spat the words now into
the faces of the three men standing opposite him : 'and that's
just what we think of anyone foolish enough to rely on the
King of Egypt!'

He drew back to give this time to sink into the minds of
Hezekiah's three representatives, noisily clearing his throat
before spitting contemptuously on the ground at his feet.

'Now then,' he went on, 'if you think your God will protect
you from Sennacherib, then you are nitwits. Use your heads,
men. This God Yahweh of yours, what about Him? You're
all crazy, and none more crazy than this King Hezekiah of
yours. Didn't Hezekiah tear down this Yahweh's altars and
high places all over your country, and then tell you you've got
to come to Jerusalem to worship? Can you think of anything
more stupid than just that? He tells you you've got to worship
this Yahweh of yours, and then all your altars and incense-
burning censers he ripped up and tossed into the Kedron
valley! If that's all Hezekiah thinks of his God, then how on
earth does it make sense to behave like that?'

And the Rab-shakeh threw back his head and burst into
great guffaws of mirth. And I burst out laughing too, because
I can't think of anything more ludicrous than a Rab-shakeh
making an ignorant attack on faith. Have you ever noticed
that quite often men who are really very great in their own
place in this world's affairs in thinking can still be extra-
ordinarily wide of the mark when it comes to matters of the
faith? I remember some few years back reading a book by
H. G. Wells in which he made some delightfully biting
witticisms at the expense of Christianity; and I was almost
bewildered, as I chuckled, to realize that Wells simply didn't
know what he was writing about. He was writing about

Christendom, or about some organizational elements in church affairs, apparently without any understanding that the personal faith of a man in Christ, his Lord, is something of an entirely different order. How many times did the inimitable G.B.S. seem to reach a point suggesting that perhaps at last he did just know the simplest rudiments of real Christian doctrine; and then miss it altogether? And if this is so clearly the case with Wells and Shaw, who write and think so well, don't be in the least surprised if you see the same thing in even greater display in Big Business or politics. Just being a twentieth-century Rab-shakeh, loud mouth and all, doesn't give a man any insight into the working of the Spirit of God in human affairs.

And the Rab-shakeh threw back his head and laughed and laughed and laughed. And whether it was the break in the spate of verbiage or whether it was something that the funny joke stirred in his mind, I don't know; but the Tartan leaned over and tipped the Rab-shakeh's shoulder and gabbled something in Assyrian. At which the two of them clapped each other on the shoulder and stood there rocking with laughter. The Tartan turned, and choking back his mirth, blurted it to the Rab-saris. Whereupon he let out a wild cackle (I detest the Rab-saris; can you think of anything worse than just being a sort of second-class devil?) and shouted it to the guard, who passed it up and down the Assyrian lines until there was a wild confusion of ribald yelling and baying and catcalling and the like, in which the surrounding valley seemed filled with myriad, echoing, coarse Assyrian voices all raised in a vulgar pandemonium of jeering, mannerless, derisive contempt.

It was all so sudden, so unexpected, so spontaneous, and withal so fiercely passionate, that the three Jewish envoys literally recoiled a half-step as if the blast of Assyrian mirth were a sirocco of searing human hate. They obviously had not heard what had been said, but no-one could possibly mistake the overtone of mocking contempt in the ribaldry of the army detachment. And as I glanced up at the people on the wall I thought I saw the look of sheer panic beginning to appear on quite a few of the faces there.

At last the Rab-shakeh wiped the tears from his mirth-contorted cheeks and held up his hand for silence.

'Listen to this!' he managed to burst out. 'This is the best I've ever heard! I'll tell you what we will do – and the Tartan makes this promise on the authority of King Sennacherib himself. We'll do the decent thing by you. We'll make a bet with you – we'll bet you two thousand horses if you can simply find enough men to ride them. Then we'll have a real, fair dinkum fight! What do you think of that? Isn't that terrific? Come on, you crowd of punks! Can't you find the riders? Can't you make a decent scrap of it? Do you have to rely on the Egyptians for every single fighting man? Where are your horsemen? Where are your charioteers? You just haven't got any, that's how it is, isn't it? Yes! that's how it is, and don't we know it!'

There was not a trace of laughter now. This was the bitter contempt of the big man for the little man – perhaps the most un-funny situation in all nature.

The Rab-shakeh jutted his chin out that little extra bit that in all such men betokens the outburst of some particularly aggressive statement. 'Yes,' he literally hissed, 'and every single junior captain in the whole of our army could take the whole bunch of you on one-handed. And yet you have the nerve to hold out against us. And your tinpot God – what has your Yahweh done about us so far? We are here right slap up against the gates of your miserable little city, and you just can't do a single thing to stop us, and neither can that God of yours!'

And this time he spat deliberately at the feet of Eliakim.

There was an absolute silence now that was perhaps more terrifying than the babel of mocking laughter of a minute before. The whole of the Rab-shakeh's harangue had been in Hebrew, which he spoke fluently, and his had been the only voice which had been heard all this time.

And as he stood there, hands on hips, feet apart, leaning slightly forward to give as it were a physical impetus to his words, the silence was suddenly broken by a quiet, rather choked voice speaking in Aramaic.

'Sirs' – and it was Eliakim, good for him, though goodness knows how he managed to get it out through his quivering lips – 'your servants speak Aramaic, and we should prefer to discuss this in your language. We prefer that the people in our city remain uninformed of our deliberations.'

I could hear, and so could anyone in the whole of that company hear, the hiss of indrawn breath as the Rab-shakeh stamped his stocking-gaitered foot so hard on the pavement that I was surprised that the jewels decorating it were not dislodged.

'You dog!' he bellowed, in a sudden new passion of rage that he had not even hinted at before. 'You miserable cur! Do you think that my great and noble master has sent me here to talk to you and your tin-pot little pip-squeak king alone, and not to all these men clinging on the wall up there?' And as he spoke, cheap little agitator that he was in himself, I had that awesome sensation that I and many millions of men had in the late thirties, when another little paper-hanger agitator assumed the fearsome title of Führer of the Reich. Never, never underestimate the Rab-shakehs!

'You are all to hear it, and hear it you will! You are all of you doomed, and I promise you that before you die we will make you all eat your own dung and drink your own urine!'

There was that stunned silence that only a shocking exclamation like this can produce. The crudity, the obscenity, the sheer evil, seemed to hang over the whole assembly in a choking, sulphurous pall. The Rab-shakeh's face was ablaze with the passion of the moment where a man realizes, almost in surprise, that he has suddenly ripped off every single layer of social veneer, to expose the arrogant malignity that only man can be.

Eliakim stood so still and so ash-white that he looked like a carved wax figure, only the tears collecting in his staring, unblinking eyes showing that he still even lived. And up on the wall the only single sound was the horrible noise of people being physically sick.

There was a pause, as the Rab-shakeh noticed, almost in astonishment, I thought, the shattering impact his outburst had made. It was all spoken in such a loud ringing tone that if it had not been entirely in the Hebrew tongue I am sure the whole Assyrian detachment would have been convulsed with laughter. And isn't it true that on such occasions Assyrians always think it just the most excruciatingly funny thing that they have ever heard? Let us not be a bit embarrassed in admitting that to the man of God it is just too sickening to take.

And now the Rab-shakeh waved it all to one side with a great beckoning sweep of his hand as he changed his tone altogether. 'Listen, you fellows up there on the wall. I'll tell you what is really good for you. The King of Assyria is really your very best friend, if you only knew it. Don't be taken in by Hezekiah and all his guff. What can he do for you? Not a single thing. All he says is "Rely on Yahweh. Yahweh will get us out of this. Yahweh won't let the Assyrians take us." What rot! What a miserable little punk he is! Now listen and I'll tell you what the King of Assyria says. He says, "You be friendly to me and I'll do the decent thing by you."

'Would you like a nice little place all for your own, with a lovely grapevine growing big sweet juicy grapes? How about a big fine fig-tree to give you plenty of soft cool shade in the middle of a scorching day, and the tender purple figs almost popping themselves into your mouth? How about that? Doesn't that sound pretty good? I'll say it does.

'And none of this water down at the cistern at one end of the city – oh, we know all about your conduit and your city water supply, you may be sure. We know everything. But what about a nice deep water tank in your own garden? That's a lot better still, isn't it? Then that's what we will promise you. That's our programme for you. We've got some glorious pastureland, plenty of grain and crops, and wine and vineyards and olives and honey – the things you've always really longed for. All simply laid on. And it's yours if you want us to give it to you. That's what the King of Assyria offers you.'

And as the Rab-shakeh stopped, to dab his brow with a beautiful piece of embroidered silk, I thought of a thousand TV commercials, and nearly burst out laughing as I suddenly pictured in my mind the script-writers snatching up their ball-points and making hurried notes. 'Use that for our soap and cigarette ads . . .' 'Just the plug we need on the gasoline stunt . . .' 'should sell at least another ten million cans . . .' 'try it in the next chocolate series . . .'.

And I wished that Eliakim, or at least even one of the multitude on the wall, had in fact burst out laughing at this Assyrian nonsense. Had they had just a trace of that strong wisdom of Jesus, who on several such occasions had the clear wit to turn the laughter of good common sense against the

churlish wickedness of His attackers, they might even then
have still saved the day.

But no. With another swift gesture (Hitler used to sweep
back his forelock, do you remember?) the Rab-shakeh's voice
snapped into a veritable snarl: 'and don't let that liar, Hezekiah, mislead you. He says, "Yahweh will deliver us." Yes?
Rubbish! Has any God ever yet delivered any nation in the
world from the hand of the King of Assyria? Not one. Not a
single one. Hamath and Arpad, what about them? Where
are the Gods of Sepharvaim and Hena? Or of Ivvah? Those
are the very people we planted in Samaria, don't you remember? And wasn't your God the God of the Samaritans too?
A fat lot of help He was there! Come on, tell us. Which
country can you name, whose God has saved it from Assyria?
Can you name one? Just one? No! You can't, and you know
all too well you can't! Because there isn't one. And now tell
us just why you expect your Yahweh to deliver Jerusalem out
of our hand.'

And without even the slightest sidelong glance at Eliakim,
Shebnah and Joah he stalked back to his waiting canopied
chariot in obvious, open contempt and disdain. A sudden
staccato command from the Tartan, and with the smooth
precision of a Guards brigade the whole Assyrian detachment
swung into a lyric of motion and wheeled up the highway to
the Fuller's Field.

The suddenness of it, the unexpectedness of it, most of all
the almost unnerving smoothness of the whole army movement, left me as open-mouthed and staggered as it did
Eliakim, Shebnah and Joah. The last standard-bearer was
already well past the conduit of the upper pool before any
one of the three gave the first sign of returning life and action.

What a scene! What a day! From their first appearance to
the last sign of the departing Assyrian horsemen was barely
an hour of time. And what tense agonized ages that hour
expanded into in the emotion of the Jewish people. I thought
for a minute or two that Eliakim and Shebnah and Joah
would never move again. But the shock-recovery mechanisms
came good at last, and back into the city they turned, almost
running as they passed the gates to speed to Hezekiah and
tell him all about it.

What a conference! The three envoys, their robes now

torn in ceremonial token of abject humiliation and grief; and the king, hearing it all, tearing his royal cloak too and covering himself with sackcloth as he recognized his own utter defeat and dismay. Can't you feel, even after two and a half thousand years, the pathos and misery of that day? If it had been a matter of blood and sweat and fisticuffs and the like, then perhaps they could have played the man. But this sneering, taunting, boasting braggadocio, backed as it was with the enormous fire-power of Assyria – that was a shame and a disgrace which left them ashen in despair.

Hezekiah sat there with his mind spinning. What could he do? How could he have known how the Assyrians were going to play their hand? That was always their greatest ability – no-one ever knew their next move. This time, the air sulphurous with bitter, cruel blasphemy. Next time, perhaps, the same sky black with arrows. But always only ever one aim : conquest, conquest, conquest!

And God – what about God? Could God do anything? Could He really help? Isaiah had always insisted that Yahweh, the God of Abraham and Isaac and Israel, would stand by them and deliver them. But had God heard what the Rab-shakeh had said? The taunts and sneers and vulgar blasphemies – had God heard these?

'Listen,' he said at last. 'Go and tell Isaiah all about it. Make him realize what a day of distress and rebuke this is. A day of sheer disgrace. Find out what he thinks about it all. Ask him does he think that Yahweh, his God, heard what the Rab-shakeh had to say. Tell him about the mocking sneers of the King of Assyria, ask him does he think the living God will rebuke the blasphemies which Yahweh, Isaiah's God, must have heard. Ask him to pray to God for the few of us who remain out of all the tribes of Israel. I think that is the best thing to do – you go and talk to Isaiah like that.'

I don't think Hezekiah was embarrassed by sending a message like this to Isaiah. He was in too much trouble to be over-concerned now about pride and protocol – mere saving of face. A man in a slit trench is quite unashamed as he prays, 'God, get me out of this.'

I remember a man coming along to church one Sunday morning for the first time since the day he was married twenty-odd years before : the previous Friday his doctor had told him he had cancer and had three months to live. I am quite sure he was not embarrassed. Men as worried as he just can't afford to be embarrassed. (He lived just two months.)

Hezekiah, God didn't send the Assyrians up against your little city just to make things awkward and to tease you. Listen to this, Hezekiah : 'Do not be bewildered by the fiery ordeal that is upon you, as though it were something extra-ordinary.' Hezekiah, you don't know this, as you sit there with great tears quietly coursing down your cheeks, but your life span is nearing an end and it is only a few short years now before you will know, and know in full, that 'it gives you a share in Christ's sufferings, and that is cause for joy; and when his glory is revealed, your joy will be triumphant. If Christ's name is flung in your teeth as an insult, count yourself happy, because then that glorious Spirit which is the Spirit of God is resting upon you.'

Eliakim, Shebnah and Joah crept their gloomful way to the Temple, to the little private office of Isaiah. The great pro-phet was sitting at his desk writing, so intent on his work that it was only a respectfully restrained cough from one of the envoys that drew them to his attention. Haltingly, pain-fully, shamefacedly, the whole story came out.

Isaiah heard them through, interrupting only to add a prompting question or two, never a hint of rebuke or distress in glance or voice. There was a moment of silence before he replied. His words were unhurried and his whole manner quietly serene.

'Thank you for telling me, and would you please take this message back to Hezekiah? Tell him that this is in fact a message from Yahweh, our God. God says that Hezekiah has nothing whatever to be frightened about in any of the Assyrian revilings. God says this : "So far as the King of Assyria is concerned, I will entirely upset all his plans. These Assyrians will be disturbed by some rumours they will hear; and ultimately Sennacherib will go back to his own country and in fact he will finally be assassinated in Nineveh itself." That is God's message. Tell Hezekiah to remember that his true refuge is in God. Good afternoon, my friends.'

The old prophet bowed gravely and picked up his pen again.

Just like that. As simple and as complacent as that. Much as if he were concluding the instruction for the running of some trifling piece of temple ceremonial. No blood pressure and adrenalin and tension at all. Just the Assyrian army. Just Sennacherib being re-routed to his final destruction by murder. And Isaiah went back to his writing, altogether too absorbed in awe at the truth he was learning about God to be chilled by any fear of mere Assyrians.

Isaiah was right again. God tangled up the Assyrian wires so simply that it sounds almost childish. But men, wicked men, are so little, so puny, when squirming in the strong hand of God, that history is just full of such examples of this.

It seems that the Rab-shakeh and company were hardly round the first corner from the city before a rumour reached him that Sennacherib was leaving Lachish. There was no walkie-talkie and short-wave intercom equipment then. Not even a morse heliograph. A man on a horse was the fastest communication in existence. So the Rab-shakeh decided he had better go back to Lachish and find out just how the war was really getting along.

Now make no mistake, I admit I'm guessing here again, but on pretty reasonable grounds. I guess the Rab-shakeh was secretly very glad of the alibi. Jerusalem was only a tiny little city, true enough. But it was a very difficult little fortress to attack, and the lines of communication to an assailing or besieging force were a military nightmare. And I'm also quite sure that the Rab-shakeh had such a one-hundred-per-cent contempt for the whole place that he just couldn't work up enough steam to order a full-scale attack. He heard the rumour and moved accordingly. Back to Lachish he raced, to find that he had been quite right after all – Sennacherib had planned to move to Libnah.

And Sennacherib in his turn was also in something of a dilemma, for army intelligence had reported that Tirhakah, the new black Pharaoh of Egypt, was preparing for war with Assyria. Sennacherib was certainly not finding the time dull and the days leaden-footed.

And Hezekiah, up in the hills to the north-east, what of him now? Will Assyria just pass him over? Will they just forget all about him? Oh no! Assyria was never like that then any more than it is now. They may be stalling for time, but it is only because they like to move in their own time.

Sennacherib barked out an order and an office secretary was called in. 'Take this down.' The secretary poised his writing point over the parchment.[1] 'The Rab-shakeh will dictate it to you. Write it up as an official document and bring it to me for my personal seal. Rab-shakeh, outline the essential gist of your speech at Jerusalem. Make it pretty strong, and don't drop a hint about our being tied up here. Make it sound as though we are ready to spring. I'll leave it to you.'

And out he went, to superintend the troop positions, to give his personal directions concerning the mopping up of Lachish, *etc., etc., etc.* While the Rab-shakeh slowly and carefully dictated the text of an official document ridiculing Hezekiah, his God, his faith, his stand; and demanding his immediate surrender.

'He wrote letters to cast contempt on the LORD the God of Israel and to speak against him.'

As you read that statement in the Old Testament the print on the page is nice and even as befits the publication of a modern major printed work; but can't you still picture in your mind the slight tremor in the hand of the old Chronicler as he wrote about it that first time, thousands of years ago? Can't you imagine his astonishment and concern as the messengers of Sennacherib arrived with the king's document at the city gates? Can't you hear him muttering in his long beard as he wrote 'And they spoke of the God of Jerusalem as they spoke of the gods of the peoples of the earth, which are the work of men's hands'?

This time Hezekiah himself met the messengers. This is a much more humble, much more spiritually great Hezekiah than the one of a few hours ago. Read, if you please, of how this time Hezekiah himself took the message to God. Pray, if you have such a heart, the prayer that came from Hezekiah's own heart, as he humbly admitted to God that the vaunted might and boasted strength of Assyria are indeed

---

[1] Chosen for the sake of narrative simplicity. It might have been a wax-covered wooden writing-board or even a papyrus scroll.

real might and terrible strength as seen by the king. But join, if you will, in his confidence that now he is surely in the will of God, and in that measureless strength 'all the kingdoms of the earth may know that thou, O LORD, art God alone'.

I feel I am beginning to breathe more freely, and the rather tight clammy feeling I have had ever since the death of Sargon is beginning to lift, as I see the stature of this new, this really great, Hezekiah.

But I must not stop and ponder on Hezekiah, with the work of grace going on in him as it has been in every saint in all history. It is the Assyrians I am still studying, and I must not let Hezekiah make me forget that. Hezekiah was still prostrate before God, lost in the wonder of adoration and humility that all such praying involves, as I tiptoed out of the room and raced through the Temple court to find Isaiah.

I found Isaiah at his desk, writing, still writing. He rose as I entered, courteous, composed as always, not for a flickering moment indicating the annoyance he must have felt at this unannounced intrusion.

'Sir,' I burst out, 'I have just left Hezekiah and he is praying. He has a message from Sennacherib – it is really just the same as the loud-mouthed speech the Rab-shakeh made to Eliakim and Shebnah and Joah; but Hezekiah is not in the terrible flap he was in that time. He is praying now, and it really sounds as though he expects God to repel the Assyrians. What do you think, Isaiah? What would you tell Hezekiah?'

They tell me Isaiah was really of royal blood, but that is not the thing about him which always held me. It was his eyes. He describes his prophecies as 'the vision . . . which he saw' and I could never read them without feeling myself under the piercing spiritual scrutiny of the only Jew in all Old Testament history who dared say 'my eyes have seen the King, the LORD of hosts'. I feel the same about St. John, and a bit the same about Thomas à Kempis. But I felt it never more keenly as I stood there in the old prophet's study.

'Would you like to take a message back to Hezekiah?'

I had no need to answer. A man who can see the great spiritual truth that Isaiah saw can answer a simple question like that for himself.

'Then you go and tell Hezekiah that the LORD, the God of
Israel, has heard his prayers about Sennacherib, King of
Assyria.'

There was something about the way he said those four
words 'Sennacherib, King of Assyria', there was an intensity
in it, that almost made me jump. Indeed, I felt a sudden
strong feeling of pity for Sennacherib – I felt I should just
hate to be the man whose name Isaiah spoke in that way.

There was quite a pause. I didn't have anything to say, and
Isaiah seemed reluctant to say anything further. But I could
see easily enough that this was not his whole message. He
was intensely moved by some deep feeling, and I felt myself
to be playing no direct part in it at all. He turned, and sat
down at his desk again; then picked up a parchment. He
stared at it a full minute, a minute that seemed an eternity,
before he brought himself to speak. He was reading, now,
from the parchment:

    ' "She despises you, she scorns you – " '

Can I ever describe in words the intensity of emotion in those
mere half-dozen words? Or the depth of the caress as he
added

    ' "the virgin daughter of Zion;" '

I swallowed a big lump that formed in my throat as into a
flashing second of time was kaleidoscoped that whole fateful
morning with the Rab-shakeh outside the little city walls;
and I swear there was a tear in Isaiah's eye as he repeated the
theme:

    ' "she wags her head behind you –
        the daughter of Jerusalem." '

Isaiah was still sitting at his desk. His voice had dropped
to a mere whisper, and his gaze had also dropped as if he
were shielding his eyes from some most unwelcome sight.

But now he drew himself up to his feet, standing ever so
straight, old and hoar-headed though he was, and his voice
was suddenly the clear clarion call of the ramshorn.

    ' "Whom have you mocked and reviled?
        Against whom have you raised your voice
        and haughtily lifted your eyes?" '

I recoiled for an instant before I realized that he wasn't even seeing me at all. He was seeing the Rab-shakeh and the Tartan and the Rab-saris and Sennacherib and all the Assyrians in human history and now there was the sharp snap of the whiplash as he himself answered:

> ' "Against the Holy One of Israel!
> By your servants you have mocked the Lord,
>   and you have said, With my many chariots
> I have gone up the heights of the mountains,
>   to the far recesses of Lebanon;
> I felled its tallest cedars,
>   its choicest cypresses;
> I came to its remotest height,
>   its densest forest.
> I dug wells
>   and drank waters,
> and I dried up with the sole of my foot
>   all the streams of Egypt." '

He had reached the end of the writing on the parchment in his hand and as he looked up at me the sudden pause gave me that moment for some lost memory to spring to conscious notice. It was something I had heard, but I had forgotten I had heard it until his words reminded me.

Isaiah. Wait. I've heard that before. I'm sure I have. That bit about 'the tallest cedars, choicest cypresses'. That line about 'I dried up with the sole of my foot all the streams of Egypt'. I've heard that just recently. Where was it? Yes! Isaiah, I remember – that was one of the Assyrian battle songs. They were singing it as they marched up to Jerusalem that morning. It's out of their army song-book, isn't it?

The prophet nodded.

I now babbled on. Sir, I've heard quite a lot of songs just like that. You wouldn't know this one, but I grew up on it – 'Rule Britannia'. That was very popular and we stuck out our chests ever so far as we sang it. And another like it – we used it for our recruiting campaigns for two world wars – 'Land of Hope and Glory!' There was another one, also just as popular, but a wee bit nostalgic, I thought – 'There'll always be an England'. And right round here on the other side of the world, we have a rather tin-pot thing called

'Advance Australia Fair'. We have scored it up for full orchestra and hope it sounds impressive enough.

Isaiah stood quite still, looking directly at me; and whether it was his gaze, or whether it was because I had for the first time stopped to think just what these arrogant songs were really pretending, I don't know. But thinking of them I suddenly felt rather like a foolish child who climbs up on some dangerously high ledge and then boasts, 'Daddy, I'm bigger than you.'

He waited patiently and courteously for me to go on. Isaiah has always this strongly disciplined patience that is so disconcertingly God-like.

I now faltered: Sir, there are lots and lots of songs like that. There was a very popular one in Germany, 'Deutschland Über Alles'; and across the Atlantic they sing 'The Star-Spangled Banner'.

My head was somewhat awhirl, as I stopped now to ask him directly: Sir, we all think we did it on our own. We think we built our own greatness. The Assyrians sing 'with my many chariots', and of course that is really what we all claim for ourselves. But did God know about it? Does He have any real say in what goes on in human affairs? These bitterly aggressive people like the Assyrians – what has God got to say about their rise to power?

Isaiah handed me the parchment from which he had been reading, and then walked quietly over to his desk. He picked up another scroll.

'Take this to Hezekiah,' he said, handing it also to me. 'This is God's answer to his prayer. Read it, if you like.'

I took the manuscript roll and began to read:

'Have you not heard
    that I determined it long ago?
I planned from days of old
    what now I bring to pass,
that you should make fortified cities
    crash into heaps of ruins,
while their inhabitants, shorn of strength,
    are dismayed and confounded,
and have become like plants of the field,
    and like tender grass,

like grass on the housetops,
    blighted before it is grown.'

I paused to turn the roll and as I did so there flashed into my mind those most horrifying scenes of Assyrian conquest. Men impaled on stakes, men being agonizingly skinned alive, men being dragged to their hideous death by hooks through their noses and bits rammed into their broken mouths.

'I know your sitting down
    and your going out and coming in,
    and your raging against me.
Because you have raged against me
    and your arrogance has come to my ears,
I will put my hook in your nose
    and my bit in your mouth,
And I will turn you back on the way
    by which you came.'

I had been reading it aloud. As I came to the end of the message I looked up straight into the eyes of the old prophet. And I swear there was in his gaze an expression of exultation that only heaven or hell can impart to man – and hell certainly had no part in Isaiah!

'Here,' he said quickly. 'Take this too. This is the covenant sign by which Hezekiah can be certain of the truth of this prophecy.'

He handed me still another parchment. As I glanced at it I could see reference to crops and season's growth and so on – obviously in an idiom and image that would mean a lot more to a Jewish king than ever it would to an Australian medico.

Isaiah sensed my incompetence as he now spoke very directly to me. 'Would you like to know what Yahweh says about the King of Assyria? Listen. He will not come to this city. He will not shoot a single arrow into it. There won't even be a single Assyrian shield outside the city and no Assyrian earthworks will ever be heaped against our wall. He will *not* come to this city. He will go back to his own country along the same route by which he came out.'

The prophet's voice had risen through this impassioned staccato message until it now seemed to thunder to the very peaks of the far-off hills. Until it seemed that it must be

almost from heaven itself that I heard the words : 'God will
defend this city, for His own sake !' – the prophet moved over
and took me by the arm as he led me to the door, adding, in
sudden quiet warmth, 'and for the sake of His servant David.'

Surely, I said to myself, that is the most wonderful bene-
diction that any departing worshipper has ever been privi-
leged to hear : 'for the sake of His servant David.'

I could not get away from it. Over and over and over again
these words kept running through my mind. 'For the sake of
His servant David !'

It was 'for the sake of His servant David !' This was the
thing that had me in its grip. 'God will defend this city, for
His own sake.' Yes, I could understand that easily enough.
I had already begun to experience a feeling that was half awe,
half terror, as I thought of Sennacherib up against God. How
right, how altogether right, for God to defend the city, when
a mere man had pitted his strength, however Assyrian that
strength might be, against God. Surely this is now a city God
must defend. His honour, in one sense His very Being, is at
stake. Ah, yes. I could understand that. And the more I could
understand that, the more I felt a turmoil of heart for Sennacherib. I could understand now that sudden frightening sense
of utter and final dismissal in the voice of Isaiah as he had
referred to Hezekiah's prayers about 'Sennacherib, King of
Assyria'. It was a gesture of spirit akin to the gesture of hand
with which one might brush away a speck of dust that had
settled on a royal robe.

But 'for the sake of His servant David'. Just what of that?

It was now nearly sunset, and these words were still racing
through my mind, as indeed they had been every moment
since I had heard them in the Temple that morning.

Here I was, again standing on the city wall, this time looking down over the city gate where the Rab-shakeh had hurled
his abuse and contempt for God into the face of Hezekiah's
envoys, only a few short hours before. But what a difference
those few hours had made. I remembered, in every vivid
detail, the dramatic impact of that morning – an impact
which had left me nearly as stunned as the puny little people
against whom it had been hurled.

C

But now, how different. Now I had heard another voice, and this time it was the answering voice of God. This voice had claimed all knowledge, all mastery, all power. 'Have you not heard that I determined it long ago? I planned from days of old what now I bring to pass. . . .' 'God will defend the city, for His own sake!'

Rab-shakeh, I wanted now to cry out. Don't do it. You are not big enough, not strong enough – only foolish enough. Rab-shakeh, a mere hundred volts will sear your flesh to the bone, yet you are setting yourself to tackle all the multi-million volts in existence! Can you be so utterly foolish as to try to clench your fist on a galaxy of heavenly cyclotrons? But, Rab-shakeh, your life need not end like this. God is the Great Architect. He is the Builder, not the demolisher. And you, Rab-shakeh, you are Assyrian enough not to make the sloppy, sentimental mistake so many people make in my own time, in thinking that God will abandon His building just because some miserable little man like you (or me) is standing in His way. No, sir. Light is not to be limited and confined by darkness.

But may I tell you this also, sir? God is not *against* men, He is altogether *for* men. This may sound utterly fantastic to you, but the God who built and operates this whole universe will Himself one day become a man. He is so greatly concerned for man. That is what God is really like. He says He 'will defend this city' not just for His own sake, but for the sake of His servant David. He is so much concerned for that one man, a man of His own choosing, that He will utterly crush every tiny detail in human experience which may stand in the way of that man's destiny. Love is like that. Love is always like that. For the man of God's will, not even life or death itself will be allowed to separate him from love. Oh no! A thousand times no, Rab-shakeh! God is not against men. It is for the sake of His servant David that He will defend this city! God is utterly for man, and this only ever seems to be a paradox because of our human reluctance to allow God to show His love in our own lives.

The evening had set in; the moon was rising, full and clear. The cool chill of the night air on my cheek matched the chill in my heart as I thought of the Rab-shakeh and God. I remembered the same chill in the heart of Jesus as He had looked on this very same city seven hundred years later, in His tragic lament at their equal rebellion against God.

Could I not warn the Rab-shakeh? Could I perhaps even gain audience with the great Sennacherib, and make him heed his desperate danger? Surely some, at least, of the common troops in the Assyrian lines would be glad to call off this madness. Surely any reasonable man would rejoice in the knowledge that God is so much on the side of His servant David! This is the greatest news man has ever heard. And they must be told this in the Assyrian camp. Can I, then, be the messenger?

I had already given the parchments to Hezekiah, and told him all that I had learned from Isaiah. And had I not come to Hezekiah once before, to warn him about the death of Sargon? Why not now do the same for the Assyrians, and warn them of the fate that is worse than death if they withstand the claim of God? Why not?

Down the Lachish road, into the night, through the night, to the vast Assyrian encampment I sped, driven by fear and dread, spurred on by the elation of hope.

What a night that was! The fear and the dread of each moment dragged me down to hell itself, as I thought of men against God. Yet the hope and elation of each moment set my heart soaring into the highest heights of heaven, as I thought of God *for* His servant. It was only a few short minutes' distance as the helicopter flies, only a few seconds in a super jet; but each turn of the winding road, each climb and descent of the mountainous track, seemed only ever to be leading to another just like the last.

Dawn was breaking as I was still on the road, but now I was nearing the besieging Lachish army. And in the grey shadows of early day I could see that the camp was astir. Yet even from the distance and in the half-night, it was clearly no ordinary army reveille. The sluggish reluctance of every waking in every such camp was missing in this one. There was activity, but it was much too active. And there was oddly little of it.

Tired and all as I was, it was at full pelt that I now came dashing down, my heart pounding as I half guessed the answer even before I knew it.

What had happened? I do not know. No-one knows. The

Assyrians never let out the secret, as they wrote up the official history of this campaign. That official history is now in the British Museum; but no tiny hint of this night's tragedy and its terror was scribed in their cuneiform text. That was a night such as has never been known in this world before or since. That was a night of battle between the vaunted might of the most bitter, brutal, blood-drenched army in human history, and God. That night 'God defended the city for His own sake, and for the sake of His servant David'. Of that night the Assyrians tell us not a single word. And of that night's encounter God has no need to tell us more than to insist that He won as He must always win. God is love; and love does not gloat in victory any more than it dare be too sentimental to join battle.

If you read the story in the Old Testament, the laconic Hebrew literary style is to our twentieth-century western minds tantalizingly unimaginative. But that is because we have been conditioned to a literary style where in fact all the imagination is supplied by the writer, and the reader can skim along in almost total detachment, in the escapism that is the main stock-in-trade of mass modern literature.

But God is not like that. God is the one single Author of all being, and His voice in the affairs of men will always cause men to give heed, to consider, to make answer. This is always His call to men to stop their escape: to stand up before Him, puny creatures and all that they are, and answer Him face to face. No wonder men love TV and racing and sport and music and such means of escaping the terrible responsibility of answering the voice of God as He speaks in the affairs of life. And no wonder the Assyrians have shut their lips and guarded for ever the bitter story of that night when they were made to hear God speak.

Isaiah, speaking of that night, reports merely that 'the messenger of the LORD went forth, and slew a hundred and eighty-five thousand in the camp of the Assyrians; and when men arose early in the morning, behold, these were all dead bodies'.

When I was a youngster, and the sermons in church were too long for my short patience, I would often thumb through the stories of the kings in the Old Testament and this particular paragraph in the text would nearly make me chuckle

out loud. For in my mother's Authorized Version I would
read the near absurdity: 'and when they arose early in the
morning, behold, they were all dead corpses.' I knew that of
course this couldn't mean what it said, but I used to think
then how very funny it must have been to have been there.
To see all these men get up wearily in the morning, rubbing
the sleep out of their eyes, and then suddenly find out that
they were all dead corpses! And the whimsy of it would
shorten the longest sermon in a most satisfying manner.

And then in early high school I was introduced to Stevenson
with his *Kidnapped* and his *Treasure Island* which I would
happily bracket with the only thing of Byron's which really
appealed to me: 'The Assyrian came down like a wolf on the
fold, and his cohorts were gleaming in purple and gold'; and
I would smack my boyish lips at the tang of adventure and
death.

But many added years and a life now always lived in the
shadow of suffering in some form or another has dried up
that boyish chuckle and soured that adolescent lip-smacking
utterly and for ever. Even if I were able to forget that about
one-fifth of all of my days on earth so far have been lived while
my country was at war, I am still so much involved in the
fears and the tears of my fellow men that I can never again
find death amusing or exciting.

Oh no. And neither does God. Stepping in and, in His
sovereign will, writing *finis* to the account of 185,000 lives is
not just His way of getting a laugh or of keeping the game
interesting. A thousand times, no! When St. Paul reminds
us that 'the created universe . . . was made the victim of
frustration, not by its own choice, but because of him who
made it so', it is not because God has some rather distorted
sense of humour – what blasphemous nonsense – it is 'because
the universe itself is to be freed from the shackles of mortality
and enter upon the liberty and splendour of the children of
God'.

When the writer of the Epistle to the Hebrews says so
bluntly 'it is the lot of men to die once', it is not because God
is enjoying it all with the detached interest of a grand-stand
spectator. Far, far from it. This writer reminds us that this is
a lot that God Himself assumes. Listen: 'Christ was offered
once to bear the burden of men's sins, and will appear a

second time, sin done away, to bring salvation to those who are watching for him.'

What a tremendous concept! 'God will defend the city for His own sake', for the Son of God is the Son of man. It is His own city as in the fullest truth it is His own world and He will defend the city for the sake of His servant David, for, wonder of all conceivable wonders, David is now son of God too!

That is how much concerned God was when those 185,000 Assyrians died that night. That is why Isaiah writes so simply, 'the angel of the LORD went forth, and slew a hundred and eighty-five thousand in the camp of the Assyrians.' It is only to men that this is a matter for excitement and specula-tion. It is to God the unfolding of a design of which every tiny detail was planned. As Isaiah says equally simply, 'Have you not heard that I determined it long ago? I planned from days of old what now I bring to pass.'

And you don't need to have the imagination of a Jules Verne or a Hans Andersen to picture the turmoil and the excitement and the dismay in the Assyrian camp that morn-ing! As the ghastly toll of the dead was mounting and ever mounting. As from tent after tent, company after company, division after division, a seemingly endless stream of bodies was slowly collected. As the first black scowl of annoyance on the face of Sennacherib, when he heard of the initial few deaths, became the cold, set stare of brittle rebellion by the time the whole truth was known. Yes, a day of the bleakest excitement in all human history.

'But what was it?' you ask. 'Herodotus said it was field mice. He said they chewed up the bow-strings and the leather shield straps, and when the men went into action they were hopelessly unarmed. Do you think that is what actually happened?'

That's not a bad guess really. But it's not the only one.

'Probably plague', I hear someone reply. 'Sure to be plenty of rats about in a long siege like that. And plague took a terrific toll in London in 1665.' 'Might be pneumonic flu,' says someone else. 'Think of what happened in 1919 to 1920. Fifteen million, altogether.' 'Malignant tertian malaria is my suggestion.' This is a very thoughtful voice indeed. 'The sudden troop movement from the heavily infested plains into the cold mountain night air can trigger off a deadly rigor in just this way. Remember, that was a big detachment that was sent up to Jerusalem, into high hill country.'

But does it matter? If you stop and think carefully is this the thing that is most worth knowing? If God had told us that He had destroyed the Assyrian campaign by a malarial parasite, would that make men ponder their ways and seek to know the mind of God? Of course not. It would merely remind them to spray the locality with DDT and put the troops on Chloroquin. When the Serbian army was virtually wiped out by typhus in World War I, did the Germans or the British stop and ask what was the lesson God was teaching in this horrible infestation? You know as well as I know that they didn't. They simply recognized it as an object lesson in the wisdom of preventive medicine, and insisted on better bathing hygiene among the troops and encouraged the chemists to produce a really effective anti-louse chemical; and they are well pleased to relate that in World War II this loss was not repeated.

And let me admit very readily that I find this just as tantalizing as you do. Don't you sometimes almost gnash your teeth? If only God had written a Complete Encyclopaedia of General Knowledge instead of writing the Bible! How much more valuable it would really be! Just think of the laborious scientific probing and research it would save! What a speed-up it would give to all our plans for improvement and progress and advance in world betterment! I have thought like that, as any human may well think like that, conscious of the limitations of a mind which has merely some thirteen hundred and fifty grammes of brain as its working machinery. And even as I do think like that I am humbled and stop dead in my thoughts, as I remember that knowledge doesn't save a man. Even knowledge of the Bible won't save a man. It is faith, that unique obedience in a man–God relationship that is called faith, that saves.

And it is in this turmoil of emotion and thought that I remember the Rab-shakeh again. Let me get to him and ask him all about it. He will talk all right. He'll answer my questions; I am wondering very much as to whether he has answered God's questions too. I'll find the Rab-shakeh again.

It is no trouble. You can pick out his tent a mile off. All

decked out in trimmings and fancy bits, there it is on a nice southerly slope in the most lavish of all possible settings. It is in a lovely little grove of almond- and fig-trees which the Assyrians have taken over and turned into officers' quarters for their very top brass. But I barely spare a glance at all this glamour as I rush to the tent door. And even as I put my hand to the flap, a sudden fear grips me – is he here? Is he, too, perhaps . . . ?

Yes. He is here. In a sumptuously appointed inner chamber I find him. There he is, surrounded by a group of busy attendants – and I turn away feeling just a little sick – doctor and all that I am. For these attendants are not valets, not doctors – but embalmers.

And everywhere I now turned it was the same. The Rab-saris, grade two devil and all that he was, how I should have wished to meet him again, even for a moment. But he had gone too. And the Tartan. And so many, many others.

The old Hebrew chronicler, writing up this spiritual record of the Jewish people, reports it even more simply than does Isaiah. He tells us that 'the LORD sent an angel, who cut off all the mighty warriors and commanders and officers in the camp of the king of Assyria. So he returned with shame of face to his own land.'

That is all. No high-power reporting. No TV interviews, no on-the-spot photographs, none of the big headline write-up of our day. And most important of all, no gloating.

I went away a little and sat down in the shade of an olive grove as the heat of the day began to beat down on the stricken army. The campaign was, of course, at an end. Sennacherib could afford to lose 185,000 men and still soldier on. But not with all his high-ranking officers gone. Lachish had fallen, as indeed had every other fortress in Judah except for Jerusalem; and now even the bitter Sennacherib had to postpone his assault on Hezekiah as he gave the evacuation order and the remainder of his army set foot on the return road to Nineveh.

I had no inclination to speak to Sennacherib. It is always very difficult to speak other than technically to men like that. These are men who have clearly made up their minds that their own plan, their own intention, is the only one. To challenge them is only ever to enrage them. It takes the greatness of a Moses to go and speak to Pharaoh. And I have nothing of the greatness of a Moses to equip me to speak to a king whose heart was as hardened as Sennacherib's. I just waited and waited, until at last all the movement orders were drawn up and the return was under way.

No. I didn't want to talk to Sennacherib. I think I could even have guessed what he would in fact say. For he does actually tell us about his successful campaign and the forty-six walled towns he destroyed. He tells us of the 200,150 prisoners and all the spoil he took in Judah. He tells us about how he himself took part in the actual attack on Lachish. And he has his artists and sculptors make a bas-relief for his palace walls, showing the capture and sacking of Lachish.

But about Hezekiah and the city which God defended for His own sake and for the sake of His servant David – I had half hoped that he might have kept just the tiniest possible element of humility, just that hint of modesty, that would make him omit any reference to it at all. It would be asking far too much to hope that he would admit defeat. He did, of course, admit it in fact. But to write it in his official army records, that is asking the impossible! But I had still hoped that he might have had enough grace simply to shut up and say nothing at all about it.

But no. You would never believe this unless you really understood the heart of Assyria – but in his official history of this campaign Sennacherib said, concerning Hezekiah, 'I shut him up like a caged bird in his royal city, Jerusalem.'

Surely, as you read this, you want to drop your gaze and hide the blush on your cheek, as you reflect on such arrogance! Such pride as to claim to be restraining the city which God is defending! But then I remember that this is always Assyria, in all ages. 'I shut him up like a caged bird in his royal city.' Hezekiah, the God you serve, the Master you are obeying, will one day walk those very streets you are treading now. And the Assyria of His time will talk the same blasphemous nonsense that is ever rebel man's answer to God – 'Crucify Him! Crucify Him! Shut Him up for ever in a sealed tomb.'

God didn't write that boastful claim of Sennacherib in His Word. The archaeologists have found Sennacherib's campaign history, and there it is inscribed for all to learn and stand aghast. God simply reports, through His ancient record, 'Sennacherib king of Assyria departed, and went home, and dwelt at Nineveh. And as he was worshipping in the house of Nisroch his god, Adrammelech and Sharezer, his sons, slew him with the sword.' That is all God needs to tell us. He has no need to keep writing the tale of man's ever-repeated vanity and pride. God recorded that for us in the third chapter of Genesis, and what is true of Adam is true of every unregenerate son of Adam ever since – and of course it is just as true of Sennacherib, King of All Assyria notwithstanding.

And so the tale is told. I am still down at Lachish, if that is what you can call the burnt-out heap of rubble that was once Lachish. Everywhere I look I see destruction and death. And as I think again of the rich glory of Nineveh and Nimrud, I remember the price of 'greatness'. I think I can understand just a little bit more clearly why Jesus said so simply, 'Do not store up for yourselves treasure on earth. . . . Set your mind on God's kingdom and his justice before everything else.'

It is hard to express the elation at seeing God deliver the city. And it is hard to bear the feeling of misery as I walk past the huge graves in which so many Assyrians were massburied. I am on my way now, and hardly knowing where I am going. But I do know that I want to be out of here. I never want to see Lachish again. And I most certainly never want to see Nineveh or Sennacherib again.

Yet a half-formed question is in my mind, and has been for days and days. So much has been happening that I haven't previously stopped to let it come to clear conscious notice; but now it flashes into my mind, clearly, strongly – it is the question I must put to Isaiah. And I now recognize that it is a question I wanted to ask the very first moment I saw him; but it was then swept away in the turmoil and dread of the Rab-shakeh's visit.

For now it is something I must know. Tired I may be, but not too tired to tread the winding mountain road back to Jerusalem. Back to the Temple, to ask Isaiah a last single question. To find, if I may, the last secret in the story of the man of God and the Assyrians.

There is this time none of the haste or urgency with which

I raced down this road before. There is much on my mind and I am glad of the chance to think.

It is a long trudge, and it is steeply uphill. Lachish is nearly down on the coastal plain, and Jerusalem is right on a mountain ridge. I have plenty of time to think; and some of the thoughts seem to be more disturbing as they become more clear. For the clearest single view of Assyria that I can frame in my mind is of men forever fighting. War, conquest, capture, oppression, death. This is the picture; and every other glimpse is a superimposed image on this constant background. And I close my eyes to the scene of centuries gone, and now look up into the bright blue sky of twentieth-century Sydney. For there, any day now, almost every day soon, may be seen man in orbit, surely the most incredible of all military developments in the ghastly picture of the history of man versus man. If man can find no easy way of attacking his God, then let him find every possible way of attacking the creature most like God – his neighbour.

Yes, this is Assyria today. The siege apparatus, the engines of assault, the captives led in chains – these were the tools by which Assyria shaped her greatness in days of long ago. And what puny tools these were, when compared with Assyria of today. Our orbiting satellites, our intercontinental ballistic missiles, our endless stockpiled atomic war-heads, our nuclear-powered submarines – these and all the multi-billion dollar skill and talent and mind poured into the great maw of 'defence' give today's Assyria a mien of such fearsome evil that we sneer down our noses at poor little Sennacherib and his hard-toiling troops.

Sennacherib, a whole campaign and some two hundred thousand, one hundred and fifty prisoners to show. Kid's stuff! Why, we have hundreds of pre-set underground missiles ready to go at any one moment in time – and each one of them will kill more in a single burst than you killed in your whole campaign. And lots of them will bag ten times that number at least! Sennacherib, you make us laugh! Your dad took over three years to conclude the capture of tiny little Samaria, and even then had to chop down forests of trees to burn the place out because he couldn't break Ahab's walls! And one well-placed shot today would not just knock those walls down – it would 'vaporize' the whole city into actual nothingness! And, Sennacherib, you remember how you used to get a lot of fun watching your victims skinned alive strip by strip; or wriggling to tortured death on spears and spikes? But just think of the fun we will have as we intend to see our victims slowly rotting away with the necrotic burns of radiation; as we may well hope to see the offspring of such victims enter life with all manner of amusing deformities from genetic damage by radioactivity. Sennacherib, you have to hand it to us – we have a far better Assyria than ever you even imagined!

And, Sennacherib, I said I didn't want to talk to you ever again. But if I am going to talk about war at all it is very hard today to find the real king. With you it is easy. There you are, all pomp and glitter, up on the highest public gallery in your mighty palace, for all your world to see. But we have only Rab-shakehs up there today. You know, those brass-mouthed insincere loud-speakers whom we vote into position in job-lots without really knowing the slightest personal detail about any of them. We talk of 'parties' and pretend that there is some intrinsic difference between a Liberal Rab-shakeh and a Republican Rab-shakeh. We admit, if you press us very hard, but only most reluctantly indeed, that a Labour Rab-shakeh and a Conservative Rab-shakeh and a Democrat Rab-shakeh are really identical birds simply with plumage lacquered different gaudy hues.

That's why I have to talk to you, Sennacherib. The real king in our world today is the depersonalized monarch variously known as Progress or Culture or Standard-of-Living or some such euphemistic eponym. But however subtly he camouflages his true intentions we can still see him to be the old aggressor of your day, Sennacherib. And his resources for 'defence' are so vast, so utterly devastating, so overwhelmingly horrible, that even the Rab-shakehs themselves are terrified by their master.

But, Sennacherib, you wouldn't possibly understand this today any better than you understood it two thousand, seven hundred years ago: God is still defending His city, for His own sake and for the sake of His servants. Exchanging arrows for atomic war-heads hasn't brought God to His knees in the way it has brought mankind to its knees. You remember that awful sick look on the faces of your enemies, when they saw the streaming banners of Assyria bearing down on them in battle? That look which made you feel so hot and proud inside, as you remembered that this was your doing? 'While their inhabitants, shorn of strength, are dismayed and confounded', as Isaiah expressed it for you? Of course you remember that. Then that's why you would find it hard to understand our world, where the fear is so real, so terrible, that men have even given up feeling afraid. With all the colossal arsenal that comprises the modern world, the always higher-looming calamity is now so altogether vast that we just don't dare glance at it – we watch Westerns on the TV and listen to Hi-Fi and concentrate on sport and even tune in 'music while you work'; we dash madly about our world at the highest possible speed by any and every available means of transport – anything to avoid even a single moment of quietness which might give us the tiniest glimpse of the real aggressiveness that is so basic to the story of man in revolt.

Sennacherib, I have learnt a lot by stopping and looking at you and your people. But, Sennacherib, what a tremendous lot you could learn by watching us!

And yet there is still this other thing that you didn't learn in your time and will never learn in all time or in all eternity – there is a City of God in this world even yet. Isaiah said in your time, 'Out of Jerusalem shall go forth a remnant, and out of Mount Zion a band of survivors. The zeal of the LORD of hosts will accomplish this.' And Sennacherib, the Master Himself has reminded His people : 'On earth nations will stand helpless, not knowing which way to turn from the roar and surge of the sea; men will faint with terror at the thought of all that is coming upon the world. . . . When all this begins to happen, stand upright and hold your heads high, because your liberation is near.'

I track on, up one steep slope, down another, yet always getting higher and higher, on the road up to Jerusalem and Isaiah. And again I have time to think, time to re-think, the world of my day as I find it challenged by the Assyrian world God has exposed to our view. And I see something else, something just as horrible as the blood and death of war.

For this time I see an Assyria ever on the grab. Pillaging,

plundering, grasping, snatching: ever on the grab. I remembered the beauty and the grandeur and the lavish wealth of Nineveh, now to ask myself where it all came from. All the skill and the education and the inventiveness that Assyrian culture had so richly exhibited in its palaces and temples and royal cities – is this entirely Assyria? Is this her contribution to her world? Or is it in fact the wealth she has taken out of her world, is it in awful truth the blood she has sucked from the economic veins of victim nations she has bled white?

No need to ask Sennacherib this question. No need to revisit Nineveh, to study the trade-returns and bills of lading for the State Departments and big merchant houses. Not this time. I'll get this answer from the common soldiers, for this is no secret at all; every yokel in Assyria knows this. Listen – it's that song again:

> 'With my many chariots
>   I have gone up to the heights of the mountains,
>   to the far recesses of Lebanon;
>   I felled its tallest cedars,
>   its choicest cypresses;
>   I came to its remotest height,
>   its densest forest.
>   I dug wells
>   and drank waters,
>   I dried up with the sole of my foot
>   all the streams of Egypt.'

That's where it really came from. No secret at all. I just went up and took it. I liked it, so why not have it? I wanted that straight-grained cedar planking. I felt I could do with that cypress-pine for timbering. 'With my many chariots', of course. Sure, that's how it's done. If you have the chariots, if you have the fire-power. If you can out-blast, out-kill your neighbours, then you can loot and grab and just make off with every single thing that you like the look of. And who is going to stop you? Come on, tell me that! 'With my many chariots' we have done it in Assyria. And unless you can match us at that you can just take what is coming to you and we'll certainly dish it out. And we'll take the lot!

Yes. That is the voice of Assyria. Greedy, more greedy, always more greedy still.

And I remember the nice young sales manager in his middle thirties. I was not one tiny bit surprised to observe that he was paying me good money to try and find help for the stress symptoms from which he was suffering. For he told me that in two and a half years he had raised the sales in his division of his giant engineering masters from two thousand pounds per month to two hundred thousand pounds per month. I felt like saying, 'Good for you. It's a great record. Keep at it!' But I have learnt a lot from Nineveh; and instead I pursed my lips and said very seriously, 'Yes. That's your problem, without a doubt. Next year they will expect it to be two hundred and fifty thousand.' And I shall never forget the look of real fear in his eyes as he came back : 'No, Doctor. They are expecting it next month.'

Big Business, we call it. Expansion, sales promotion, merchandising methods, *etc., etc., etc.* We have all sorts of impressive words, we have a whole new vocabulary of such jargon, all interspersed with smooth clichés telling ourselves just how good and progressive and clever and successful we are. But what we will not admit is that this is really just Assyria. Just the same insatiable greed of Assyria in all the ages.

Two hundred thousand this month. Then two hundred and fifty thousand the next. What about three hundred thousand by Christmas? Half a million in the next two years? And so on and so on. What's the limit? What is your target? 'Oh, we haven't got a limit. Our target is always bigger and bigger. Nimrud wasn't big enough. That's why we built Nineveh. Our own cedars weren't big enough to meet our aims, so we took them from Lebanon. The Tigris was a mighty fine river, for sure; but we wanted more than that so we just dried up with the soles of our boots the streams of Egypt.'

Sure! It's easy if you have the chariots. And if you have a sales manager who can't ride the chariots, don't worry. Kick him out. Get somebody better. If he sleeps soundly every night without a sedative and has time to be with his children as a proper father, then he's slacking. He is no good to us. We want the executive type who really wants to go big places. None of this small-town thinking in our group. Tell you what, boys! There's always room at the top! Doesn't that make you keen to drive faster? And boy, oh boy! You just see that you make those chariots travel!

The take-over, we call it. That is one of the fastest, most merciless chariots we drive. If he's little enough, if he's in your way, if he has something you want – then take him over. It's legal. There's nothing to stop you. We've always done business that way in Assyria!

Sure, it pays to advertise. Get the line across. Hire yourself a top executive to do it for you. Don't call him your Rabshakeh, somebody might get squeamish. Call him Sales Promotion Director and make it sound very important and proper and all that. He'll sell it for you. Never mind two bits if they don't want it. Tell them they do. Tell them that all the smart people have it. Write it up big. Put a pretty girl in the front of the picture so that they'll be sure to stop and look at it. Sell the idea to the kids if you can. They can work on their parents, remember. Get the kids to think that they ought to have it in their home; the Joneses do next door. Tell them it's got to be the new model. Not the crummy old last year's model. Tell them that that old timer might be good enough in little old tin-pot Zion, but it's no good in Assyria. Of course it must be new. Never mind about whether it's good or any of that line. You don't make the big dividends by taking notice of things like that – just see that it sells, and that we get the sales rake-off. We've always done business that way in Assyria.

The miles are slowly tramping by and now I don't seem to notice them at all. For my mind is filled with thought of the power and the strength of Assyria. The ruthless organization of bitter male aggressiveness and the insatiable greed of a people who concede no rights because they have no neighbours. In their world there are only ever Assyrians or victims. In their driving motives there are only ever the things they want – and if they want them then they must have them. Not much business for the psycho-analysts in Assyria, not too many repressions in their psyches. Concentrate on the id, make the super-ego take back place. If you like the taste of sweet things, then just you feed yourself on sweet things to your heart's content. Do you want it? Then take it.

For my mind is still in a turmoil from the things I have heard, the things I have seen, most of all from the things I have felt. And as I trudge along, thinking over all that has been happening in these last few days, I sense something else altogether again. Not the fearsome aggressiveness, not the big, hungry greed – but something warm, sensuous, alluring, enticing.

Listen – there's the Rab-shakeh again – 'big, ripe, juicy figs, eh? Grapes? Grapes that'll make you smack your lips for days – and bunches and bunches of them? We're just the boys to come to. Rich soft olives? O.K. We've got them. Come in with us and stuff yourself on them. Pleasures and appetites and passions – we thrive on them, we never check them. Never mind about this City of God stuff – all that repressive business. That might go all right in Jerusalem but not in Nineveh. Remember, Nineveh is big time. Why don't you drop your poky little wowserish Hezekiah and his narrow-minded pettiness and come along with us and play it up to the limit? All this self-restraint will make you sick – give you guilt feelings and all sorts of complexes and goodness knows what else. We know better than that. We get rid of our inhibitions – if we are weak enough to get them in the first place, ha ha! And it's lots of fun. . . .'

For now I am hearing properly, understanding properly, something I did not really take in when we were all peering over the city walls that terrible morning a few days ago.

'Quarrels, contentious temper, envy, fits of rage, selfish ambitions' I had never been in any doubt about. But this was now a new approach, one that seemed to be so much more overwhelming – because it was so completely attractive. The Rab-shakeh hurling insults and threats, offering death and torture, is clearly an enemy through and through. But this new alluring Rab-shakeh with his lip-smacking and his over-tones of rich banqueting and warm comfort and soft sensuous ease is hard to conceive as an enemy at all.

Surely this is just the thing we do want. Isn't this indeed the thing the whole body-chemistry of man is asking for? What is the point in having a good healthy appetite without the sweet-tasting tit-bits that meet its clamorous call? Why the warm passionate emotions if they cannot lead to satis-faction and fulfilment?

Rab-shakeh, you talk of the lovely coolness of the fig-laden shade-tree in the heat of a Mediterranean late summer day. But, Rab-shakeh, you ought to come and see our glorious sun-drenched surf beaches, right at the doorway to our beautiful city. That's all we want in Sydney. We'll settle for that. Nice girls, plenty to eat and drink, and long summer days to laze away on the sand, or in the rolling surf. Now you're talking sense, Rab-shakeh, it's our sort of sense, and perhaps Assyria is not such a bad place after all. Perhaps the little City of God hasn't got much really.

For now I am listening again to the great booming clamour of the Rab-shakeh – and yet the warm, alluring strength of his Assyrian voice is disturbed by another voice. It is hard to hear, but I think I can pick it out – listen. 'My friends, all that is true, all that is noble, all that is just and pure, all that is lovable and gracious, whatever is excellent and admirable – fill all your thoughts with these things.'

It is St. Paul I am hearing. But his voice is lost again in the swelling Assyrian chorus – 'whale of a party . . . best show going . . . great sport . . . don't miss out on this . . . let's make a night of it . . .'. For now a thousand voices are around me, as my pulse beats faster and I am swinging into step with the dancing feet and the cheering throng – when there is a moment's lull and I hear again, so clearly that the voice could almost be my own, it is so near, '. . . drinking bouts, orgies and the like. I warn you, as I warned you before, that those . . .'.

But St. Paul's words are drowned now in the voice of the Rab-shakeh himself. And this time it is a voice more attractive, more seductive than any voice I have ever known. It is the lilting voice of warm-blooded youth, and singing now to the stirring beat of the drum and the soft blowing of the coolest of all cool reeds, as the song and the dance go on.

For the flush of cheek and dilated pupil in each Assyrian face around me tells me the excitement of the mood. Every pulse seems to be beating in time as the chorus takes it up.

It is infectious. It is lilting. It is enchantment as only Assyria can enchant. And as song follows song, verse follows verse, with the seductive rhythm and the insistence of enrapture, I catch only a meagre word or two from that other voice. 'Goodness', I hear. 'Fidelity.' 'Self-control.' But the voice of

Assyria knows no such vocabulary and St. Paul is all out of place in this company.

For those other voices are myriad. Even their words are now lost to me as their voices are so many and so strong and so passionate : '. . . enchanted evening'. '. . . you in my arms . . .' 'dream lover . . .' '. . . kisses, kisses . . .'. These I hear, breaking out from the ever-swelling chorus of overwhelming emotion.

Until the whole warm mountain air is heavy with the seductive alluring of erotic hunger altogether beyond restraint. And now I cry out in a tumult of elation and of horror, for I suddenly see that this is not just the Assyria of the past at all – this is the deep underlying passion of my own twentieth-century Western world, a world where the restraints of chastity, of self-control, are strained far beyond breaking-point. This is my own world, where this Assyrian voice is now almost unchecked at all. For my head is whirling and my heart is pounding as I spin around the next turn in the road – to find that at last I am in front of the little city, the city God had preserved for His own sake and for the sake of His servant David. My ears and my head are full of the passionate voices of the Assyrian courtiers, but now I am racing full pelt to hammer on the city gate, clamouring for urgent admission to seek the mind of Isaiah, to find in desperate need the answer to my last and most important of all questions.

In through the gate, helter-skelter between the shoppers and the merchants in the mid-morning trading-hour, wildly through the open Temple doorway to the prophet's study.

I am all out of breath and hot and flushed with the near panic which had filled me. And now I am even more flustered by the warm stillness of the Temple chamber and the cool serenity of the prophet himself as he rises at my clattering approach.

Sir, I blurt out, there is something I must ask you, if you please. And oh, sir, something terrible has happened to the Assyrians. But . . . but I suppose you know? And I stand there, silent, more disturbed now by my own disturbance, as I compare it with the strong self-control of the prophet. I am trying to collect my thoughts, to clarify my problem. The prophet just waits quietly, in the way God always waits for men. No-one has ever seen God rattled, even though multitudes of men have tried to rattle Him. They even put Him on trial once, and killed Him – but they didn't fluster Him in one tiny moment of it all!

I sat down on a low stool across the room from the prophet's writing-desk. Isaiah was looking at me intently, searchingly; yet I knew he was entirely kindly, altogether helpful, in his silently penetrating gaze.

Sir, I said, very quietly now, I have lived through an eternity in these last few hours. I came here to look at the Assyrians, and I saw in them only what was utterly frightening. And what is more, sir, I saw in them so much of my own world that I believe I can never now think of them as apart. Your Assyrians have a callous brutality that makes your whole world shudder. But, sir, our Assyria has such a cold-blooded scientific murder in its heart that we can't shudder at all – we simply dare not even glance squarely at it!

For a moment I began to picture mushroom-clouds and radiation necrosis; and even for one intuitive flash that most evil of all evils, the brain-washed totalitarian state. But I checked this disturbing fantasy as I pursued my tale.

Also, sir, I saw in your little Assyria a greed and lust which has beggared and degraded the whole of her surrounding world. But I must say this, sir. I saw in that just the foreshadowing of the legalized, organized tyranny of the avarice which my world deifies as Big Business; and the slavering sensuality which masquerades in our twentieth century as love and romance.

But there is one thing that I most dearly would like to know. You remember that awful day when the Rab-shakeh stood outside your little city and hurled his taunts and threats against Hezekiah and God and the people of this city? And you remember that Hezekiah sent Eliakim and Shebnah and Joah round to tell you about it? Now when they arrived here you were sitting in exactly the same place where you sit now. And you were quietly writing. Do you remember that, sir? Now I know almost for certain that all the misery of that day was no surprise to you. And I know very much more certainly that it was no surprise to God. God is not caught on the hop, men never catch God in an unguarded moment. You know that, sir; I know that.

But, sir, would you be good enough to do this? Would you please tell me what it was that you were writing when we came round that day? Can I see that? Perhaps I can learn from that some final answer to my own world and its terrible threat to my faith and the faith of my fellow believers?

Isaiah never let his eyes move from me as I spoke. And his gaze was still holding me in some sort of spiritual grip as he answered, 'I'll do that very gladly. I was writing a poem, really a Psalm, that morning.'

The prophet stood up and walked over to a little alcove in the stonework. I could see that it held many parchment scrolls, but he picked one up without hesitating, without needing to rummage around at all.

He came over with it in his hand, extended for me to take it. 'You would like to read it? You are very welcome to do so.'

I half put out my hand to take the scroll; then hastily withdrew it. Sir, would you mind reading it to me, please? And do you mind if I ask you some of my own personal questions as you read? For I have quite a problem. I had been all around the city with Hezekiah before that Assyrian assault party arrived, and Hezekiah was quite sure that his doubled walls and fortified towers and his water conduit would protect the city. But I know also that when Sennacherib had cracked the whip loud and hard, Hezekiah had jumped to rip the gold off the Temple doorposts to pay that tribute. And I think you knew something else – you knew God had another answer altogether. Am I right in that, sir?

Isaiah slowly unrolled the scroll without answering me. He looked intently at the writing on the parchment for almost a full half-minute before he began to read:

> '*God* is our refuge and strength,
>   a very present help in trouble.'

There was just that moment's pause in which the soaring strength of his faith, the emphasis he placed on the word 'God', rebuked me as it would Hezekiah, as it would rebuke all weak saints who had dared to substitute their own defence works for the defence God Himself provides.

And then he read on in the clear ringing statement of utter confidence:

'Therefore we will not fear though the earth should
    change,
    though the mountains shake in the heart of the sea:
    though its waters roar and foam,
    though the mountains tremble with its tumult.'

Through my mind flashed the racing thought of TNT and
nuclear warheads; my mouth was half opened to speak of
these; but Isaiah looked up with almost an impish smile and
quite a twinkle in his eyes as he interposed : 'I have a little
chorus for the end of each verse. It is simple, as any response
in a Psalm should be, but it is wonderfully true :

    "The LORD of hosts is with us;
    the God of Jacob is our refuge!" '

He read on :

    'There is a river whose streams make glad the city of
        God,
        the holy habitation of the Most High.
    God is in the midst of her, she shall not be moved;
        God will help her right early.
    The nations rage, the kingdoms totter;
        he utters his voice, the earth melts.'

And because the imagery was so telling, because I could
see so clearly now the grandeur of the river God supplies
when contrasted with Hezekiah's 20-inch conduit, because I
could catch something of the eternal meaning of God's purpose when set alongside the long-vanished pomp of Nineveh :
because of these and all the other truths I was beginning to
see emerging from this little page in human history I joined
my voice to that of the prophet as together we exulted :

    'The LORD of hosts is with us;
    the God of Jacob is our refuge !'

Now I had no need to ask questions or interrupt – the sheer
greatness of the whole concept was overwhelming as he read :

    'Come, behold the works of the LORD,
        how he has wrought desolations in the earth.
    He makes wars cease to the end of the earth;

he breaks the bow, and shatters the spear,
he burns the chariots with fire!
"Be still, and know that I am God.
I am exalted among the nations,
I am exalted in the earth!"'

The prophet lowered the manuscript and his eyes seemed
to search me through and through: this time, and alone, I
replied in hushed voice:

'The LORD of hosts is with us;
    the God of Jacob is our refuge!'

For now I have my answer. Clearly, simply. This is the
truth this whole story is really telling. The electric contrast
between the mighty thundering of Assyria – and don't be in
the least bit shy about thinking of an Assyria with H-bombs
and germ warfare and all the Big Business trimmings of
twentieth-century Nineveh – and the rock-fast serenity of the
man of God quietly sitting inside the very centre of the
Assyrian pincer-grip and writing the forty-sixth Psalm. That
is why this is not just Hezekiah's story, any more than it is
Sennacherib's story. It is altogether God's story.

For in the absolute sense it is the same story. It is the story
of all the challenging voices of life, and the story of that single
answering voice which insists in utter finality: *God* is your
refuge and strength.

It is the call to turn from the human voice of ageless
Assyria, the voice that forever claims answer in the so-human
terms of self-seeking, self-fulfilment, self-direction.

This, then, is why He said so simply, 'You must not think
that I have come to bring peace to the earth; I have not come
to bring peace, but a sword.' A single clear word from Him is
the immediate, undying challenge to every other voice in the
whole world in which I have grown up.

And in all the excitement of the story I have just re-lived, in
the awe and wonder that must always fill a man as he sees
God defending His city for His own sake and for the sake of
His servant David, do I hear another voice? Listen! Is it
indeed an answering voice? Weak, yet strong; anxious, yet
serene; doubting, yet confident? Yes, it is another voice. Dare
I say it is my own voice? 'God is *my* refuge and strength.'

CHAPTER THREE

DEGENERATIVE DISEASE

EVERY doctor knows all too well those occasions when he just doesn't quite know what to say. Those times when he has to pass on information that he wished with all his heart he didn't possess.

You may easily enough imagine the feeling yourself. How do you tell the young wife that the long-awaited first baby that she is expecting in six weeks' time has already died? Or the lovely, young, unmarried student that she is now nearly four months pregnant? What way is best to break the news to the father that his child is blind? Or that the pathologist says it is malignant? That the cough that made the Ph.D. thesis so much of an effort to write is in fact T.B.?

I can't tell you what I do in cases like these because I don't know myself until I start to do it. But I can say this : I keep putting out feelers in conversation – drop hints, study reactions, switch from one approach to another, and so on and so on and so on, until at last the truth is out. All doctors try to do this in some measure or other. Some, very foolishly I think, just hide the truth. Others simply blurt it out. But all of us are really endeavouring, with our varying skills and techniques, to help prepare the patient to face the ordeal ahead and give some assurance that the doctor will always be on hand with help in some form or another. Cases may be fatal; but none is ever hopeless.

And this is often a matter of much time and many visits. The word of encouragement today may prepare the ground for the more guarded caution of tomorrow. And it often needs saying over and over and over again. The art of landscape and portraiture contains no more subtle patience and resolve than this art of medicine.

And I assure you that this is exactly where I am now. I have closed my interview with the Assyrians, I have shaken hands with Hezekiah and Isaiah and turn now to my next consultation : to find it is one of these very cases.

It is indeed one of these problems. I think I understand the signs and symptoms. I know well enough what is wrong. The prognosis is no secret at all. That is not it. That is not what bothers me. The real trouble is to express it, to make the diagnosis and the therapy clear enough and simple enough to be both understandable and bearable.

For I am asking you to sit in on an interview and examination in a case that I confess I find disturbingly difficult to describe.

The Assyrians were simple enough; in this regard at any rate. The only real subtlety about the Assyrians is their sheer lack of subtlety! And seen always against a background of the dazzling brightness of Isaiah their blackness is etched out as if engraved by fire. Indeed, it may largely be because of the drama and the excitement of that last story that I have found it so difficult to find a suitable line of approach in this one.

For months and months have passed since I put down my pen and closed that interview with Sennacherib and Isaiah in Hezekiah's little Jerusalem. I have seen hundreds of patients, performed many operations, celebrated another Christmas and even inscribed another notch on a now impressively long tally of birthdays.

But all to no avail. Evening after evening I have taken up my pen; written a few lines – sometimes a few pages – and then crossed it out. Many times I have turned from my professional journals and simply picked up the Bible, to read again some of God's relevant case notes – and decided to forget the whole idea. For the case notes themselves are not even chronological. The literary critics simply say the work is not terribly badly edited – should be re-compiled. The philosophers shake their heads in disdain and say it's really much the same sort of gloomy nonsense as that Number One piece of illogical moonshine, the cross.

And all the time I feel much as I feel when facing a patient whose case is *in extremis*. Why can't this one go to some other doctor? Why not send him off for a second opinion and pretend I don't quite know what it is that I see? And all the time completely aware of the fact that that is no answer. That is not doctoring at all!

And so I have run out of excuses, and run out of stalling for time, as I take you with me now to study a case that you will at first think too utterly unreal to be true. If you came with me as we looked into Hezekiah's little walled city and saw God defend it for His own sake and for the sake of His servant David, then you may well be excused for thinking that what we are going to see now must surely be the most completely crazy piece of topsy-turvydom this side of *Alice through the Looking Glass*.

For listen carefully. Take a deep breath and hold on to your chair. FASTEN BELTS; NO SMOKING, as the airlines express it so succinctly.

We are going to watch God defend the city again, for His own sake and for the sake of His servant David. Yes, the very same little city of Jerusalem. And this time He will defend it by tearing every single thing to pieces and reducing it to a smouldering heap of rubble trampled into the dust under the feet of the all-devouring Babylonian army!

You see what I mean? If you think that this is simple, if this looks easy as pie, then you and I work on different wavelengths altogether.

But if you did in fact feel something of the exalted wonderment that I myself felt as we saw God save His city in the days of Hezekiah, then I know you will share with me something of grave foreboding awe as we see God show His unfailing love and utter faithfulness in this astonishing way

That, then, is the nub of the problem and the outcome of the story. So come with me, if you still feel so inclined, as we fill in the essential details.

The little city is really very much the same – just a little bit more fortified than in Hezekiah's time, but really little altered. And that is perhaps the only thing that is the same.

For the time is something just over a hundred years after Hezekiah and Isaiah.

And the king this time is any one of a tragic series of puppet-kings installed by command of great foreign powers, and altogether so un-Hezekiah-like as to break your heart.

And the prophet? Oh dear, oh dear! You remember Isaiah? Strong, serene, undisturbable Isaiah, of royal birth and such compelling strength of presence? Then shut your eyes to all such glimpses, for the new prophet is Jeremiah And Jeremiah is just so different that he has been more misunderstood than almost anyone in all history! So miser able, it seems; so unrelievedly gloomy, it ppears; so full of 'lamentations', it reads; so much of all these that his name has become a sort of by-word for all the long-faced wretchedness that so many people think any prophet of God must be!

Now then! To make the story and the meaning clear I must ask you to come on a sort of round-up as we collect the data. And just as I was taught as a student to begin by looking at the whites of the eyes, the tongue, the tonsils, the chest (say 99, of course), the heart and so on, then here I should like to follow the sequence I find most helpful and start by looking at the history.

I must insist that this is not absolutely necessary. I am quite sure that you could arrive at all the right final findings and answers if you just started with, say, Jeremiah himself. Or with one of the reigning kings. Or even by looking at the state of the world at the time.

But I should prefer to sketch in the historical background, if you please, partly because I like it that way in my ordinary everyday medical practice (it's the unasked questions that aren't answered and the unlooked-for signs that are not seen) and partly because God has Himself sketched in some of this background.

It seems that, after many years of failing health, Hezekiah died about 686 BC. For the last ten years or so of his reign he granted co-regency to his son Manasseh who assumed the throne on his father's death. And if you can understand the explosive reaction when Hezekiah took over the throne from that miserable insincere weakling who was his spineless self-seeking father, Ahaz, then you can readily enough understand what happened when the throne passed to Manasseh. For Manasseh had no faith. He had no intention at all of serving God, and back swung the pendulum of spiritual leadership away across to the other extreme.

I must confess that there was a time when this used to puzzle me rather. Why not be more tolerant? That is what I would mutter to myself. That is the real secret of life. Learn to live and let live. Avoid all this unseemly, un-British brawling. Let's be gentlemen at least. Anything to avoid making a scene of ourselves.

But over many years I have learnt a great deal more than that. I know now that if we could leave a dreadful no-hoper like Ahaz reigning for twenty years and nothing started to boil because of it, then we must toss out everything we have ever learned from the Bible about God and man. 'What has righteousness to do with wickedness? Can light consort with darkness?' St. Paul asks so cryptically.

No, a thousand times no!

And just for that very same reason, when you have a Hezekiah blazing out the clearest beam of faith since the time of David, then any able intelligent son of his taking the throne with a clear intention to disobey and disregard the will of God will certainly do so with the evil blackness of a Manasseh. This is the way it works. This is indeed the way it must work.

For setting out on his long reign of no less than fifty-five years this was just precisely the intention in the heart of Manasseh. Remember Isaiah? Sawn in half, the old Jewish tradition tells us, in the bitter rebellion the new king felt for his father's God and his father's prophet. But Manasseh lived under the still-mounting shadow of Assyria, whose very greatness was now beginning to spell her doom. And then, with no Isaiah to stand in all the strength of the very presence of God to guide him, Manasseh made all too tragic a picture as the great Assyrian whip cracked! Yes, the bitter worst happened. This rebellious, reactionary, God-hating king got caught up in the devouring wrath of Assyria. For there we see him next, trudging the blistering road to Nineveh, a great bronze Assyrian fetter on his wrists and a cruel Assyrian hook through his nose.

It is hard to pass by this story of Manasseh. I think it is unique in the Bible. So far as I know it is the only account where we see the endless love of God pursue a man to such a seemingly hopeless length. There, even to the bitter depth of an Assyrian prison, God pressed after Manasseh, as the aged rebel heart yielded and a life of faith began at last.

But no. It is not Manasseh we are to study, however we may wish it. However much we may like to think of what went on in the now repentant heart of the prisoner-king, bowing low ourselves as we wonder reverently before the gracious long-suffering love of the God who will still deign to accept the surrender of so bitter a foe.

But we must not stay over-long here, however sacred the

spot. For Manasseh came back to Jerusalem, incredible though it seems. Just why Ashurbanipal should release him I can only guess. My guess is that the Assyrian king was beginning to feel his world tottering beneath him, and thought that perhaps it would stand to Assyria's advantage to have an ally even in the miserable little kingdom of Jerusalem. And I think that there is very good evidence to support this idea, as I shall explain in due course.

But it was a 'converted', 'born-again' Manasseh who came back to Jerusalem, to resume his throne, to correct if possible the mistakes of all his earlier years, to straighten out all the crooked turns into which he had led his nation.

But his life was over, his time had run out. Manasseh died, leaving his son Amon a legacy of spiritual disturbance in which the new king was promptly murdered! And Josiah, the little eight-year-old princeling son of Amon, is king.

What a mess. This pendulum is not swinging, it is positively rattling! For on to the throne came perhaps the greatest of them all. Out of the background of a father murdered by his inner Court circle, of a grandfather who blew both cold and hot in successive breaths, came the delight of an eight-year-old whose heart is already covenanted to serve the will of the God he as yet so little knows. And the pendulum swung this time to the furthest mark in all the history of Judah. The boy-king set out on the most intense revival movement ever recorded, a movement so strong, so confident, so fearless, that it brought about his own death and the gravest misgivings in the heart of the still young prophet Jeremiah.

Thank you. That was most certainly the place for a break. If this were a TV script then this would be just the spot for a commercial.

For I must now stop and clarify those two statements. The statement, first, that it was his faith that brought Josiah to his death. And secondly, the much more important statement that it was the tremendous revival programme of Josiah that filled Jeremiah with such dismay. For, as far as I can understand the story of Jeremiah, the key to his personal experience and the meaning of his role as a prophet hinges on Josiah and his faith.

Josiah seems to have set out on his reign with a spiritual impact that even in his boyhood had his whole Court gasping for breath. And at the age of twenty-eight, when one of the priests, a worthy fellow called Hilkiah, discovered a copy of the Book of the Law, Josiah really changed into overdrive. The spiritual accelerator was kept flat down on the floor boards, as the king's heart sang in the exultant light of now knowing with absolute certainty what God wanted. No longer relying on mere ceremonial; no more dependent on hearsay, and inaccurate human memories; no further to be under the dictation of traditions which may or may not be reliable. Can't you feel the racing pulse of the young king as he held in his hands the priceless treasure of God's own writing? For the zeal and enthusiasm of those years of youth are now to be directed and enlightened by knowledge and understanding.

And Josiah, you are not the only one. There will be a few like you over the succeeding centuries, men who will feel very much what you feel. About a thousand years after your own time a certain priest in Rome will feel it. He will find the Word of God in his own 'vulgate' Roman vernacular, after centuries of burial in classical Greek; and he will risk excommunication for his find! And over a thousand years later again Wycliffe and Tyndale will risk execution for finding the Word of God again in their common English. And Josiah, you would never believe this, for you are just not made like this : but indeed in my time we have some wonderful access to the Word of God, not by the findings of men with strange names like Hilkiah but very twentieth-century-ish names indeed, like Knox and Phillips and RSV and NEB. And Josiah . . . Come over here in a corner, so that I may whisper it to you and not feel too ashamed at blurting it out aloud. You remember how Hilkiah brought you that dust-covered old copy of the Law? Wasn't that a wonderful day? Then I am sure it would nearly break your heart if you knew just how reluctant are a lot of our priests of today to bring out the clear, meaningful, modern translation from under all the Temple-dust that centuries of time must inevitably deposit on any text.

And Josiah, just one thing more. You will learn the truth about God, surely enough as you read His Word. That is what stirs you, that is what now drives you on in this nation-shaking revivalist movement you are embarked on. Most surely so, indeed. But mark this, Josiah. You will learn something else, too. You will learn a lot about men, particularly the arrogant, greedy men who have refused to hear the call of God to obedience as you have heard and obeyed.

And listen carefully, now. You will learn a lot about Egypt. And a lot about Assyria. And what you learn about them may well cost you your life. What do you think about the Word of God now, Josiah? You are thirty-eight, a man of mature years. It is over twenty years since you started your great reformation, it is a full ten years since you were given the Book of the Law. Will you still follow the text, when it might well prove fatal? You think that over carefully, Josiah, for the whole course of human history now hangs on your decision.

And Josiah made his decision as carefully and nobly as any martyr in all history, and died in simple consequence.

Can I tell you just what happened?

Assyria, great Assyria, was tottering. Indeed, she was on the very point of falling. Ashurbanipal, her last great king, was a scholar and probably far too much of a perfectionist to handle so dynamic a situation, calling for so much sheer off-the-cuff resourcefulness. I think that is why he had released Manasseh from his prison in Nineveh. He also freed Necho I of Egypt, whom he had managed somehow or other to capture.

And Ashurbanipal had died, died long before Josiah was even born; but this piece of strategy with Egypt had paid off.

For in the eighteen years that followed Ashurbanipal's death in 627 BC, Assyria was beginning to crumble apart in all her massive greatness, as the challenging thrust of ever-mounting Babylon brought her to her knees. Nineveh had already gone. It was from his final hold-out in Haran and in the very throes of death, that Ashur-uballit II of Assyria did just what I think Ashurbanipal was preparing for when he freed Necho I from captivity – he cried to Necho II, the new Egyptian pharaoh, for help. And the cry was heard and the Egyptians came marching to give aid.

And this was exactly the thing that stuck in the spiritual

throat of thirty-eight-year-old Josiah. The prospect of Egypt, the old taskmaster Egypt, the nation from whom God had effected so great a redemption under Moses, coming now to the aid of cruel, greedy, aggressive Assyria, was more than Josiah could stomach. He had read God's Word; to be sure he had. He knew about Egypt. He knew plenty. And he knew about Assyria – he lived right alongside Assyria. And to see Egypt added to Assyria was to Josiah sheer spiritual dynamite.

He mustered his puny troops and marched straight into the face of the advancing Egyptian army!

Of course he was a fool! Only a fool would even think of buying into a suicide programme like that! If to be sensible is only ever to take on what you know will show a safe rake-off, then Josiah was a fool all right. If the really heady play is to deal only when the cards are stacked in your favour, then Josiah was mighty dumb. If all the profit in life is measured in nice, crinkly, cash-in-hand bank-notes, then Josiah was too poor even to be lumped among the bankrupts.

Josiah, you were quite a fool to do it. You have joined a most celebrated company of fools like yourself. Crack-pots who, like you, have done all manner of equally foolish things just because they have read God's Word and started to obey what they read. Those fools who think that the things they learn in the Temple have to be put into actual practice in real life.

Sure, Josiah, you are not the only one. We know about others who 'were tortured to death, disdaining release, to win a better resurrection. Others, again, had to face jeers and flogging, even fetters and prison bars. They were stoned, they were sawn in two, they were put to the sword, they went about dressed in skins of sheep or goats, in poverty, distress, and misery . . . they were refugees in deserts and on the hills, hiding in caves and holes in the ground.' Josiah, I can't tell you this, for it is seven centuries after your day that this will happen: but God the Son will Himself come to your little city and do perfectly what you did with such noble imperfection. He will only ever do His Father's will; He will be crucified for His divine folly!

And Josiah, as you sink to the floor of your chariot with that Egyption arrow through your belly, as physiological shock-mechanisms carry you into a merciful unconsciousness from which you will never emerge in this world, I think you already know the simple accolade with which God has honoured you and all your fellow fools of faith: 'They were too good for this world.'

And so Josiah died. The brightest single beam to shine in all history, since Moses himself, was thus suddenly snuffed out in one glorious moment.

And watching it all, analysing it all, understanding it all, was the sombre, gloomy, melancholy, lamenting Jeremiah.

For now it was Necho who cracked the whip. He was on his way back to Egypt after his unsuccessful trip up to Haran.

Oh yes! He was most unsuccessful! Don't be surprised at that. Josiah might have been all sorts of a fool to blaze his life away in his madcap obedience to God's call; but he had still been one hundred per cent successful. That delaying action on the plain of Megiddo in which he lost his life had cost Necho very valuable time. For when at last the Egyptians reached Haran the show was over. The Babylonians had swept Assyria to her final doom and Josiah was still victorious even in death.

But it was now Jehoiakim whom Necho appointed vassal-king in Jerusalem. Jehoiakim, paying tribute to Egypt. Jehoiakim, the political yes-man whose whole moral fibre was measurable in terms of sheer expediency. This is the Jehoia-kim who will be ruling in Jerusalem as the great prophet Jeremiah finds himself entrusted with the spiritual oversight of this tragically run-down little city.

No wonder Jeremiah looks gloomy. Think what brazen spiritual nonsense it would be if the Prophet of God in a heart-breaking setting like this were to be found rushing about slapping his fellows on the back, exclaiming, 'Isn't this just the best of all possible worlds?' And skip lightly away, chirruping gaily, 'I am H.A.P.P.Y.' And if I never learn another single thing from Jeremiah I must at least learn this: the Prophet of God is there to explain the truth, and truth is always as honest in its recognition of darkness as it is exultant in its understanding of light.

Jeremiah, I must confess that as a doctor I should like to express my deep indebtedness to you for that reminder. The same honesty is surely so fundamental in my own world of

D

sickness and healing. How may any doctor hope to advise and treat his patient unless he is honest enough and clear enough in the first place to be utterly convinced of the real need for treatment? To ignore that tell-tale skin dimpling is not to treat the early cancer underlying. Turning a deaf ear to that ominous systolic murmur will not cure the rheumatic fever. No, a thousand times no!

Jeremiah, God has included your words to such length in His Word to us not because you were so long-faced and melancholy. Of course not. The fifty-seven chapters written by your pen are in the Bible because you tell the simple truth, so simply; and it only ever sounds melancholy and mournful to our human ears because in our human littleness we don't like truth the size of God. And it may very well be, Jeremiah, as we come to see your little Jerusalem world through your so un-rose-tinted eyes, that we may even get a truthful view of our huge disturbed Western world.

And if we can see this at all clearly as being the political setting against which Jeremiah was to proclaim the truth, we shall at least be somewhere on the road to understanding his estimate of the religious climate of his time.

For Jeremiah had a unique chance to estimate the true spiritual values of his people, and his findings there were far more disturbing to him than the mere Jehoiakim puppet-king political situation.

And what is more – remember that Jeremiah was in fact making this estimate first under the noble reign of Josiah. This may sound surprising – but it was then, in those exciting days of vast religious reform and revival, that Jeremiah's face began to fall. It was in fact then, while Josiah was in that full-blooded enthusiasm of idol destruction and religious re-formation (against which Cromwell and the Puritan reformers look very anaemic indeed), that Jeremiah first began to see the stark tragedy of it all.

For he was not in the Throne Room. He was not in the Cabinet. He was not even Finance or Big Business. He was just the Prophet of God. And he saw the thing that Josiah could never have seen. He saw the ordinary man in the street right up close. Saw him in his home, saw him in his work, saw him in his pleasure. And, yes, saw him in his trouble.

And Jeremiah saw all too well that the great faith of Josiah belonged to the young king, surely enough, but to him alone. It didn't belong to many of the members of the Court, it had no part in the lives of most of the priests, it was tragically missing in the experience of the common people of the city. Not that they didn't all feel the immense impact of it; just that they didn't in fact possess it.

Faith is like that, of course. The life of God's people is always like that. If it is the life of a king, and a great king, then his whole kingdom feels the impact of it. If it is the humblest subject, then just the tiny circle of his humble influence will feel it.

And it was very much his understanding of these simple people, it was his knowledge of their humble, unimportant little lives, that so moved the prophet to deepest concern as he saw Josiah blazing a mighty trail of reforms. Jeremiah saw all too well the indifferent apathy in the lives of the common people as their king's faith affected them but never belonged to them.

As the shrines and groves and foreign religions came tumbling down, filling the Kedron valley with a huge pile of jettisoned ecclesiastical bric-à-brac, Jeremiah realized only too well that to Tom, Dick and Harry it was still 'business as usual'. They were quite happy to be again thought of as 'the people of God', so long as it was just a matter of the religious performances. Quite happy, provided it didn't affect the usual trading. Splendid, so long as the pay packet was not reduced, so long as the dividends were maintained, so long as the fun wasn't interfered with.

But far more than that, Jeremiah saw that the priests were no better either. Jeremiah himself was of priestly birth, and he had plenty of access to their thinking and their ways. And what broke his heart was the discovery that the priests weren't in the least bit concerned with the truth of the will of God. They were concerned with getting on, with being popular, keeping on-side with public opinion.

And at last the immense and bitter truth dawned on the sensitive mind of the prophet. As he saw the utter preoccupation of the city with business and pleasure; as he had seen them using the great religious reform of Josiah as a cloak to hide them from the naked truth of the clear, known will of God; as he finally saw the sudden changes in the whole pattern of world affairs, Jeremiah reeled under the impact of the truth he now understood.

No wonder Jeremiah felt sick, sick as death, as he blanched and trembled with the awful truth! No wonder he squirmed and tossed in his so-human desire to avoid having to declare what he now knew.

But it is not to be that way, not with the Prophet of God. Jeremiah wasn't called to tell the people just what he thought they would like to hear, any more than he was called to tell the people just what he himself would like to say. Never, never, never! He is to tell the truth.

And finally, it seems, the sweeping change in the whole pattern of world dominion triggered him off. Out into the open, out into the Temple, out into the bitter hatred and opposition of this new puppet-king and priest alike, came the most terrible message the people of Israel had ever heard. *Jerusalem is doomed! The city is to be destroyed! The only hope of survival lies in slavery in Babylon. Surrender to Babylon. That is the only victory you can hope for!*

Jehoiakim was still king. He had been placed on the throne by Necho of Egypt, after the death of Josiah. But Babylon had risen as perhaps no power had ever risen in the world before her. From political obscurity and mediocrity out in the Tigris-Euphrates delta, that area where a thousand and more years before had existed Old Babylon, the Sumerian culture out of which Abraham had come, there was now rising in meteoric fashion the mighty New Babylon. Chaldean infusion seems to have brought a driving vitality that nothing, not even Assyria, could check.

Down went Nineveh. Just rubbed clean off the map of significant human history. The death of the Babylonian king, Nabopolassar, didn't halt their marching stride for a single moment. Nebuchadrezzar, the eighteen-year-old Crown Prince, was already much in control, and his father's death gave him freedom to increase the tempo, to establish a military and economic kinetic that barely felt any human resistance in his path.

Necho went. Nebuchadrezzar caught up with his army near where Necho had himself caught up with Josiah. When Necho went, Jerusalem went with him. A short four years of vassalage to Egypt gave way to bondage under Babylon.

And Jehoiakim was still king. No trouble to him at all. He could say 'yes' to Nebuchadrezzar just as readily as to Necho. The fact that the city belonged to God meant nothing to Jehoiakim. He was just as unconcerned with doing the will of God under Nebuchadrezzar as he had been under Necho. Just so long as they kept him in office, so long as he could keep his cushy job with all its perks, he was satisfied.

Oh yes. There had been some major disturbances, for sure. Nebuchadrezzar had shaken the place up pretty badly, and Jehoiakim wasn't going to start looking for more trouble by getting bothered about the will of God. Nebuchadrezzar had been bad enough; God would be much worse. Nebuchadrezzar had carried off into slavery a very valuable selection of his subjects: all the top artisans, the top intellectuals, the top administrators. That was bad, very bad. But Nebuchadrezzar had left the Throne Room intact, had left a reasonable Court, in fact had shown a genuine concern with establishing Jerusalem as something of a worthy Babylonian frontier outpost centre. And though the taxes were biting and the tribute rather devastating, it was running along smoothly enough.

And Jehoiakim was happy to play it the way it was. He couldn't for the life of him see how he could get out of the Chaldean clutches, but never mind. He and his little city were still in existence, which was much more than you could say about mighty Nineveh. And who knows, Egypt might still come back for more. Necho had been beaten, but the whole might of Egypt was still something very real, and it might be possible to work some very helpful intrigues some day.

No. No more trouble. Play it very cool. No panic move, and things would be pretty right. Jehoiakim was very satisfied indeed.

Satisfied, except for one thing. Except for a pestilential prophet, a small-time insignificant Bible-basher named Jeremiah, who persisted in saying that they were wrong, that they should find out what God wants, that faith and worship are more important than religion and business.

Jehoiakim didn't like that. He was annoyed – but not overmuch. It took him just a little bit of an effort, but it was really quite simple. A little conference with the Temple chiefs tidied it all up very neatly. No trouble at all, he found it to be. The Temple bosses were only too willing to play ball with him. It seems that they didn't like Jeremiah any more than he did.

They just banned Jeremiah from the Temple. Just stopped the crackpot from getting at the people enough to make a disturbance. Of course there would be a few they couldn't catch up with. A few who would go along with Jeremiah. There was a fellow called Uriah, who came up from Kiriath-jearim. He gained entrée one day into the inner Court of the king, bang into the whole Court-full of military chiefs and civic princes. And this fellow had come out with the same sort of disturbing Bible-banging that Jeremiah used. *My,* was Jehoiakim mad! The fellow saw in a flash how thoroughly sore the king was, and had shot off for his life, right over to Egypt. But the king had sent a hunting platoon after him. They caught up with him and dragged him all the way back to Jerusalem where Jehoiakim killed him on the spot and tossed his dead body on to the public burial tip. That ought to teach them all a lesson, even if you can't catch up with every single one of them. You can't stop the whole game. There was news of an even worse nuisance over in the Babylonian slave task force, a fellow called Ezekiel, who would have been really dangerous if he hadn't been so completely nutty and if he had not in fact gone dumb. And Baruch, Jeremiah's personal servant, was quite as bad. But fortunately he wasn't a priest, and in any case wasn't anything of a speaker. He wouldn't do any harm.

And Jehoiakim relaxed, all on-side with Nebuchadrezzar, and breathing much more freely now that the little off-side group at home had been squeezed right out of the playing area. Yes, Jehoiakim could well relax. Relax enough to look after his own affairs a bit. To put on some extra taxes to pay for those very costly private buildings he had set his greedy heart on. To keep an ear very close to the ground over in Egypt, where Necho II was obviously planning another showdown with Babylon. Necho didn't like having his Middle East army beaten up so badly at Carchemish, and Jehoiakim chuckled at the thought of possibly turning the tables on Nebuchadrezzar. And the chuckle turned to a savage frown as he remembered Jeremiah and his stupid talk about the will of God.

But what of Jeremiah himself? How did he make out in all this? The prophet could never get his eyes very far from the common people who surrounded his own simple life. And in these humble lives he saw only utter and endless tragedy. He knew, as any man of God in all history knows full well, that the nagging deep-down-inside need of every man is for God Himself. That relentless insatiable thirst in the very soul of man. That endless longing to be lifted out of the insecurity of creatureliness, to be held for ever in the strong, steadfast hand of the Creator God. And it was knowing this, knowing it so well, that Jeremiah's vision of the truth of God made him burst out:

> 'Be appalled, O heavens, at this,
>   be shocked, be utterly desolate, says the LORD,
> for my people have committed two evils:
>   they have forsaken me,
> the fountain of living waters,
>   and hewed out cisterns for themselves,
> broken cisterns, that can hold no water.'

But if that was what Jeremiah saw in the tragedy of the common people, trying to fill the parched dryness of godless living with such water-less substitutes as money and pleasure and formal religion, think what he saw in the people who should be helping them. The 'prophets', the priests, these men in places of national and spiritual trust who should lead and advise the people truthfully. Jeremiah is just hopping mad with them! Of this you may be sure – if you meet people who argue that a good middle-of-the-road compromise is the ideal answer to a problem, if you hear anyone say that true peace is a sort of half-and-half between rebellion and obedience, if it is suggested to you that reconciliation of truth with error is the ultimate in human wisdom: then you can be altogether certain that you are not listening to the truth as it is recorded in the Bible! And least of all by Jeremiah!

He was furious. And he was furious because God was furious. 'From least to greatest of them, every one is greedy for unjust gain; . . . from prophet to priest every one deals falsely.' Were they ashamed, he asks, when they committed abominations? No! They weren't a bit ashamed! 'You just didn't know how to blush! This', says Jeremiah, 'is God's way of rating you all.'

And something that is the doctor in me is stirred ever so

deeply at this – this temptation that is ever at a doctor's door urging him to take the easy way out when the news is bad, when the sickness is truly grave, when the prospect is bleak. But this is spoken to the spiritual doctors, says Jeremiah. 'It is to you who tend the spiritual health of God's people that he says this: "You have healed the wound of my people lightly, saying 'Peace, peace,' when there is no peace."'

Time rolled slowly on, season after season, year after year, always the same theme, always apparently the same response. And now no pulpit, even, to preach from.

But the truth must be proclaimed! This Jeremiah knew, and since he knew it he had to do it.

I don't know what you would do in a situation like this, and I am sure that I don't know what I would do myself. I spend most of my waking hours talking to people, talking mostly to the ones and the twos who all add up at the end of any one single year to several thousands of individuals. I can't think what I would do if I couldn't talk to them – but I can tell you what Jeremiah did. And I won't be a bit surprised if at first you laugh out loud at what happened, because it does at first glance seem to make such a comic little incident out of what is really such a tragedy.

Jeremiah called in Baruch, good faithful Baruch, whom Josephus describes as of noble family, but who seems to have been Jeremiah's 'Gentleman's personal gentleman'. It was the fourth year of Jehoiakim's reign, and Jeremiah called in Baruch, and started dictating.

Ha! I say. That's the stuff. Shoot off a letter to *The Jerusalem Times*. Come on Baruch. Snap into it. We've just got time to get this in on the two o'clock mail. Not a second to lose.

Not a bit of it. Our twentieth-century high-speed frenzy isn't God's way at all. God is never in any sort of a frenzy. Not that God can't move fast. Terribly fast. Isn't that in fact the most utterly disturbing single thing we know about God. You know – the way a man can get life really under control, just fix it so that he can relax. Can stretch out his legs in front of the fire, smack his lips at the smooth roll of the sip of Scotch and soda and say to himself, 'Man, you have plenty of good things laid by, enough for many years: take life easy, eat, drink, and enjoy yourself.' And bang! It's a coronary.

Or a drunken idiot straight through a red light. Or a stroke of a pen in some government office revoking certain import licences and he's out of business. Or that exam paper with just those questions he did not have time to learn. Or any or all of the thousands of ways God finds to move like the flash of lightning into the tiny world of a human life. Oh yes. God can move fast.

For Jeremiah missed the two o'clock mail. And the midnight mail too. In fact, there they were again the next day. And even the day after that. Jeremiah dictating, Baruch carefully writing away.

I always imagine Jeremiah as a highly sensitive, emotionally taut man who would today almost certainly be on some sort of tranquillizer or other. But not Baruch. We know very little about Baruch, yet I have no question but that Baruch was a quiet, rather stolid, unimaginative man of endless tenacity and courage. This is not the place to tell you why I think Baruch was like that. But please remember that Baruch was in fact like something. He was a character in history, not a character in a novel.

And it was two real men, the prophet and his attendant, the dictator and his scribe, who were sitting there day after day, week after week, month after month.

Jeremiah poured out all his heart as he poured out all his message. And faithfully Baruch wrote it all down. Spoken, written. Read, re-written. Word weighed against word, truth against truth. Until finally, there it was, a scroll filled with perhaps the most carefully compiled writings in all Bible literature. Well over a year it was, in preparation and perfecting.

But still not a soul had heard it. Baruch was not the sort of man to start questioning and protesting and impatiently jumping up and down. But Jeremiah could readily enough sense the question in his helper's mind.

'Baruch. This is for you. I am not allowed in the Temple, so it is up to you. I want you to go and read this so that God's Word will in fact be heard. But listen. Not any old day. We must wait for just the right day. It may well be that there will only ever come one single chance for you to read this, so it must be the best possible occasion.'

The New Year came and went. Summer turned to autumn,

and autumn became winter before that special day arrived.
That day when the prophet was sure it was right to declare
the naked truth.

We may need to speculate a bit on the mechanism of this
special event, but it seems it was a big religious feast, called
possibly because of the looming terror of Nebuchadrezzar and
his army almost on their doorstep. The Babylonian king was
in fact down at the Mediterranean coast just west of Jerusalem
making final and utter destruction of Ashkelon, whose doom
Jeremiah had also predicted. And Jehoiakim and his Estab-
lishment were doing just the very same sort of thing that
leaders do today in such times of crisis. 'Call a national day
of prayer.' 'Have a Commemoration Service.' 'The situation
is desperate and the Prime Minister (or the President, or even
the Pooh-Bah for that matter) has called Church leaders to
support the nation in special religious ceremonies.' Doesn't
a war, or a pestilence, or a drought, or an earthquake inevitably stir this reaction in the administration? For it was into
this atmosphere of national panic and calamitous upheaval
that Baruch was to burst with the scroll of the writing of God.

I am sure they had rehearsed it and discussed it in every
possible detail and from every known angle. Jeremiah was
far too mature in his faith, in his understanding of God and
His ways, to fall into the simple mistake of just leaving
Baruch to stroll over and hope to be 'guided'. You know the
naïve 'prayer' you must at times have heard : 'And, oh God,
make the supper a success', when the committee-man concerned has not even bothered to find out if there is hot water
available to make the tea with !

No ! Jeremiah was not like that. And Baruch was not like
that. 'Baruch the son of Neriah did all that Jeremiah the
prophet ordered him about reading from the scroll the words
of the LORD in the LORD's house.'

You can still study the mind and care in this planning, even
now, twenty-six and a half centuries later. For Shaphan was
still alive. He had been State Secretary back in Josiah's time.
Indeed, it was he who had taken that precious Book of the
Law that Hilkiah had found. He actually put it in Josiah's
hand. It was he who had read the Book out loud to Josiah, as
the young king's eyes were so filled with tears of penitence
that he could never have read it for himself.

And Shaphan's son Gemariah had his office right there in the upper court of the New Gate Temple entrance. And it was in Gemariah's office, in full hearing of all the fasting onlookers in the courtyard below, that Baruch read the message.

Yes, you say. That's very fine. But what about the king? What about the princes and chief state advisers? There is good old Baruch reading steadily away in Gemariah's office, and probably quite a collection of open-mouthed yokels outside listening. But this is not much to show. If Jeremiah is *the* prophet, his message must get squarely through to the king and the Court if it is really going to count as the voice of God in the land. And even Gemariah himself isn't there, and he's one of the 'keen' ones. You'd think he at least would be there to give a bit of official support. It seems rather as though the scheme was a bit of a flop. This isn't going to get far in determining the doom of the nation.

But not so fast, please. Not quite so fast. For admittedly Gemariah wasn't there. He was in the palace, with Elnathan and Delaiah, the only other big shots in the whole place, it seems, who could be counted on at all in a show-down like this. And there were all three of them, sure enough, hobnobbing with the whole bunch of anti-God leaders over in the palace, the while you would think good stout-hearted Baruch was needing every ounce of weight he could gain in his support.

Doesn't God know all the answers? For Gemariah (and Elnathan and Delaiah) may not be there – but Micaiah was there. Young Micaiah, Gemariah's son. And I have no possible question that it needed just his sort of dynamic to spark the whole thing off properly. For Micaiah was still quite a young man, and as his young ears heard all the stirring message of Jeremiah's scroll it made his head spin and his heart pound. And isn't it sometimes necessary to invoke the stirring and pounding of youth to reach the calculated measure of the middle-aged and elderly?

For this is exactly how it worked. Micaiah was stirred, I think, as he had never been stirred before. And out he shot, through the Temple gate and into the palace itself, into the council chamber where all the leaders were assembled.

Protocol may be quite essential for smooth business management. Courtesy may be altogether necessary for maintaining dignity and decency. Tradition may be utterly invaluable in promoting orderliness of procedure. But that rare occasion does at times arrive when protocol and courtesy and tradition must give way to transcending authority. And into the roomfull of assembled dignitaries exploded young Micaiah, just bursting with the awful significance of Baruch's message. The utter seriousness of the young man; the sheer simplicity of his account; perhaps most significantly of all, the presence of his own father, Gemariah, and the warm support of Elnathan and Delaiah – all these carried the day. In all that passion and emotion that is both the strength and the weakness of youth, out poured the account of Baruch and his frightening warning. That statement of doom and death that he had just heard in the Temple.

The official business was forgotten. You can imagine the tension, the sense of conviction, and the silence that followed.

'Jehudi', a spokesman called to one of the official attendants. 'Go and get Baruch.'

There was that silent yes, that invisible nod, that only ever in such moments of great crisis can express so much. One spokesman was speaking, but all the princes were approving. 'Tell Baruch to bring the scroll. We must hear it ourselves.'

Hurrah for the Baruchs of the faith. Those utterly solid men who just stick to their instructions, deviating never a hair's breadth to the right or to the left, no matter what the provocation. I am absolutely certain that Jeremiah himself couldn't have done it. Facing such a congregation, seeing such a unique opportunity, I just can't imagine Jeremiah keeping to the text. He would inevitably have started to expand and modify and develop. Of course he would. So would you, probably. So would I, certainly. But not Baruch. Carefully, steadily, he started on column 1 and read it exactly in the form that all those weeks and months of thought and prayer and practice had perfected.

The seriousness and the doom of the message was only too clearly reflected in the faces of the princes, reflected even more in the embarrassed foolishness of the questions that finally trickled out.

'Tell us how you got this.'

'Yes. How did you come to write all this?'

'Er . . . r . . . r. . . . I suppose . . . that is, was it at his dictation?'

Baruch looked squarely into the eyes of this questioner as he answered.

'Yes. It was at his dictation. He dictated it, and I wrote it on this scroll.'

No need to say who 'he' was. 'He' was the man they had banned from the Temple. 'He' was the man who challenged the right of the king himself. They knew who 'he' was.

And then action! These were men used to action, and after the first stunned reaction they moved fast.

'Baruch. Go and hide, you and Jeremiah. Hide carefully. Don't let a single soul know where you are. Don't trust anybody at all. Leave us the scroll, and off you go for your lives!'

'Elishama. Lock the scroll away in your office. Quickly.'

'Gentlemen. We will go and tell the king.'

'Yes. Let's go.'

It was winter. The king had a cosy winter palace, and there he was in his little court chamber, reclining back in a soft-padded lounge, feet stretched out to the warmth of a glowing brazier in front of him. We can only guess at what was in his mind before the princes were admitted; but I have no doubt at all that Jehoiakim wasn't over-pleased at this intrusion. He heard their story through.

'Jehudi!' I am sure there was quite a bite in his voice, smoothly, quietly though he spoke. 'I suppose we will just have to hear this thing ourselves. Go to Elishama's office, fetch the scroll. Bring it here and read it again.'

Can't you imagine that minute or two of waiting? The king there in the centre, disinterested, scornful, seemingly much more concerned with the glowing ember he leans over to turn in the brazier than with this uninvited group. The princes themselves, standing around, trying to look comfortable. Perhaps there was a decanter and glasses – cigars would have been a very useful diversion, if only they had had them. Sure to be someone starting to tell some rather lewd joke, half whispering in the embarrassed manner from which such men can never escape.

But thank goodness, Jehudi is soon back. The scroll is unrolled, and he begins to read.

There is an electric stillness in the group, the voice of

Jehudi sounding very loud and very clear, with just an occasional crackle from the little fire to punctuate the reading.

The king is just looking into the fire, indifferent to it all. Beside him is a handsome side-table and on it an exquisitely carved writing-set, with which the king is absently toying. There is a moment's diversion as he throws a small coal on to the fire, but that is all. Jehudi reads on.

He is holding the scroll in his left hand, reading the written columns one by one, taking the free end in his right hand to hold the parchment steady as he unrolls it. Column succeeds column – perhaps it is now four that have been read, as Jehudi pauses to re-roll with his right hand the part he has just completed. The king has not been looking at him at all, but before Jehudi can take up more than the first turn of the roll of parchment, the king has moved. It is all done in a mere second or two of time. From the beautiful writing-set beside him his hand has slipped out the penknife, and in a single deft movement he has swung round and in one cut parted the parchment clean across. And before Jehudi can move his hand or even see clearly what is happening the king's left hand has flashed over and flicked the cut end of the roll out of the attendant's right hand and tossed it into the fire.

It is all done so smoothly, so neatly, so quickly, that it could easily be mistaken for some simple little parlour trick. That is, if it were not for the sudden flash of black rage in the king's eyes as for that second they looked up from the fire. That is, if it were not for the fallen face of Jehudi as his right hand blankly gropes for the severed end of the roll in his left hand. That is, except for the sudden cry :

'Oh, sir ! . . .'

'Please. Don't destroy it . . .'

'Sir ! You can't do that. . . .'

But what can Gemariah and Elnathan and Delaiah do? The words of protest die on their lips as the flames lick up the parchment, as the quick impatient toss of the king's head gives the gesturing signal to Jehudi to read on. And this time it is all done so deliberately, done with such cold-blooded coolness that it hurts where before it had shocked. The few columns read, calmly sliced off, dropped in the fire.

Until the scene that a few minutes before had been so tense with sheer drama now degenerates to the level of mere pantomime. Jehudi looking and feeling so foolish as he reads on, holding out the scroll now for the king to cut it across; the king barely stifling his yawning disapproval at the boredom of it all; the embarrassed confusion of Gemariah and his two friends as they see the message of God reduced to the level of sheer farce; and the half-smothered guffaws of the others, as they stand watching the little play run its course.

And so it is over. The last column has been read, the last piece burned, the whole thing played out. There is that moment of inaction that follows any such scene, where in a theatre there is the falling of the curtain as the applause breaks out; when on the TV the sponsor bursts in with his cackling appeal to 'Buy King-sized !'

But this time it is the king who breaks it up. Gone, in a flash, the boredom, the tedium, the half-hearted interest. He is on his feet, the stamp of rage equalling the scowl of face and bitterness of tone.

'What impudence ! What cheeky lies ! How dare this fellow say this ? What right has he to say the Babylonians will destroy this city ? Fancy anyone pretending to be a prophet of Yahweh writing nonsense like that !'

'Jerahmeel !' One of his own sons snaps to sudden attention. 'Seraiah ! Shelemiah ! Seize Baruch and Jeremiah. Grab them both ! We'll end this treason ! Get going, the three of you, and bring them in. I won't stand another moment of it.'

And in my imagination I watch the Celestial Operator tapping out the incoming answer : 'Message received stop message understood stop no action stop signed Jehoiakim.'

I have left Jeremiah. Jeremiah and his faithful Baruch, as they fled into hiding, as they set about their faithful task of doing-it-all-again ! For the purpose of God is not changed just because the king didn't like what he heard. God is not forced back on Plan B simply because some mere man, whether king or serf, raised his human objections to Plan A and burned it to ashes in a fire. Fie to all such blasphemous nonsense ! 'Jeremiah took another scroll and gave it to Baruch the scribe, the son of Neriah, who wrote on it . . . all the words of the scroll which Jehoiakim king of Judah had burned in the fire; and many similar words were added.'

Yes, I have left Jeremiah and his Jerusalem of over two and a half thousand years ago. It is now Sydney, throbbing high-speed Sydney of the mid-twentieth century again. It is my own city, the city of jack-hammers and high-speed riveters, of skyscrapers and expressways, of soaring concrete shells and sprawling satellite towns. A city of urgently preserved life in the pressurized oxygen chamber, of wantonly squandered life on the highways and byways, a city of sunshine and sport and pleasure unlimited, of tablets and tranquillizers, pep-pills and sedatives.

It is home again. It is work again. It is hour after hour, day after day, week after week, always people in need. Often tiring to near-exhaustion, never once tiresome or near to boredom. It is Sydney.

And it is autumn. Days when the warm sunshine and the stirring breeze make pleasure out of toil and contentment out of effort. Yet days which turn to evenings with the sheer caress of stillness and calm. These are days when a man may tackle the toughest of tasks, and well feel ready to do it. And evenings to spend in the coolness of the garden, to relax and reflect.

For it is in the relaxation and reflection of just such an evening that I ask you now to join me. This is a very particular evening. A very particular evening indeed. I have been thinking and pondering and musing about my world and about my country and, yes, about myself.

And I want to share these thoughts with Jeremiah. With the man we last saw carefully re-compiling all the message that Jehoiakim had burned in his brazier. Jeremiah had never seen an electric light, to be sure – and here I am standing out in the garden looking out over the mirror-smooth waters of our lovely harbour at the myriad lights of a big modern city. Jeremiah had never travelled at a speed faster than a galloping horse – and I look up at the droning whine of the super jet overhead. Yes, Jeremiah had never seen TV, never heard the tinkle of a cash register, never been treated by an anti-biotic, never known a single bit of sensible modern science, had never even had the simple pleasure of a nice warm shower!

And yet it is to Jeremiah that I should now like to talk. It is Jeremiah I should like to have here with me now. To have him bring me the revelation of his insight into the purpose of God as it may still apply most aptly to my so-different centuries-later city.

Then why not? If I may turn the clock back and revisit Nineveh and Jerusalem, talk to Sargon and Sennacherib, why not invite Jeremiah here? Isn't that indeed what I am supposed to do? Has God preserved these writings and experiences of His prophets merely to give us an interesting *critique* on past history? Nonsense! 'All these things that happened to them were symbolic, and were recorded for our benefit as a warning,' says St. Paul concerning comparable matters.

And this is why it is such a very particular evening. This is an evening in the company of Jeremiah. This is an evening I shall never forget. . . .

Jeremiah, I said hesitantly, before I can ask you any questions at all, there's one thing you must make quite clear, please. That is your idea of God. For I know that there are just about as many ideas of God as there are people in the world. Sir, there are some psychiatrists – plenty of them in fact – who are complete atheists and yet they are very insistent that they believe in God. Yes, God, and spelt with a capital G. But, sir, we want to understand what *you* believe about Yahweh, your God. For we live in a world of almost unbelievable inventiveness and creativity. Craftsmen in your time used to make beautiful little works of art, carving wood and overlaying it with gold and adorning it with jewels. But just catch your breath as you look at the circuitry of a modern electronic computer.

Your wood-carvers were artists enough, for sure; your goldsmiths were craftsmen enough; but think of the countless myriads of electrons which our workman today can produce and toss about in such utter mastery that you can sit back in a sponge-rubber spring-bottomed lounge chair and actually watch in your own centrally-heated and air-conditioned home a football match being played in some distant ground at this very moment. And, what is more, Jeremiah, step into a modern jet and part-circle the earth and you can see it in full colour! And we can put our Telstars in the sky and bounce this fantastic wonder round and round the world just as much as ever we like.

Here – look over in that corner of the night sky. See that

tiny moving speck – that's a man circling the earth. And that other one further over to the right – that's another. That wisp of cloud – that's not a cloud at all, Jeremiah, that's the vapour trail of a rocket on the way to the moon.

There is not a smile, but I am sure I can detect just the slightest movement of his lip-line, as he stoops and picks up a handful of earth from the garden beside us. 'Your chemists have learned a lot about soil. Your trace elements, your spectro-analytical methods, your electron-microscopy. Great knowledge. Have they learned that it is He who made this by His power?'

He stopped and let the soil trickle away through his fingers, as his gaze moved across the headland where we were standing and over the harbour to the opposite bay. The low roar of the surf as it pounded in on our sparkling ocean beaches was just to be heard through the soft rustling of the leaves in the light breeze in the evening air. 'Yes.' He paused, obviously in deep reverie and emotion, as he continued to speak. 'What truths your geologists have learned. What secrets your geophysicists have revealed – they even probed a mile and more below the earth's surface to find oil for you. Think what unique wonders you have discovered in the physical properties of simple water itself. Did your teachers at school and university tell you that this is altogether due to the wisdom of the God who established it? And look up. You Australians are world leaders in radio-astronomy. These radio-waves your men are measuring tonight from the explosion and energy of stars were actually flashed out into space thousands of millions of years ago. This vastness and complexity of grandeur that makes the greatest of minds reel back in awe – did your astro-physicists tell you that it was the limitless understanding of God's mind that stretched out the heavens?'

I didn't know what to answer. No man has ever had an answer to questions like that, as Jeremiah so well knew.

'Let me use your jargon, perhaps. Speaking to my people, with their simple cosmology and humble science, I used their language and imagery to tell them this. But it fits your twentieth-century terminology just as easily. Those clouds over there – "Condensation of water vapour on the ionized particles in the outer atmosphere . . .", your experts say. Listen. That is in fact God speaking. That is God communicating through His creation to man the ultimate creature. That is not a mere meteorological phenomenon, any more than it is just science; that is revelation. The accumulated electrostatic charge which constitutes the mega-voltage lightning flash, the thermal and gravitational mechanisms which are involved in the soft touch of the night breeze on your cheek, or in the lashing buffet of the tornado – I would tell you, just as I told my own people in my own time, to think of them as provisions God is bringing out of His divine storehouses. God knows what you want but He also knows exactly what you need. And He has just the thing stored away to meet that need.'

The prophet half turned away, and I could sense a sudden rise in his emotions. But I was quite unprepared for the shock as he turned and almost bellowed at me, staring me full in the face : 'Every man is stupid and completely ignorant; every technician is put to shame by the very instruments he looks after. His gadgets are false. They are not life-giving. They are worthless, a work of delusion !'

He stopped, and again I could sense the sudden change of mood. I am getting just that touch of middle-aged deafness which made me listen ever so carefully as he now barely whispered – 'Your scientists have indeed discovered great truths. I have heard it said that they expect very soon now to be able to make life itself. They will group their amino-acid chains with the DNA protein helix and bring life into being. Yes, that may well be. But it is God who provides all the raw materials. It is all His equipment, and it is all His invention that they are simply investigating and exploring.'

Again he paused and this time he was holding back his words, as though marshalling his thoughts for some final remark. It was perhaps a full half minute before he spoke. 'You want to know how I understand God? God is not a mere super-scientist. God is not just a master technician. He is not the ultimate calculator and electronic brain. He is the one Creator who formed everything in all existence.'

I was thinking furiously. Trying to adjust my twentieth-century thinking to this so old and yet so timeless truth. And I swear Jeremiah must have read my mind (doesn't God always read my mind?) as he continued, speaking now very smoothly, very confidently.

'Your problem is not the least bit new. It is the same old problem, as old as man himself, but just clothed in the new apparel of twentieth-century culture. This was the problem in my time. This was the first and the greatest problem. Our own plans, our own inventions, our human projects loom so very large in our lives that we find it very difficult to concede that the whole objective of life must be one hundred per cent of God's directing. That was really all I had to say to my own people, if they had just been prepared to stop and listen. They always had some sort of political manoeuvres going on, but when I asked them what direct authority they had to support their ideas, they just laughed at me. The politicians said that it would work best that way, and the people just supported their politicians – their business methods gave some of them a comfortable enough living – and just for that single reason they saw to it that their methods were retained, and even the whole religious organization was geared to suit the ideas of men just trying to look after their own affairs.

'Now look at your own world. Are you any better? Your Western world is at this very moment engaged on the most lavish, spendthrift, single project in all history. You think of the selfish pride that bled Egypt to provide her enormous pyramids; think of the man-power in my own time spent in building the lush tropical "hanging" gardens of Babylon. The Colosseum at Rome, the Parthenon at Athens, the Taj Mahal, the grandiose palaces and temples and all the rest. Add them all up – multiply them together if it suits you better – and then see them for the peanuts that they are compared to the sheer insensate pride that drives your world into the madcap race to place a man on the moon. Surely this is so nearly incredible that you must need to keep pinching yourselves to be sure that it is really and truly happening. And what for? Well, for thousands of billions of dollars, that's what for! But for what purpose? For no purpose at all. Does it feed the hungry? Does it heal the sick? Does it bring love and warmth to the widow and the orphan? These are not even thought of. It is done for cheap, common, mean-spirited human pride, and nothing more. Just for the miserable self-satisfaction of being able to say that a Russian got there first, or an American got there first. It's that still-persisting little-boy mind which says "I'm bigger'n you. My father can lick your father. Ours is a brand-new one." And if you question the whole horrible plan, you know only too well what answer you will get. Don't even bother to ask the politicians – ask the common workman. "We'll lose our jobs." That's what they will say. "We are working things for the army." "This is a big government job." "Canberra is interested in this show." (Or Washington, or Whitehall, or the Kremlin – it's the same wherever you go.) The people don't want to stop it, the bosses don't want to stop it. But just you try asking them, does God want it? Is this something they honestly believe God wants them to fashion from the matter of His creation, and you'll get a very cool reception indeed. I know. I tried.'

There was a low sandstone garden wall terracing the lawn where we were standing in the cool evening air. I moved over as Jeremiah was speaking, and sat there, chin cupped in hands, lost now in a reverie of thoughts his words had evoked. I thought of a little instrument I had been holding in my hand only that morning – a tiny, innocent-looking piece of stainless steel, and yet one of the most wonderful of all our modern surgical wonders. For it was radio-active. It gave surgical access to tissues within tissues. It may be deployed to achieve surgical excision of a nature that to the men of the few years ago that was Lister's time would have seemed the wildest pipe-dream. Think, if you please, of what the forthright Lister would have said as he sprayed his life-saving carbolic acid into his operating-theatre atmosphere, had you told him that you could place that little steel circle on the surface of a tissue and selectively destroy the damaging proliferating cells in the structure below. I seem to remember, from the little scraps of medical history which I still retain, that Lister would have had you out of that theatre with even more zeal than that with which he despatched the unwanted bacteria!

I had felt so proud, just that morning, and yet so humble, as all surgeons do, handling these wonders of our modern science. And now I felt just a bit sick, as I admitted in that moment of honesty as I faced Jeremiah, that this was only a by-product. Oh yes, a wonderfully useful by-product. But the main product of all our nuclear research is that huge stockpile of war-heads and missiles which represent the real end-result. Science hasn't poured such vast treasures of men and money into atomic physics just to produce radio-active isotopes, to

design reactors for power generation, to provide beta and
gamma ray sources for surgeons. Oh no! These are just the
tasty crumbs which have fallen from the table of the rich,
stuffed-belly War Lord at whose feet we sit hopefully.

And the jet roaring overhead, lights twinkling as it flashes
round the world in the super comfort of our unbelievable
transport. That, too, is part of the same. The real advance, the
supreme effort, is a long, long way ahead of that. The real
spearhead of all such progress is in fields very different from
that big plastic-lined jet. Very different indeed. As different
as an I.C.B.M., as different as manned space stations, as
different as war on the moon. Those hundred and more
travellers up there in the sky are simply part of the rich
reaping that Big Business can make from harvesting some of
the same crumbs from that same loaded table.

And I turn back quickly to something else in my own
world. To the world of wonder drugs and modern therapeutics. This, surely, I say to myself, must be something else.
This is better. This is the warm love of man for his neighbour,
the self-denying Samaritan in modern form, if ever there
could be such. But I remember with dismay that in one (at
least) of our mighty Western nations the drug houses spend
each year four times as much money on merely promoting
their products as that nation spends on providing and running
all of its medical schools combined. And I then remember
that great heap of lavishly produced advertising pamphlets
and blotters and booklets and even leather-bound books that
come in my mail every single day of my life. And I think,
now, of the few black-and-white photo-micrographs which
must serve to illustrate the scientific articles in the medical
journals, those same journals that are so often bloated to
publication obesity by the full-colour art-paper contributions
of the advertisers.

Jeremiah, I want to say. How right you are! There is
disturbingly little that stems from a genuine desire to use the
wonderful secrets of matter in this world of biochemistry for
the supreme honour of Him who made it all. If we search
diligently and honestly into the motives of our world we are
not going to find anything much that we can claim to be the
will of God, any more than you did two thousand five
hundred years ago.

But I don't say that. I hide that away in my inner shame and change the subject. Sir, I reply at last. Australia is a vast country, and yet we have a greater proportion of our population living in cities than they have in England. Tiny little old England is more rural than Australia. And yet, sir, city-dwelling and all that we are, we have a larger proportion of our population actually owning their own dwellings than any Western country that I know of. We think this is a very good thing, and I am sure you will agree. But it makes a very great economic challenge to our young people setting out in marriage; and indeed sometimes proves too great a challenge for them to withstand. It's not a bit good for the self-respect of the aggressive male to have to call on his wife to help him make his place in the world. That is a very deeply felt humiliation which is not made any easier to bear just because it applies to all his friends too.

And it makes for a very disturbed little wife, as she finds that her fundamental emotional birthright to be woman, to be dependent, to have her security made for her by her man in all the strength of his manhood, is simply not there for her to receive. Instead of that warm dependent security, she finds all so commonly that she is called on to sally forth into her workaday world to help provide this very thing which should properly be hers to receive. This is not rightly hers to give. Yet it is demanded of her. It's no secret at all, sir, if I tell you that I and my colleagues make a lot of money indeed out of the stress that this throws into so many lives. Of course this is not like the work the women in your time had to do. Your womenfolk tilled the soil and worked very hard indeed by our labour standards. But ours today have to come out into the aggressive world of men's business. Into factories and offices and shops and the like, and fight there in men's fights. And in a lot of categories they even do so on what they call equal pay – they slug it out with the men pound for pound, dollar for dollar, no speck of true femininity recognized at all in the struggle. Sir, this is a very grave problem in our time, one you never ever contemplated.

I have seen this so often in the troubled lives of so many patients that I just can't pass it by. St. Paul was so right when he set up the Christian ideal of teaching 'the younger women to be loving wives and mothers, temperate, chaste, and kind, busy at home, respecting the authority of their own husbands'. But, sir, this is terribly hard for the young woman today. How can she be 'busy at home' if at the same time she has to punch a typewriter or operate a loom or reach her departmental sales quota, knowing all the time that if she cracks up, if she can't hold her end up, the home front will collapse? This is not just a difficulty of social structuring – this is a challenge to the fundamental make-up of human personality as it belongs to woman.

Sir, it is no balm at all to know that this is nation-wide, even Western world-wide. That may perhaps remove the social hurt, but it most certainly does not solve the emotional hurt. You didn't see anything like this in your time, and no major civilization in history has ever seen the like, so far as I know. But the repercussions on home, marriage and children are threatening the whole foundations of our Western world. Could you tell us something about this? To answer this for us is to give us the answer that every social worker, counsellor and analyst in the land is seeking. Can you help us?

I had changed the subject all right, but I had not disturbed Jeremiah in the least by this long-winded outburst. Even the most run-of-the-mill doctor who still cares at all deeply for his patients will know something of the profound depth of this issue. And I knew that to one of Jeremiah's sensitivity and insight it would not be out of place in the least.

'I should like to tell you of one of my problems, and you may perhaps get your answer from that.' He paused just a moment for my assenting and approving nod. 'Surely you have learnt something from your background in biological science? Haven't you had it made crystal clear that if a creature is to change then it must change genetically? The skills and culture of your Western heritage are not born in your children – they are acquired after birth from their environment. And do you think that man, the ultimate creature, has changed at all since my time? Why do we read in the Book of Moses that Adam had a third son, Seth, "in his own likeness, after his own image"? Isn't this to insist that this is the story for each of us? It was true of Seth's son Enosh. And of Enosh's son Kenan. And so of Mahalalel. And of Jared and Enoch and Methuselah and Lamech and Noah. And of David. And of me. And of you.'

Yes, sir. I know that. St. Paul has expressed this in the most graphic words: 'The man made of dust is the pattern of all men of dust.' I do know that, sir. And while our geneticists are beginning to unearth some almost incredible wonders in the enzyme mechanism of reproduction and the freak events we call mutations, we do know that no major discernible mutation has been discovered in *Homo sapiens*. No, I'll go all the way with you on that, sir. I think it is as absolutely basic to all good human biology as it is to all good doctrine to insist that man has not changed at all in the thousands of years he has been on this little planet.

Jeremiah looked at me for just a moment before he replied. And I suddenly felt just a little bit silly, for even in the half-light of a little garden lantern, I could see on his face that look which told me that he had seen through me! For of course! From his knowledge of the Scriptures, Jeremiah knew the truth about man the unchanging rebel. And I had been just that little bit too warm in supporting him, because the little bit of evolutionary science I know was so parallel in its support of this important concept. How silly! Does the Word of God need the corroboration of science? What nonsense that is! As foolishly evil as the thought that the Word of God is in conflict with science. Truth is never in conflict with truth. Never, never. Is not Truth one of the noblest of all God's names?

I felt embarrassed, but as Jeremiah replied I realized that he did not intend the embarrassment. Did he perhaps know that I am old enough to have come through student days when all too tragically often our theologians had bellowed against the clearly-known truths of science? And scientists had equally often bellowed back in denial of the God of all truth! So that there is in me, as in so many of my contemporaries, an eagerness to leap into the arena to stop the fight of truth against truth.

I don't know whether Jeremiah may have guessed something of this or not. It doesn't matter – I was at least certain that God knew it in every detail.

But the prophet continued, and there was no hint of rebuke in his words. 'Then if you remember that men and their motives are the same now as then, you will probably be able to get your answer from this story. It concerns Jehoiakim. He was the son of Josiah, you remember. And Josiah was a noble king if ever there was one.

'But Jehoiakim, during his whole reign, was really only a slave. We were placed under the yoke of Egypt; and Jehoiakim was on the throne on those terms. And if ever there was opportunity to show true kingliness and leadership it was then. But what did he do? This may sound incredible, unless you know the real nature of man – but he promptly set to work building a new palace! We were desperately hard pressed just to keep alive and meet our terrific tribute dues, and Jehoiakim decided to build a new palace!

'Not just any old palace, either. It was a very specially ornate, highly decorative, snug little affair indeed. You will smile when I tell you this, with five- and six-hundred-foot buildings going up in your city, but his was two storeys, and to us that was very elaborate. And to get it he had to cheat and rob and work all the crooked deals in the world. He bankrupted the contractors and refused to pay a lot of the workmen. I told him straight out that he was building the whole thing out of crooked dealing and that the upper floor was simply an edifice of injustice!

'And Jehoiakim had the sheer audacity to announce: "I have built a splendid house for myself. It has fine spacious upper rooms with properly framed-up windows." (Don't laugh; we didn't have your curtain walls or anything in the least like it, remember!) "I'm panelling it throughout in cedar and the whole palace is beautifully painted in the most lavish colour scheme."

'I said to him, "Does that make you a king? Are you a king because you compete in cedar? What about your father? Did he compete in cedar? Wasn't he a very great king? But he was content just to eat the food that was available, to drink what was needed to quench his thirst. Wasn't his whole objective always to do what was just, to do what was right? That is surely what it means to know God. But what about you? You have eyes and heart only for your dishonest gain, for shedding innocent blood, for practising oppression and violence!"'

Jeremiah stopped for a moment, and I could see that he was almost boiling inside. He went on again, speaking so strongly and with such feeling that for a moment I was glad of the high garden wall which separated us from the occasional passer-by on the street outside! 'I knew the mind of God well enough to be able to tell him straight out that when he died not a single person would mourn for him as for a brother or for a sister. In fact no-one would even bother to work up a purely formal lament like, "Ah, His Lordship. Poor fellow." Or, "Ah, His Majesty. What a pity." No! I told him that he would be buried like a dead donkey! Just dragged from Jerusalem and dumped outside the city gates.'

This time it was Jeremiah who was slightly out of breath! And well he might be. I had listened almost aghast at the sheer audacity and the courage which had carried him to such lengths.

But I had no time to speculate for long. He pulled my thoughts back to my own question and its significance as he asked, very deliberately, in the almost stern tone that a doctor may occasionally need to assume as he asks some deeply personal but all-important question. 'Could it be that you Aussies are competing in cedar?'

Do you sometimes find that while you are talking to people some remark or other will slip you into neutral, as it were, and off you coast on a series of associations that in only a few seconds of time can carry you through a long, intricate network of ideas? I know I sometimes do. And then some further remark rather clicks me back into gear and I am back on conversational earth with a slightly blank look and an even more blank unawareness of what has just been said during my daydream.

Because that remark of Jeremiah's did just that. 'Competing in cedar?' he had asked. He went on speaking, I know, but I was not with him. Cedar? Competing in it? Aussies? Our nice young people setting out in the warm passion of affection and finding themselves up against this terrible hurdle of thousands of undiscoverable pounds.

Yes, I thought of Australia, perhaps *the* nation most properly to be thought of as living in the economic palace of the world. And yet beggared and enslaved by the tyranny of Western materialism that always demands cedar. The elaborate home, all mod. cons., the automatic kitchen, the TV, the motor-car, the this and the that and the other that all costs so much money and that can't be left out and that we simply must have and I don't see why we can't afford it we are just as good as the people next door and they have got wall-to-wall carpets and a swimming-pool too.

And the baby that is so much the richest fulfilment of all that love and romance can bring – why, the darling wee mite is the greatest complication of all. So expensive, babies are. So much money, so very much time, babies require. Mother has to leave work to have her baby.

And into my mind flashed a picture of the young mother I had been speaking to just a few hours ago in my consulting-room. Her thirteen-month-old daughter was the patient, and a little blue-eyed treasure if ever there was. 'When are you planning your second?' I had asked casually. And how can I describe that sudden bleak look in the mother's face as she faltered – 'Not for a few years, Doctor. We can't afford another. I'll have to wait till this one goes to school and I'll go back to work and earn some more money so that we can get a proper home together.'

I had run my fingers through baby's little blonde curls as I said, 'But money doesn't buy the really rich things. You are in love with a good man who loves you dearly. You have the loveliest little daughter, and warm friends and devoted parents. These are things no money in the world will buy.' And even as I said it I knew it wasn't true. Not for her, it wasn't. She just wanted the few thousand pounds, and wanted it ever so badly. She just wanted the cedar – the Aussie palace must be panelled in cedar.

And the pieces all suddenly seemed to fall into place. With that sudden flash that doctors learn both to practise and to prize so highly – that flash where a jumble of signs and symptoms suddenly sort themselves out into a clear diagnostic syndrome – I felt I had my answer.

Jeremiah stopped saying whatever it was that he had been saying, and his silence broke my reverie.

Sir, I said very sombrely, and quite unmindful of the complete *non sequitur* my words must have been to his last remarks, I think I do indeed understand. And I think the only answer is a courage and fortitude that doesn't belong to ordinary young people at all. It belongs to God, and if they belong to Him then they may well ask Him in His grace to supply them with it. No wonder so many marriages break under the strain, trying to carry this load without the strength of God to support them. Competing in cedar!

For now it became plain. So terribly plain that I felt something turn over inside me. The teenagers and the adolescents and the young adults with their unrest and their promiscuity and their ever-mounting rebellion. What else can we expect? What else can they in fact do? With all our cedar, all our rich chromium-plated electronically-controlled cedar, what other path can possibly lie open to them?

For we make them. They are not the biological product of nature. Nature doesn't have any adolescents; *she* transforms the child into the adult at a speed that leaves all of us parents almost gasping. The boy of yesterday is today almost as tall as his dad. The little girl who romped about, all freckle-spangled and in tousled pigtails, is suddenly the lissom, shapely young woman. The hormonal drama of that sudden transition is as exciting as anything known in the whole magic of endocrinology. Yes. Nature does it that way.

But twentieth-century Westernism doesn't do it that way. Twentieth-century Westernism deals altogether in cedar, and the kids can't have cedar just for the asking. No, sir! Cedar costs a packet, and it's got to be cedar, see. All the proper grown-ups have got cedar and if you think you can slum it in boxwood or deal or pine then you had better go some place else. We're all cedar here.

Sure, if you can't afford cedar, then just don't buy in at all. Kid, you're just playing. Don't let them think you are really a man at all. Gang up with a bunch of fellows like yourself and stay outside. It's so nearly hopeless to try and get inside that you might just as well forget all about it. And those hormones that pushed you up from being a boy so fast, that drive you like a dynamo all let loose inside, they won't be slowed down just because you can't get cedar. Those hormones are too strong. It takes far too much strength to hold back those surging adult hormones. Don't even bother trying. Just play along with them, make love to your girl, cuddle up so sweetly to your boy, make plenty of dates, be hanged to all the corny old self-restraint and hands-off jazz. And, say, fellers, remember you are only kids – that's what the big outside world keeps telling you, so you just pretend they're sure right this time.

Remember, that's the big world of cedar outside, and you've only got hormones, not cedar. Dress yourself up in funny tight pants and long hair so that they won't ever think you are a man – men have to deal in cedar. Sing all your songs in a funny little bleating sort of croon so that no-one will suspect that you've really got a big man's voice coming up inside you. And remember, the girls know you must play it that way – they know you daren't even pretend to be a man, because men are measured in cedar, and you've only got hair on your chest. Sure, grow whiskers if you like, it might make you feel better – but of course you don't see any men in whiskers – certainly not the cedar men.

And listen, kids, don't let it worry you at all. Even go and get married if you like. You're only kids, and kids can get married now. Lots of them do. In the U.S. most of them do. Never mind if it's a flop later – you can always wash it up and get married again when you've got a bit of cedar together. And notice how the big men do that too. Lots and lots of them. Start out with one wife – pick up another later on. It's no trouble today. Even the biggest cedar merchants in the world do that often enough now. Lots of doctors and lawyers and politicians and tycoons do that now. And ever so many of them have little affairs going on in the office or on their trips and conferences and congresses and the like. They've got the cedar to pay for it, of course. But don't let that put you off. Just you find a girl to make love to – isn't that what hormones are for? No dice to this all-clammed-up-inside wise-guy repressive stuff the religious jerks are nagging about. If you can't get cedar then at least get your girl.

But I can't keep you with me any longer as I talk to Jeremiah, as Jeremiah talks to me. As I asked him why he always spoke to the political and civil administrators and chiefs as though they were really tied up in religious duties – didn't he think there was a separation of life into some things that were secular and some that were sacred? And he didn't reply – he just looked me straight in the eyes until his gaze seemed to bore right through me and my eyes fell and my heart felt like lead. For of course – which part of life may any man dare to presume belongs only to himself when he himself is in fact a creature of God? What blasphemy! What pagan idolatry is this that has ever been allowed to creep into Christian thinking?

But these and such questions are better kept between me and Jeremiah, for they are indeed between me and God. For the prophet insisted ever so simply and ever so sternly that they are between all men and God. Greed in the throne is of the same substance as greed in the back lane. Adultery in the monarch's palace is still the same adultery that it is in the rich man's mansion or that it is in the meanest dwelling of the poor. Any man confronted by God is only ever man.

For that is the way it must always be. To meet Jeremiah at all is truly to meet God. And while for me that must be in the living of a twentieth-century doctor in his Western culture, for any other man it must always be in the day-to-day life in which he himself is the central figure. So that I shall not ask you to share overmuch in my own personal discussion with Jeremiah; I do instead want you to come with me into an experience of his own, and from that find the final pieces in our search for information.

If you could just bear to take that short moment to wriggle or have another drink or light up again or whatever it is you do at a point like this I should be very glad, for I find that this is exactly where I have to do this myself in terms of the meaning I am trying to make. To make it easier at my end, I have even turned the page to start writing on a fresh sheet.

For surely you must be beginning to feel that my original reference to Jeremiah as apparently 'so miserable, so unrelievedly gloomy, so full of "lamentations", that his name has become a sort of by-word for all the long-faced wretchedness that so many people think any prophet of God must be', was entirely right. For in just about everything I have said about him this is true enough.

The political leaders, who tried to buoy up the hopes of the people, he labelled 'false prophets'. In other words, 'plain liars'. The religion of the day, which tried to catch the interest and support of the people by means other than those written in the Law, he branded 'idolatry'. The morality of leaders and people alike, which had an almost twentieth-century Western broadmindedness in its conventions, he insisted was simple 'adultery'. And all of this and always, he thundered, God would answer in dire and disastrous judgment, a judgment such as they had never known in all their history, a judgment that would finally end in their utter destruction and total slavery.

Now you are right in insisting, and I am ready enough to admit, that this is indeed unrelievedly gloomy. It is altogether bleak, stern, unrelenting, deadly serious. And if this were all of Jeremiah that could be discovered, if this were the full measure of the mandate of his message, then his critics would be as right as the critics of Christ would be right when they declare that a life following Him is too utterly long-faced and spoil-sport to be worth another thought.

No. Make no mistake about this at all – this is in fact the most widely held and most sincerely held misconception in all our society. It is so narrow-minded, we are told. So like the awful Puritans. So unnatural. So often the collecting-point for misfits and psychopaths and crackpots, that no normal sensible man who wants to enjoy life would ever be silly enough to get really caught up in it. No, sir. Not for little old me. Good for the women, especially the lonely old ducks, and helps the kids get a grip on themselves and learn to behave. But count me out – I'm going off to golf.

And how utterly and tragically wrong they really are. And no-one can show more graphically and dramatically just how wrong they are than Jeremiah himself. For the truth is only ever understood when you learn the other part of the story – the part you can only ever learn by experience. Not that Jeremiah didn't chat about it, write about it, preach about it. Of course he did. But nobody much took any more notice of him than they did of Christ after him or than they do of His disciples today.

So that I am not particularly interested in asking you to come and listen to Jeremiah talking or read what Jeremiah wrote about it. It's there, if you like to look it up for yourself. But I am asking you to come with me and actually observe it in the life of the man himself. See it as if it were engraved into the deepest fibre of his being. And, what is more, see it glowing in all its dazzling brilliance of assurance and hope in a setting that is an utter heartbreak of misery and despair.

For this is just what God has done, in the account that He has preserved of the life of Jeremiah. God has invited us to come and see this wonderful truth in the actual lived-out record of the prophet. And so we go back again, to the reign of Zedekiah, to a Jerusalem actually besieged by the irresistible army of Babylon, to a jail in the middle of the little city, to Jeremiah in the jail itself.

For this is an event in the very last few months of the life of Jerusalem. The city of Jebus that David had captured and re-named Zion, City of God, Jerusalem, was about to be destroyed. Surrounded for the last time by hostile, devouring foes. And not this time by the sneering, filthy, brutal hordes of Assyria, but by the stern, relentless, irresistible might of Babylon.

It is over twenty years since Josiah's death, and all those long twenty years Jeremiah had been insisting that this was the inevitable doom. The people God had called to worship Him with their obedience had instead tried to fob Him off with their religion. He had saved them from Egypt and from Assyria for all the centuries before, for the sake of His servant David and for His own sake. But now the point of no return had been reached. In the love and the purpose of God the only way of keeping His people true in their faith was by wiping their city out; by destroying the Temple which the subtle arrogance of a faithless Solomon had built as a Phoenician architectural jewel in their midst; by ending their royal dynasty and eradicating the proud tradition of indestructibility.

Jehoiakim had gone. Gone years ago; gone as a miserable cheat who escaped bondage in Babylon for his lying perfidy only by ignominious death from illness. His adolescent son Jehoiakin lasted only three months. Nebuchadrezzar saw at a glance that this was no sort of teen-ager to have administering a proud and turbulent city-state like Jerusalem, and off into captivity in Babylon went Jehoiakin. And Zedekiah, his uncle, Josiah's last son, was placed on the throne.

And if ever you want to study the quisling to end all quislings, the Mister-Facing-Two-Ways of all time, it is Zedekiah. Forever trying to stay in the good graces of his Babylonian bosses, yet trying to cook up alliances with Egypt and any other possible anti-Nebuchadrezzar ally – this was Zede-

E

kiah. Always currying favour with the Temple masters and the powerful religious hierarchy : yet sneaking off time and time again to see if just perhaps Jeremiah might have some relenting message or less determined statement of judgment – this was ever Zedekiah.

And perhaps nothing tells the utter tragedy of the life of Zedekiah so much as the account of the last thing he saw on this earth. Jerusalem destroyed, every warning of Jeremiah fulfilled in terrible detail, himself in Babylonian chains and on his way to death in slavery, he saw his sons lined up and killed in front of his eyes. And so that no further sight or picture might ever arrive to take this torturing vision from his memory, his own eyes were gouged out by the Babylonian conquerors. I don't know of any biblical post-mortem that has quite the horrifying awe that is found in the account of Zedekiah.

And it is in the very last days of this final defeat that we are going to see the reality that is the heart and spirit of the man of God.

For Jerusalem is besieged. The great Babylonian assault forces are slowly and relentlessly driving their irresistible way through the defences that centuries of time have seen built around Jerusalem. The vast man-made ramparts that in Hezekiah's time were shown to be altogether unnecessary when *God* is defending the city, are now proving so altogether inadequate when God's hand is withdrawn. And the walls are slowly being breached and the city is tumbling to her death.

There, in the heart of the fortified city, is the further fortified palace of the king. And in the heart of the palace courtyard is the king's prison. And inside that very prison is Jeremiah.

There is almost a comic-strip, TV-cartoon quality that must make you grin just a bit as you think of it. You know the kid's show – the hero is bound in weighted fetters in a lead-encased iron trunk expelled from a submarine a mile below the surface in mid-Atlantic. Will our hero escape? Can he survive this terrible death? Tune in next week for the thrilling climax.

For this story is like that, and yet so unlike that as to make your heart leap! For Jeremiah is in bonds, in the guardhouse,

in the palace courtyard, in the palace walls, in the city ramparts, in the surrounding Babylonian army. And you smack
your lips at the taste of heady drama, and mentally flip over
the pages of *The Count of Monte Cristo,* of *The Scarlet
Pimpernel* and of Houdini and of *The Wooden Horse* and of
all such Great Escape stories you ever read, as you wonder
just how Jeremiah will make it.

And then you can really catch your breath as you find that
it's already over – Jeremiah is free. Jeremiah is no more
imprisoned than the mighty Nebuchadrezzar himself is imprisoned. Is the exultant grandeur of the finale imprisoned in
the Beethoven Ninth? Is the star imprisoned in endless
space? Is the soaring eagle imprisoned in the vaulted heavens?
Why, if that is what you mean by imprisonment, then that
was the limitless freedom in which Jeremiah was bound and
fettered.

Come and watch. . . .

Jeremiah had come to a decision. He had thought and
prayed hard and long, and now he knew just what to do. He
would buy that piece of land in Anathoth. Yes, he must buy it.

In the Jewish law of his time you couldn't ring up the local
Land and Estate Agent and say, 'Mr. Realtor, I want to buy
a couple of acres of land down in Anathoth. Would you mind
sounding out the current owner and finding out whether or
not he is interested and at what price?' Because in the first
place land was held in family title only, and unless you were a
member of the family you had no honest access to it at all.
And secondly, between Jeremiah in fetters in jail in the court
in the palace in the city in the Babylonian army, and Anathoth, there was not – repeat not – any telephonic or other
kind of link at all. For Anathoth was out in the hinterland
outside the city, just about at the very spot where the Tank
Corps or the Tenth Light Horse or some such Babylonian
unit was right at that very moment parked. And Jeremiah
was preparing to buy that land in Anathoth! Jeremiah,
imprisoned? Fie!

But the land belonged to his cousin Hanamel (the son of
Uncle Shallum); and to a man in fetters in jail in the court,
etc., etc., family meetings for business negotiation are tradi-

tionally somewhat difficult to effect. But not to Jeremiah. To a man as free as he, to a man whose only final bondage was to the will of God, this did not matter in the least.

So Jeremiah collected up his cash, the seventeen shekels which was the market value of the land, and prepared for business.

And you don't need me to tell you, do you? The knock at the guardhouse door, the rattling of keys and clank of chains and there, sure enough, was Hanamel. 'Hey, Jeremiah, visitor to see you. Stay as long as you like, mate. He's a good prisoner. We've never worried about him trying to escape. Ha ha! Wouldn't we all like to escape? There you are — squat on the corner of the bunk over there — you'll soon get used to the dark. Just pound on the door when you want to go.'

I must confess I have often chuckled to myself over this deal. I may be quite wrong but I don't think so. I think Hanamel was the meanest, low-down skunk of a cousin that ever visited a miserable jail-bird in history. Because it was he who brought the subject up. Jeremiah was all prepared — had his seventeen shekels, all counted and polished ready. But he didn't say a word about it. It was Hanamel who made the offer. And if you can persuade me that it was out of his generous-hearted nature that cousin Hanamel had come prepared to sell up the family estate out there in Anathoth, right under the hooves of the Babylonian Tenth Light Horse, to a fellow who was in jail because the king hated and feared him as much as Zedekiah did, then you just come and visit me in Sydney and I'll guarantee to sell you our Harbour Bridge! You are just too naïve for this tough little old world.

No, sir! This is just plain, greedy, crooked Hanamel coming to con his poor, dreamy, head-in-the-clouds cousin out of the price of a completely useless bit of land for which he held an even more useless title-deed.

What a pair. Jeremiah, knowing the inner heart of man more honestly than any man in all history except Christ Himself — knowing the craftiness of his cousin and knowing the real object of his visit and yet mastering his excitement as he must wait for Hanamel to make the move. And Hanamel, working through a very smooth line of patter that he had been working on for weeks. You can guess with me how it goes: 'Well, well, well! Jeremiah, old man. Glad to see you.

Just like old times. Snug little hide-out, ha ha! Bit cramped though I suppose . . . how's the rheumatism? Be good to have a bit of a run in the open country, eh? Remember the old family homestead down in Anathoth? Great times we had there as kids, didn't we? Don't get much of a chance to get out there, especially with these Babylonian skirmishes going on. I'm in charge of "Q". Keeps me so busy I haven't time for family affairs. Only wish I could unload the old property responsibilities. I'd practically give the place to anyone in the family who was free to look after it. A pity you can't get out yourself. Do you the world of good to get a bit of fresh country air and sunshine after all this time in a pestilential little dog-house like this. What? You? Oh no, I couldn't possibly! My dear Jeremiah, it's frightfully decent of you, and all that, but I mean to say, in your position? Well, I suppose that if you insist I can't possibly refuse you point-blank. It's really no use to me at all, I know, but if you actually feel you'd like it? Oh, don't worry about the money. You can have it as far as I'm concerned. Still, I suppose I'd have to charge *something,* just to make it look respectable and honest. H'mmm. . . . Let's see. . . . I suppose its full value is something like a couple of hundred. But make it some token sum only. Say fifty. No. Make it twenty. Twenty. . . . Twenty. . . . Listen, could you rise to seventeen? I don't give a hoot about the money for myself, but it's the look of the thing. Must think of the rest of the family and all that, you know. We can't give the impression that we think the family estate is just a bagatelle, can we? What do you say to seventeen? How does that suit you, Jeremiah?'

Just as well it was half dark! Hanamel couldn't see the widening pupils and flushing cheeks as Jeremiah exulted in the wonder of the ways of God.

What did it matter that it was half dark? Jeremiah needed only the light of the knowledge of the greedy, selfish heart of man to see in clearest ugliness the craftiness of the angler adroitly casting his snare.

'Baruch!' It was Jeremiah now, banging on the door. The guard slowly and noisily slid back the heavy bolts. 'Would you call Baruch for me, please?'

Good old Baruch. Still with Jeremiah, still standing by in his master's need.

'Baruch, I want you to draw up a proper official deed of purchase to the title of the family estate in Anathoth.'

Baruch had been too long with Jeremiah, too close to the mind of God, to be surprised. It was Hanamel who was breathing rather thickly.

'And Baruch. I want it in duplicate. And would you ask the guards if they would mind acting as witnesses? And I want the official scales for weighing the money. It must be altogether open and above-board and legal.'

I don't know how long it all took to get organized, but it must have been an hour at least. And what an hour! For Jeremiah, that was an hour of the tranquil serenity that is still the dynamic of the surging will of God. For Hanamel an hour of that agonizing suspense of the angler who has brought his fish alongside, whose gaff is ready – but whose hand is trembling and whose heart is thumping until the fish is really in the bottom of the boat. For Baruch a busy hour indeed – you just try scratching out a bit of Hebrew prose long-hand, and you'll soon see what I mean. And the buzzing of the guards as they collected up in rather amused and sympathetic interest. And of course the inevitable gaping passers-by who all craned their necks to peer into this funny little going-on in the prison yard.

And there, in the very doorway of the prison cell, the deal was completed. The title-deeds of transfer duly drawn up in duplicate, signed by purchaser and vendor, counter-signed by the witnesses. The seventeen shekels counted *and* weighed on the official city scales in the presence and under the hand of the duly constituted authority at law. And Jeremiah, the seeming prisoner, the man who is sealed in the cell from which there can be found no possible escape, is in fact away out in the freedom of the open spaces of Anathoth – Zedekiah and Nebuchadrezzar and all Babylon (and don't forget crafty Hanamel) notwithstanding!

'Baruch! Take this official title-deed, and the open copy and seal them in a really strong earthenware jar. Seal it with wax, and make it absolutely watertight and airtight. And then bury it. Bury it so deeply that it will never be dislodged or destroyed. And listen' – and here he paused to look, one after the other, straight into the eyes of Hanamel and the guard and the witnesses and most searchingly of all into the eyes of faithful Baruch – 'Anathoth will be yielding crops and pasturing flocks again for the people of God. Oh yes, Babylon will destroy everything there is in this city – you bury that jar safely, Baruch, so that they won't ever reach it as they overrun the city – but God still owns the title-deeds of this sad city and in His own time He will bring us back into possession.'

And urged on by the excitement and drama of that fascinating but altogether tragic little episode, Jeremiah was lifted to a height of revelation that was never to be exceeded in this world until resurrection Sunday itself. There, in the pitiable setting of fetters and human wickedness, in sound of the thunder of the enemy assault mounds and battering-rams, the man of God could see at least the shadow of the greatness of the purpose of God in the destiny of man. A destiny that must finally be explained only in a new type of city, a new type of country, a new type of nation. For it meant a new type of man, a man with the law of God in his very heart. A man who 'knew' God, a man whom God Himself 'knew'.

For this is the real measure of Jeremiah, of any prophet of God, of any man of God. This is the only person who can face the darkness of the bleak heart of man as he really is, face it honestly and critically and without embarrassment, for this is the only one who can see through that and past that to the dazzling spectacle of the people of God as they are in the fulfilment of their ultimate destiny. This is not monasticism, this is not escapism, this is not mysticism. This is realism. This is the realism that is prepared to rot life out in a dungeon cell, if need be; the realism that pays out precious cash for worthless return, if called to do so; the realism that sees the world for the hard, bitter place that it is and still comprehends the measureless love of God. This is the realism of obedience, that serves God who alone holds all the title-deeds.

You may not agree with me, for this is conjecture on my part. But I feel very strongly convinced that those title-deeds are still there. I am not an archaeologist, I'm not a historian, I've never even seen Jerusalem and for the life of me can't imagine any single inducement that might ever make me want to see it. I'm just a doctor. But it is perhaps because I am a doctor, because I do know something of the character of the greatness of the humble Baruchs of this world, that I say this : I think that scroll is still there.

I feel altogether confident that if ever the archaeological treasures of Jerusalem were to be unearthed, Jeremiah's title-deeds to Anathoth would be among them. Our Baruchs don't settle for any old cracked partly-glazed jars for storing title-deeds. Not a bit of it. That jar is still as good a jar as can be had. And no slapdash daub of wax sealed that jar, either. When Baruchs seal those deeds in jars they seal them thoroughly and for keeps. And no dog scratching up last week's bone is going to unearth that jar, of that you may be sure. It's there all right. But you'll have to dig for it. Baruchs always bury their treasures properly, right down deep on the very rock face and out of the way of the curved spade and pick-axe. I suggest you had better bring along a bulldozer, hire a back-ditcher or drag-line, if you want to dig it up; for I say that package is still in safe keeping.

Yes, that is conjecture, I admit, and it's a conjecture which has quite a flavour of excitement about it, you must agree. But the conjecture is in itself quite unimportant. The real importance of that day's transaction is the truth it symbolizes, a truth that will outlast time itself.

And if some day some ordinary human behaves in the twentieth-century pattern of what human behaviour has been through all the centuries, and drops a hydrogen bomb on little old Jerusalem, then I will continue to insist that those title-deeds still hold good. Oh, sure enough, Baruch's little jar and Jeremiah's parchment will revert to photons and gamma rays and beta neutrinos and all the little what-have-you particles that the experts tell us about. But the title-deeds will still be there! God holds them as He has always held them. Let Babylon flood in. Greek and Roman, Mogul and Ottoman, Saracen and Crusader, Arab and Israeli, let them all come. God doesn't drop His claims on their account. And even let the Moloch of Western science wipe the whole face off the earth – for as the mushroom clouds clear away and the radio-active dust settles in deadly destructiveness over the whole of this little globe, you will still see those title-deeds in the hand of God.

That is what this little story is really teaching. That is the glimpse of the truth that the penetrating eye of Jeremiah could see six long centuries before it burst in full clarity into human sight. That is the allegory, that is the parable, that is the moral, that is the symbolism – that is the *idea* – you just use the noun of your own choice. . . .

Jeremiah, no wonder our Lord quoted your words more than the words of any other writer in the Old Scriptures. As you looked into the heart of your people, with all their petty greed and spiritual apathy; as you saw the advancing engines of Babylonian destruction slowly and inexorably pulverizing your city walls, you knew the answer. You didn't know the form the answer would take, but you certainly knew something of the sheer vastness of the size it must assume. As you looked into your people's history, as you looked even more closely into the black littleness of man-the-rebel as he lived in your little city, you knew. The God who, in His endless love and mercy, had preserved you *from* death for century after century, must just as surely preserve you *through* death in ages to come.

Certainly, Jeremiah, you didn't know about the resurrection. You were six hundred years before that day when God's purpose for man was to be made known. That supreme revelation was long, long centuries after your time. And you were wise enough and honest enough to refuse to guess. But you were also honest enough and wise enough to know that no paltry shekel, no earthly title-deed, was worth a moment's further grasp when the treasure and inheritance of God's people might be received in exchange. You knew just how lavish is the hand of God, who is Love.

And, Jeremiah, as I take this last look with you into the vast technological and material and cultural wealth of my own world and my own so-exciting Australia, may I thank you for your brave example and strong courage as you help me to declare, with bowed heart and exultant hope : 'I count everything sheer loss, because all is far outweighed by the gain of knowing Christ Jesus my Lord. . . . All I care for is to know Christ, to experience the power of his resurrection, and to share his sufferings, in growing conformity with his death, if only I may finally arrive at the resurrection from the dead.'

CHAPTER FOUR

PROGNOSIS EXCELLENT

IF one midsummer day I were to find myself standing on the bank of a wide subtropical river, and there to see a great rolling storm cloud sweeping up into the heavens, full of dazzling flashes of coloured lights and bronze-burnished flames; and if I then saw weaving out of this awesome spectacle four gigantic creatures each with four heads and four wings and the four feet of a calf, I can assure you that the very next moment I would be dashing to the nearest phone to persuade a psychiatric colleague to come racing to my aid with tranquillizers, insulin, little black box and all. Shades of Aldous Huxley and his mescaline! One dose of that experience would go quite a long way with me, thank you, and I am more than happy to carry right on in the most humdrum routine in the world, if that should be the only alternative.

But when it happened to Ezekiel, for it was in fact his experience, he tells us that he bowed his face to the ground and listened intently to God speaking!

Now I have said this right at the start of this chapter, because it helps me myself to understand why for so many years of my life the Book of Ezekiel was sheer spiritual desert. This prophet and I work on such entirely different frequencies that for many years I just felt our spiritual antennae were quite incapable of any intercom hook-up.

I like the negro spiritual, of course. You know:

> 'Ezekiel saw dem wheels,
> Wheels, way in de middle ob de air.
> . . . An' de big wheel go by faith
> An' de l'il wheel go by de grace ob God.'

And I have heard an occasional sermon preached from a text or passage in Ezekiel's prophecy. In fact I have heard quite a few sermons based on the great statement the prophet makes, and then later repeats, on the duty of the watchman. And I must say that I have never heard yet, and feel quite sure that I shall never hear in the future, any sermon that can match the sheer impact of Ezekiel's own words. They are their own sermon, and don't need any build-up from a pulpit.

But that didn't really help. For even the craziest man in the world may just occasionally come out with a completely sensible comment, and it does then sound more particularly sensible because of all the other quaint things he has been saying. Oh yes, I could understand the duty of the watchman. I could all too easily appreciate its tremendous spiritual challenge to my own life. But Ezekiel himself was not one tiny bit nearer.

And may I add this, which is said with the most kindly motive, even though it may at first sound utterly uncharitable? I have heard occasional sermons on other parts of Ezekiel's writings, sermons on Ezekiel's Temple – sermons by the most delightfully stout-hearted fellows in the world, but men so altogether without imagination that they contemplate the whole imagery in yards, feet and inches. You may yourself have heard something like it. Lots of maps, diagrams, charts, and the like, with elaborate calculations to determine the exact site overlooking the valley of Hinnom (or is it the valley Kedron?) or with a nice up-to-date Kodachrome showing just how it will take in the Church of the Holy Sepulchre and yes, there it is, due west of the Mount of Olives. And giving the impression that the Risen Christ will conduct Divine Service at 11 and 7 each Sunday in a heaven that is so earth-sized, glory that is so obviously merely man-made, that Ezekiel himself could never possibly recognize it as having any remote connection with his visions.

Now I don't say that meanly, in the least. I say that because Ezekiel is just so different, so apart, from most of us that he needs very sensitive understanding and very careful handling indeed.

And let us remember this, too. There is quite a trace of Ezekiel in several of the writers of Bible text, and their 'apocalyptic' statements make much of our good, solid Anglo-Saxon eschatology look rather tawdry.

And having said that, let us get back to Ezekiel and his vision, for it came to him one day early in July when he was standing by the side of the river Kebar.

And that wasn't the end of the vision, either. Not by a

long, long way. For Ezekiel stopped and gave very careful scrutiny to the four 'creatures'. For you couldn't call them animals, not with four heads and four wings and four legs each. And you couldn't possibly call them human, just because one of the faces was human, or just because two human hands were tucked away in among the skeletal architecture. (And if ever anything could be dreamed up as a comparative anatomist's nightmare, then surely this is it!) So Ezekiel calls them 'creatures', for he wants it to be very, very clear that they were not divine – they are of the category of creature, not Creator. But he says that these creatures were all joined together and moving in formation; they were in fact arranged in a square and they kept their square-formation as they moved.

I rather gather they were facing outward, backs to the centre of the square; and that meant that the eagles' faces were facing in, for Ezekiel says, 'the four had the face of an eagle at the back.'

Further, each had two of its four wings outstretched, and its wing-tips met those of the next, thus completing the square. And all the time in the centre of this square there was a blazing fire which kept throwing out lightning flashes!

'Now', says Ezekiel, 'as I looked at the living creatures, I saw a wheel upon the earth beside the living creatures, one for each of the four of them.'

You see what I mean? Ezekiel is the sort of man who is quite prepared just to go on looking at all this. You probably, and I certainly, seeing all this going on up in the northern sky, would by this time have been racing south just as fast as humans can travel. But Ezekiel simply went on staring at it. And I confess I find it somewhat hard to grasp just what it was he says he saw.

For the wheels themselves were fantastic. All around their rims they were studded with eyes. (Am I right in assuming that all these swivelling eyes were equipped with eyelids?) And the whole entourage was castoring. Ezekiel doesn't use that word, for of course the castoring wheel had not as then been invented. But it was able to move and pivot in any direction through the agency of its wheels. And then when the engineer in you starts getting excited at the idea that perhaps Ezekiel should at least be given credit for originating at any rate the concept of movement on castors, he upsets it all by seeing the whole thing rise and fall too!

And now over the top of the whole phantasmagoria he saw a great, glistening, crystal canopy, and all the time there was a deafening roar that was a mixture of huge, tumbling waters and the tumult of an army in action!

And then, literally to cap it all was a great sapphire throne mounted on the crystal canopy, and lastly – listen carefully, for this is what brought Ezekiel falling to the ground on his face – there, seated on the throne and utterly resplendent in all the glory of the rainbow, was 'a likeness as it were of a human form'. And Ezekiel may well pause, he may well fall in awe, for this One, this who had a likeness as it were of a human form, was not God – as the apostle John points out, 'No one has ever seen God' – but 'such was the appearance of the likeness of the glory of the LORD'.

This, then, is the remarkable man I want to interview with you, as we study him, try to understand him, most of all as we try to learn from him the very great spiritual lesson God is seeking to teach through him. Like all the other Bible stories, this is not there to provide amusement or light entertainment on an otherwise dull, wet weekend. This is writing to instruct, to advise, to warn.

Come, then, if you will, and join me as we meet with and learn from this extraordinary man, Ezekiel. I assure you that I myself will be stirred, as I have seldom been stirred, by the sadness and hope, the courage and despair, that we shall discover in Ezekiel. These wonderful qualities that I and my medical colleagues see at times in the lives of the men and women we care for, we may come to discover in Ezekiel as we have never seen them before.

And so that we may be clear where we are, where it all happened, and most of all what it's all about, let me explain as simply as I can something of the setting and background of it all.

The location was a slave-labour encampment, probably in the Tigris-Euphrates Delta area, probably a hundred miles or more from the Persian Gulf. The river Kebar, where Ezekiel said he saw these visions, is not today known at all.

It was very probably a man-made canal, adjacent to a huge irrigation scheme that was under way in that whole area. Today we could probably recognize it only as a slight undulation in the arid desert plain. But Ezekiel most certainly saw the thing as a ghastly, heart-breaking, endless experience of mud and digging and backache and sweat and heat and general hell-on-earth.

For he was one of the slaves. And no-one will ever persuade me that the visionary Ezekiel was the sort of man who should be thought of as a good, steady, six-buckets-an-hour mud-digger. No, I just can't see Ezekiel like that at all.

And if that was *where* it was, then *when* it was was about 592 BC. Of course Ezekiel couldn't have told us that, but he could certainly have said it was in the thirteenth year of the reign of Nebuchadrezzar. Everybody knew Nebuchadrezzar, everybody in Ezekiel's whole world. Everybody knew when Nebuchadrezzar came to the throne, everybody knew just exactly what Nebuchadrezzar meant in current world affairs. Nebuchadrezzar saw to that.

So it was easy for Ezekiel to tell us just when it happened. But he didn't. He didn't tell us like that, because he didn't think like that. Now I and my colleagues are often rather piqued by this Ezekiel-ish quality in some of our patients. You know, perhaps, the rather exasperating sort of situation. How long is it since you've had your gall-bladder removed, Mrs. Smith? Oh yes, Doctor, I remember that so well. It was the year after my mother died. I nursed her right through to the last and the doctor said I had overstrained myself, and that had brought on the gall attack, and there was nothing else for me to do, was there Doctor, really? Of course not. You did what was quite right. But what year did your mother die in? Oh, it was awful, Doctor. It was the same year my sister had the twins, and she was terribly sick carrying them, you know, and she couldn't lift a finger to help me with mother, the poor dear. And the relief you now feel as you ask simply, And just how old are the twins now?

Ezekiel is like that. That is why he says, to make it so emphatically clear to us : 'it was in the fifth year of the exile of King Jehoiakin.' And, because it is a matter of much more important precision than just that, he tells us it was the fifth day of the fourth month of that fifth year.

Now from this you may just begin to piece a few threads together. Jehoiakin was the miserable son of his miserable father Jehoiakim, the man who had built the cedar palace and whose body had been just dumped outside Jerusalem like a dead dog, when he died. Jehoiakin had been installed on the throne by Nebuchadrezzar, but he had lasted there only three months. The Babylonian king didn't approve of him, and had had him deported to Babylon. His uncle Zedekiah had been put on the throne in Jerusalem in his stead.

Fortunately, the experts can work all this out, and they tell us that it was 592 BC, in Nebuchadrezzar's thirteenth year as king.

And Jehoiakin had been five years in Babylonian exile.

And to Ezekiel that was the operative number, because it seems that he had been transported to Babylon at the same time. And if you asked Ezekiel how he counted the date then you would be just too silly if you expected him to answer in terms of Nebuchadrezzar and the Babylonian calendar. To a young priest just twenty-five years old, suddenly uprooted from his dearly-loved Jerusalem and man-powered into a works' gang digging irrigation canals in Central Babylonia, then that is most certainly the date you measure time by. Because that is the date life dried up.

And those five, long, dreadful years of slaving drudgery were an aching wound in the very heart of the young man that nothing could ever fully heal.

Not that life was altogether hopeless. It had been five years, five terrible, endless, dreary years, sure. But it was not going to be for ever. The slaves would keep reminding each other that it would come to an end. It would not go on indefinitely. There was always just the tiniest ray of hope. You know how it is – those little bits of rumour, whispers of subtle gossip, tiny nods and slight sidelong glances, all of which would escape their Babylonian overlords. And in the evenings in their encampments, in the tea-breaks and smoke-time that belong of physiological necessity to any and all such groups of working men, the hope would brighten further as they talked together.

Ezekiel knew this, knew it well. He was a priest, and most of it came from the priests. Nebuchadrezzar was very sympathetic to the religious experience of peoples he conquered, and a significant, even though greatly modified, form of their Jewish religion was left to them.

And this was the big role of the priests among the slaves. It has always been their role, seen from any such human viewpoint. Why does the army still insist on its padres? What are naval chaplains for? What are they for, if it's not for this? Morale was as valuable to the slaves in Babylon as to any other comparable group in any history. And this was the priests' message, then as now. Ezekiel heard them, perhaps joined them, as they moved around among the group. 'Stick to it, men. Keep a stiff upper lip. It won't be long now.' 'I'd say two years at the most. Some very hopeful rumours on the grape-vine last night.' 'Yes, I heard it too. About Zedekiah and you know who?' 'That's so right! Pass the word around quietly. Tell the fellows the end is in sight.' 'And don't forget this, men. God is on our side. We are His people, you know. God won't let us down.' 'We should never have been in this mess, and God will crack this little nut wide open, you see if He won't.' 'Thank goodness Egypt is still good, tough old Egypt, and Zedekiah is no fool at all. He'll tie up with Egypt. And what with God on our side and Egypt coming right in, too, these smart alec Babylonians won't be in it. They'll just snuff out and we'll be back in our nice cosy little beds at home again.'

Oh yes. There was always hope. Hadn't God saved them through the long centuries? Hadn't Jerusalem seen Nineveh, the proud heart of mighty Assyria, come and go? They were the chosen race. Theirs was God's own city. Of course there was still hope. A year or two at the most—God would see to that!

And listening to this, sharing in this, troubled and hurt and all-mixed-up-inside as any sensitive, imaginative man must be, was Ezekiel. The priest, Ezekiel. The man whose thirtieth birthday meant so much. For at thirty a priest began his active public ministry. That was the age at which he assumed the responsibility of spiritual leadership. That was when he had to search his heart and know for sure whether he was in fact just expressing his own ideas and his own hopes, or whether his words were declaring the mind and purpose of God.

And thirty was this critical age. Ezekiel had been waiting,

preparing, learning, trying to understand his place in it all. The history of his people and the history of their relationship with God had been engraved into the very substance of his mind as he sought this answer. The birthdays came, one by one, these last five in the wretchedness of slavery and exile. But his priestly call could not be denied or postponed just because he didn't feel like taking on the job or because the conditions were not to his taste. No. You will never understand Ezekiel if you think of him as being that sort of a man. Intense, yes. Imaginative, for sure. Eccentric and quaint and an oddity and all the rest of it, I grant you. But casual? Indifferent? Take it or leave it? Don't let's get too serious about all this religion stuff? Not one tiny little bit!

No, a thousand times no! If you can't feel the sheer breaking-point tension in the four simple words which begin his book, then you get right out of our company altogether, please, and go straight back to the mere bolts and nuts or bits and pieces where you belong. 'In the thirtieth year.' That is all he says, but Ezekiel could never possibly say more than that. 'In the year I did my finals.' 'When I enlisted.' 'At the time I became General Manager.' These are the real date-times in a man's life. And Ezekiel was about to set out on his heaven-sized task of being a priest: 'in the thirtieth year.' That was the supreme moment of life. The years of exile were bad, big and bad. But this is something altogether vast: 'in the thirtieth year.'

And now Ezekiel was at the place where he simply must know the real truth. The rumours that the priests were spreading, the stiff-upper-lip, cheer-up, never-say-die, look-for-the-silver-lining sort of line that the men were being given – was this what God was saying or was this just the optimism of the endless buoyancy of normal human personality?

As he studied their history, searched their Law, pondered their record of the long-suffering love of God, could he find the proper answer?

And God spoke. God gave him His own answer.

For that was what this vision really meant to Ezekiel. That was why he looked, looked again and just kept on looking. That was why he tells us that after this vision came to him among the exiles at Kebar, 'I sat there overwhelmed among them seven days.'

Overwhelmed is the word. What other word would you choose? Because if you do choose another word it must at least equal Ezekiel's own word. Say he was knocked for six, if you are a cricketer. Say it was the K.O., if you are a boxer. Say it in your own idiom, say it in every idiom, and you are only too right.

For coming through this vision, searing the whole spiritual being of the young priest, was the terrible message : It is all false. There is no hope. The people will not be freed from slavery. They will be here in bondage for all the remaining days of their lives. They will never get away. They will die here.

And Ezekiel is to be the one true prophet to tell them this. He is the lone watchman appointed to take the sole responsibility for the spiritual warning of the whole encampment. If they are not warned, if he fails in his task as watchman, then their doom lies fairly and squarely on his shoulders. Young, inexperienced, timid and shy as only such hyper-imaginative people can be, Ezekiel is to stand out in the middle of the slave encampment and tell them this terrible news. Tell them that all the hopes that all the other priests had been building up are in fact false. Tell them that Egypt will never save Jerusalem. Tell them that Zedekiah will never save Jerusalem. Tell them that *God* will not save Jerusalem – that He will save some of them, the slaves, but only because He will destroy Jerusalem. Tell them all that – and tell them so clearly that their blood will not be on his hands ! Tell them that if they are looking for life and hope then they have it – this mud and slush of the irrigation scheme is in fact God's way of salvation and life for His people !

Don't you sometimes pause in sheer awe at the wonder of the voice of God in human life? I confess I do, time and time again. The storeman who played the sax four nights a week in the dance band, who told me that three years ago he had nearly died with meningitis – 'God spoke to me, Doctor, and I have been reading my Bible ever since.' That old Jewish financier in our city, more money than he knew what to do with, whose younger brother had dropped dead with a coronary – 'Doctor, I have made a great deal of money in my lifetime; but I am a poor, disillusioned old man.' The young father, tears on both cheeks, whose two-year-old son had died within twenty-four hours from a fulminating staphylococcal pneumonia—'Joan and I had planned great things for our little Bruce. But we had never planned anything as wonderful for him as to bring his own father to God.' The man I went through school with—'John, I have had nothing but success after success. Every single thing I have touched has turned out right. I don't know anything about religion, but there must be a God. It's not just my doing.'

Yes. The voice of God, calling, challenging, entreating. And let me speak of this in all humility: for He speaks to me, too, listening in, as it were, so often, as He speaks to men and women who have placed themselves under my care.

Yes. He speaks.

And I confess further that He has spoken to me, again, as I have been writing and reading the story of Ezekiel. Seeing this sensitive, retiring young man flung suddenly and inescapably into the vortex of this social and spiritual maelstrom by the extraordinary appropriate medium of a summer's day's vision. How right, how completely right, are the ways of God.

Come, then, and have a chat with Ezekiel, as he sits there overwhelmed among the slaves in Kebar. He looks as though he could do with some real friends, some genuine sympathy and support. Of course there are the inevitable gossips and hangers-on, with their ideas and advice and explanation. Job had them in the earliest of times and Ezekiel had them, you may be sure. Can't you hear the babbling of the unthinking optimists? 'Don't let it get you down, Ezekiel old chap. Just a touch of the sun. Nothing that a couple of nights' good sleep won't fix. Soon have you back on deck, giving us all a cheerio shot-in-the-arm and the buck-up talk. . . .'

And the equally unthinking mumbling of the pessimists, the groaners who revel in such episodes. 'H'mm . . . looks bad. Last one I saw taken like this finished up in the mad-house. I always said he was too serious. I can't see this one getting better, can you?'

And we can't help overhearing the rather high-pitched voice of the scientific type, the know-all who is ignorant enough to believe that if you can explain the workings of the machinery then you can explain away the One who operates it. 'Rather fascinating example of the katatonic state, what!

I mean, just sitting there, day after day. Metabolism quite undisturbed, you observe. And I must say the association of hallucinations is unique. Visual and auditory, quite a nice combination. But gustatory too – you remember that bit about the *book*? He thinks he ate it, you know, and says it tasted like honey! Isn't that priceless! That is well worth recording. I hope he gets written up in the psychiatric journals.'

And I brush aside the mere garrulous gossips, with their 'I told you so', and their 'Let me tell you what I heard from a friend the other day', and all such love-less unhelpfulness, and come and sit quietly beside the young man himself.

Ezekiel, I say at last, is there anything I can do to help? I know the meaning of God's message to you, and I think I understand how difficult it is going to be. But I should dearly love to be of use to you. Would you care to tell me your plans? Is there any problem where an older head may be worth sounding out? Any detail you would care to discuss?

I think it is only right to tell you, Ezekiel, that in our modern world God only very rarely speaks to us Westerners in visions like yours. It does happen, I know; but it is highly suspect. It can just possibly lead to a work of grace, but it is much more likely to lead to a course of shock treatment; or, worse still, to some new false cult. And another thing, Ezekiel – you have been stuck out there in the Persian desert in a spiritual isolation that must be as heart-breaking as it is soul-destroying. But today we have the whole revelation of God in our hands. In His sovereign will God has seen fit to make this available to us in book form, telling us every single necessary detail concerning ourselves and concerning Himself. And this must make your ears tingle, Ezekiel; we may have all this in superb modern English prose at a cost that is only a fraction of a day's wage for a common labourer. Oh yes, Ezekiel, visions like yours are highly suspect, properly suspect, today. Indeed, the faith of many has been deeply disturbed by people who say they have had visions like yours. People too lazy, too stubborn, too proud, to take the care and time and effort necessary to check their visions against the Word of God.

But God has chosen this way to speak to you, Ezekiel, and we are just as thrilled to know that you can understand it as we are concerned at the difficult task it has laid on you.

John Wesley had a task like yours, in a godless, eighteenth-century England, and he trod the length and breadth of the land time and time again, preaching sometimes for forty hours in a week, as he carried out his commission. Will you do that, do you think, Ezekiel? Is it your tradition that Wesley will be re-enacting nearly twenty-five centuries after you? Just what are your plans?

I am sitting right there beside him, speaking much as I have spoken to many, many thousands of other troubled people. And as I watch for the slight nod, the tiny movement of facial expression which can be so valuable a guide, I see a sudden movement of his lips, a catch in his throat, a bead of perspiration on his forehead.

And I feel my own face blanch, and my tongue is suddenly parched, for now I know the rest!

Ezekiel is dumb!

I think now you will be beginning to understand why I said that the story of Ezekiel has so deeply stirred my own heart. As I stop to ponder this most shocking, bitter hurt, my heart begins to pound and I feel my breath caught in my throat. Oh yes, I admit that I have the advantage of experience in the handling of problems like this. That moment when a doctor sees in a flash that it is malignant – a sentence of death. That finding which tells him in a single instant that there is a tumour in the brain; that the kidneys have packed up; that some essential body function is never to work again; that the child's life is beyond hope. These, and all such as these, which so greatly challenge his skill and his sympathy and his honesty.

But, in a world of problems, Ezekiel is something new altogether. I am out of my depth. I have no suggestions to make. Even to ask questions is just to rub salt into wounds that are already cruelly sore.

Of course if Ezekiel could visit our world, instead of us visiting him, it would be very different indeed. We could snap him out of his hallucinations, doctor up his katatonic state, analyse his aphonia, do all sorts of helpful things. What with euphoriants to counteract depression, hypnotics to inhibit mania, stimulants to give pep and sedatives to go slow, with an ever-swelling flood of all such drugs which are now so numerous that we can't even hope to learn their names, let alone evaluate them fully : oh yes, we could do a lot for Ezekiel. In fact we could turn him over to some of our super-experts who could persuade him that the vision didn't really happen at all; that God didn't really mean to upset him at all; that God isn't even God, but is a nice convenient noun to apply to such a significant grouping of personality mechanisms, so convenient a noun that it deserves spelling with a capital G, God.

But Ezekiel is not in our world. He is almost as far from us as it would be possible to get in time and space. Ezekiel is in fact sitting there, overwhelmed, in the slave encampment by the river Kebar. And on him, and on him alone, rests the whole weight of the responsibility of the spiritual future of his people. And the message he has to give is the most shockingly unacceptable truth that could be imagined. And he has only just turned thirty; and he is dumb.

This, then, is the man we are going to watch. Here, in a setting that is bleak and stark and altogether without relief, is the man of God in a hostile world if ever there was one.

But what will he do? How can he convey this dreadful message when he is dumb? No John Wesley here. No tiny trace of a Billy Graham, with his dedicated team and his hi-fi P.A. system and TV hook-up and radio network. Oh dear no. Ezekiel can't even slip down to the jobbing printer on the second corner on the right and order a few thousand handbills to spread the story through the camp. No; he can't even order a single handbill at all, let alone a few thousand. There is no jobbing printer and there is not even a local stationer to give him ready and available writing-material.

For Ezekiel is a slave. He is just a mud-digger, a hopeless, unpaid toiler in an irrigation project, without any remotest possibility of finding the wherewithal to circularize the neighbourhood with his grim message of inescapable captivity.

Not that he won't write it down. He will somehow find the time and the material and the sheer endurance necessary to write it all down. But that is likely to take years. In fact, it is likely to take all the rest of his life of slavery.

But that is not his call as a watchman. A watchman guarding a city isn't there to write a thoughtfully compiled monograph on enemy deployment and assault tactics. No! His duty as a watchman is to alert the city, and that means now!

Sure, Ezekiel. You will write it down. We are more than grateful to you for making that effort, for the patient tenacity you had to show to get it down. And you weren't to know this, as you laboriously and carefully recorded the tale of your visions, but God Himself wanted that writing finished, for He planned to include that in His own Word. Just imagine that, Ezekiel! Right alongside the writings of Moses and David! You are only a young priest in a desolate mud-camp, but in His wisdom and providence God will preserve your story as 'The Book of the Prophet Ezekiel'.

Yes. That is the book we now have, and I have no doubt that it was in his much later years that Ezekiel found time and strength and patience to compile it. But to the bewildered young man sitting there overwhelmed among the slaves at Kebar that was probably miles and miles away from his immediate thoughts. His problem was not how to write a book – his problem was how to warn the people, when he was friendless and speechless.

And the blood of his whole company is on him if he fails to warn them!

And Ezekiel – just this one word before we leave you and move back among the busy crowd of slaves around you. We have come two and a half thousand years to see you do this. We come from a world where the sheer incisiveness of God's truth is almost completely obscured. A world where the words Christian (noun) and Christian (adjective) are used to cover so many quite different categories of people and variations of qualification that they mean nothing in the way we are looking for meaning. Ezekiel, our Master told us that our place in our society is like that of salt used in cooking – it is to bring out all the piquancy and the tang of the finest savour. We are called to be the light of our society – to 'reflect as in a mirror the splendour of the Lord', to use St. Paul's daring imagery – and our Master again insisted that the lamp that is lit 'is not put under the meal-tub, but on the lamp-stand, where it gives light to everyone in the house. And you, like the lamp, must shed light among your fellows.' You see what it means to us, Ezekiel, to come all this way to watch you. You have no meal-tub! The only meal-tub you can hide your light under is the meal-tub of sheer defeat or of cowardice or of sloth.

But you won't do that, we know. You are in fact the watchman. You will by some means or other bring out the full-salted flavour of the message of God so that it can leave a taste in the spiritual palate of your workmates for time and for eternity. You will somehow manage to blaze out a light that will either light your fellow-men into the glory of the dawn of the kingdom, or have them lurking deeper and deeper into the eternal shadows.

And we may well hope to see this so clearly, so uniquely, so vividly, that we can expect to understand in our own world just what it means to be the salt of the earth, the light of the world.

And so we move away, joining the hard-working band of slaves in the canal diggings. What back-breaking, relentless work it is, now moving into its sixth year of drudgery.

It is too strenuous, too much effort altogether, to be able to keep much of a look-out for Ezekiel now. It's a full week since he fell 'overwhelmed' among the exiles, and a week is a long time to be watching someone, specially when you work in a Babylonian works gang. Slaves are pretty cheap in this part of the world, and Nebuchadrezzar's men aren't too sympathetic towards drones and loafers. You would need to be a super crack-pot to start a go-slow movement in that little piece of Babylonia. Any trade union movement there was very embryonic indeed, I should say!

But it is a full week. And I wipe the sweat out of my eyes just to see what Ezekiel is really planning to do. And I stop short and put down my bucket of mud. I stand on tiptoes. For, say, I just can't see him at all! There he was, day after day, all that week just sitting and sitting. But now he's gone!

Excuse me! I tap the shoulder of one of the older men who has been working there all this time too. But have you seen Ezekiel? You know, the chap who had a sort of collapse. A breakdown. He was sitting there all last week, and now he's gone. I wonder what can have happened to him. Have the Babylonians given him the axe? It is very important to me to find out. Do you know what has happened to him?

'Oh, he went off this morning. I don't know what was wrong with him, but he just got up and sloped off into the desert. And I reckon it's just as well he did, or the bosses would have put the boot in, you can bet. And I know some of our fellows were a bit sore about it, too. I don't hold with them, you know. I think religion is pretty useful at times, especially when life is going like it is here. But they think he's too religious, and say it makes a man good-for-nothing. I hope he's all right though. I always rather liked him, in his way . . . but I'm off. The boss is watching us.'

And I am standing alone, now. And I have just that heavy-inside feeling I get when a patient says, 'Oh, I've stopped the tablets, Doctor. I know you said they were important. But they gave me a touch of indigestion. Even made me knock back a schooner of beer the other night! I felt I'd be better without them.'

Don't tell me, I say to myself, not Ezekiel. He is the watch-man. Has he just walked out on God? Oh, I know it has been done. Jeroboam did it. Judas did it. Men in great places of privilege and responsibility have done it. Men who saw, in their own way and in their own lives, the vision of God. Men who heard the challenging voice of God. But Ezekiel? Has he just flaked out? Had he found it too hard?

No, I insist to myself. I'll wait and see. I'll just wait and wait. He's out there in the desert, for sure. But has he gone out there to get away from God, or has he gone there to meet with God? St. Paul was down this way, in Arabia, for years and years after his conversion. And how glad of that we are today, as we read in his letters the maturity and insight that those years brought to him. And Moses did just that, too. A whole generation came into being while he was keeping the flock of his Arab father-in-law. And the whole of world history was changed by those long years out in the Arabian desert. No. I'll just wait. I think he'll be back.

Now I must speculate a bit here, and it is only right to tell you that this is speculation.

For this has to do with Nebuchadrezzar, and the sort of mind he had. He was then only in his early twenties, but he was probably the most powerful king the world had as yet seen. Perhaps some of the earlier pharaohs might have come near him for sheer size, but if you think in terms of an absolute monarch, of a man responsible to nobody else at all, then Nebuchadrezzar is the number one example in history.

But tyrant and despot and all that he was, he was essentially the nation builder, not the nation destroyer. Time and motion study is something we like to regard as a modern industrial aid, but Nebuchadrezzar practised it in its essentials thousands of years ago. His was the sort of mind that would order a mountain to be torn down if it stood in his way. But it was the sort of mind that would not give the order until he had also found some unattractive valley that needed filling in, and so use up the spoil from the mountain.

Now Nebuchadrezzar built the whole of his huge Babylon in brick. He used up more bricks than anyone else in all history has ever done. Sun-dried, some of the bricks. But many of them fired in bitumen-fed kilns, and some even with fire-glazed designs on their face side.

So that I think this was what was happening out in Kebar. Digging canals is simple enough. You just get a few thousand slaves, feed them enough calories to keep them working, and a bucket and a shovel will set each slave up in business. Dig, fill, and empty. That is the whole trade. That's a trade anyone can learn in ten seconds, and then spend the whole of the rest of his life wishing he could forget it! It's just too easy to set that job up. The problem is to think what to do with the diggings. If it's like our chocolate loam, or our beautiful black-soil plains, those millions and millions of acres of our inland continent, it's simple enough. Just spread it around the surrounding pasture lands and you have a perfect top-dressing.

But if it's clay, it's a different story altogether. For a start, of course, you can heap it up on the banks and make a levée or embankment, and so increase the effective depth of the canal. But after that, what? Spread it on top of your grasslands and you'll grow the most miserable collection of bracken and spinafex in the world.

And this is my guess. My guess is that Nebuchadrezzar had the clay baked into bricks right there on the spot, and so made one labour force do two jobs at once. Add just that bit of simple carpentry necessary to set up the brickmoulds, and your canal-digging programme pays you a fine bonus in bricks. Bricks to build cities with. Bricks to build houses for the guards. Perhaps even bricks to build the humpies the slaves live in. . . . But always bricks.

That is what I think happened, and that, I think, is why the next thing happened as it did. For it was just such a working day as every other day had been, year after year after year. Just digging, carrying, emptying, bricks. It was the short lunch-time break, with the men resting wearily as they gnawed away at the hard leathery damper that was their slave meal.

Some were squatting on the ground, some lying, some sitting on the huge half-baked bricks.

And I saw him. Yes! There he was!

Ezekiel! Hurrah, it's Ezekiel.

I jumped to my feet and raced over to try and shake his hand, to tell him just how excited and relieved and yet how concerned for him I was. But I didn't get to him. There was quite a little crowd gathering around him, and I couldn't quite reach him. In fact I was glad of my few extra Aussie inches to see over their heads and watch what was going on.

For there he was, not saying a single word, but putting on a little act that soon collected the whole lunch group around him.

Right out in the middle, he was, with quite a sizable crowd clustering around. The men in front had now squatted down, and from further back we who were standing could watch it all quite clearly.

Ezekiel had one of the huge Babylonian bricks out there. None of the sissy nine-inch bricks we are used to, or the even more sissy modern modular bricks. This was a genuine Babylonian brick, something like forty pounds of clay in it. It was a new brick, still soft and undried. He was modelling away at the clay on the top and it was only a minute or two before someone in front spotted it. 'Hey! It's Jerusalem!' And now others took it up. 'So it is!' 'Yes, there's the Millo. There's the main city wall.' 'Yes, Ezekiel, put in the Temple. Don't you want your old job back again? Don't forget the Temple.' And now the air was full of the wit and the nostalgia and the pathos that such a setting can so readily evoke.

And then Ezekiel moved over beside the brick and started heaping clay up against one side of it. I could now see that he had a bucketful of wet clay there beside him. He was very deft and it seemed to be only a few seconds before his rapid daubing and modelling began to produce a vividly clear picture.

For he was throwing up siegeworks against the city. There were the assault ramps. There, too, were the mobile defence walls, behind which the attackers were advancing. And now they were bringing their battering-rams up, and the whole assault was pressing in harder and harder on the city.

It was a most exciting and graphic little piece of drama. Ezekiel was working like a beaver, and the sweat was simply pouring off him, as he spun around this way and that way and heaped up the clay mounds.

And then suddenly he darted away about six feet, bowling a couple of onlookers out of his way, so absorbed in his task that I am sure he was completely unaware that they were there at all! He had picked up his iron plate, the one and only utensil he possessed (this was the plate on which the damper was cooked, as I shall explain later), and threw himself down right on his stomach on the ground as in a flash he stood the plate up on edge between himself and the model of the besieged city. I almost burst out laughing at this, even though it was all so graphic, so dramatically clear. For it was altogether reminiscent of those dozens of scenes from each and every one of the hundred or so Westerns on the TV. You know – the bit where the goodie is shooting it out with the baddie and flings himself down behind a rock just as the bullet splats against the stone and the whine of the ricochet tells you he's still safe.

But this was not a Western. This was not entertainment. The look on Ezekiel's face made that terribly clear. This was a real life-and-death affair, and there was something almost feverish in his energy as he leaped to his feet again, raced in and pushed up some more earthworks, darted back to his hiding-place behind the plate; and then back and forth and back and forth until I felt my own breath getting short in my chest.

Until at last Ezekiel himself fell absolutely exhausted on his face on the ground, his whole body heaving with his heavy breathing, but the iron plate still shielding him from the enemy around the city. There was a tension in the whole crowd that even the hot subtropical sun could not dispel. And it was a singularly quiet group who quickly slipped back to their digging and their filling and their emptying and their bricks that afternoon.

I didn't follow Ezekiel as he went back to work too. He couldn't talk about it, for he was dumb. Yet he had said so much in those few minutes that I felt no sermon in all history could have said more. But my heart was simply glowing with the warmth of the admiration I felt for the watchman and his warning.

But what of the people? There were, perhaps, more than a hundred men there that day. What did they think? I had noticed a few priests among the crowd – how would they take it? There could be no possibility of them mistaking the meaning of the imagery. The vivid picture of Jerusalem in a state of siege, the Holy City in the menace of war, no-one could fail to understand. This was something that had never before happened in all her centuries-old history. Jerusalem had been threatened, Jerusalem had even capitulated – was she not even now under Babylonian authority? But she had never been attacked outright. She had never been mauled, her mighty defence walls had never withstood the assault ramp and the battering-ram. And now, was Ezekiel right in declaring her doom? Was he right in finding a place of safety and survival over there behind his iron platter, that miserable reminder of their slavery and their monotonous, tasteless food ration?

Oh no. There was no mistaking the message. This was a watchman whose alarum made the very earth shake. He got it through to them all right!

But what happened then? What came of it?

I don't think much came of it. And I think Ezekiel didn't think very much came of it. And he was sure God didn't think very much came of it either.

Not that it wasn't appreciated, mark you. In the dull monotonous grind of a life like theirs, a scene like that was most warmly appreciated. Even the priests who most completely disagreed with the message were only too glad of the event itself, if merely because it provided a new starting-point for the chins-up, stick-to-it, it-won't-be-long-now campaign. In fact it became quite a social item. It was talked about and re-enacted time and time again, so that those who hadn't been there to see it soon heard every detail. It almost seems a pity that Big Business missed out on the chance to cash in on it and market the 'Ezekiel Clay Modelling Set' for the kids to enjoy it too.

And everyone felt a little bit better for it, perhaps. That feeling of relief to have something out of your system, so to speak. That moment or two of terrifying soberness, that sudden realism of naked truth that so easily makes way for the more bearable tedium and lethargy of obscurantism.

And Ezekiel was getting a smile here and a nod there that he had not had ever before. It was easy to sense the feeling in the camp, especially as each lunch-hour came around. That quick turn of the head, that slight sidelong glance, that sudden lifting of the eyebrows, as expectant eyes hoped to see another little scene enacted.

But nothing was happening now. As soon as the lunch-break turned up, there was Ezekiel lying flat on the ground just like so many others of them, perhaps even more lethargic, more quiet than any.

And so it went on, day after day, week after week. There he was, lying on his side looking at the clay brick with the Holy City depicted on it, with all the surrounding assault scene still intact. It was still there, dried out now and quite firm and hard. And sure enough, every day Ezekiel was there looking at it as he lay on his side in the sun.

But wait a minute, wait a minute.

'Say, am I seeing things, Joe? But have you noticed Ezekiel? He's a queer bird, but he's really quite a deep sort of chap, and I think he's certainly up to something. You watch. He's always lying just like that. Exactly like that, just as if he had been tied in that position. You watch – he's always on his left side, he's always got that arm exposed in that identical position and his face is always turned straight at that brick model. I've been watching him for days now, and he never varies it one inch.'

'You know, Dan, I think you might be right. We'll keep a bit of a sharp watch, and have a good look again.'

And, yes, it was the same when tomorrow came. And the next day again; and the next and the next.

And now the whole camp was interested once more. There could be no possible mistake. He was always exactly in that same position. Just lying there as though tethered by unseen cords, not at all comfortable, always on his left side.

Until the whole camp was buzzing with it. 'Just what on earth does this mean?' 'You ask me! Either I'm dumb or he's dumb, but I don't get it. It must mean something, but you'd probably have to be as crazy as him to understand it.' 'Yes. And it's over three months now, and if the message hasn't got through by this I reckon he ought to give up.' 'I'll say. Here's Halek. He's the priest. He might know. Let's ask him.

'Say, Rab Halek, what do you think Ezekiel's up to this time? He's been doing that for over three months and it doesn't make sense to any of us. Do you reckon it's supposed to?'

But Rab Halek is too experienced to fall into this sort of trap. 'Don't you worry,' he replies. 'I'm sure it has a sound religious basis, but you just keep your minds on the simple, easily understood truths. Keep a strong hope burning in your hearts, and look for the deliverance of the Lord. Remember the words of Moses himself in the oldest of all our Psalms, "LORD, thou hast been our dwelling place in all generations."'

Yes. Let us admit it. This sermon was really quite a flop. Going on for months and months and nobody really even knowing the text he was preaching from! And they were all busy, and tired, and pretty dispirited, in the way slaves may well be expected to be. And Ezekiel, lying there on his left side, is now just part of the lunch-time scenery and it's really just a bit stupid looking.

So that I must confess that I am really not too sure at all just when it was noticed, but it may well have been like this, months after it began.

But one day someone watched Ezekiel rather closely as he prepared and baked his damper for the day.

Now this is something which travellers tell us can still be seen even in the twentieth century, in Bedouin and such Eastern encampments. The meal is crushed, and the ration for the day is ground into a flour in the iron cooking-plate, mixing in such herbs and flavouring as may be available; and then water is added to make a stiff dough ready for cooking. The cooking is simple enough. A tiny slow-burning fire is lit and the plate stood over the little flame, supported by a few stones. Any sort of fuel will do, provided it burns slowly and with not too much heat. Half-dry grass, small sticks, anything like that will do. The real desert wanderer may be lucky enough to come upon a lump of dried out camel-dung, which is excellent! But, of course, to the Jewish race this would be utterly abhorrent, for all excrement is unclean – his religion would never sanction that.

And Ezekiel was cooking his damper. And somebody began to notice that there was something about it that was different. In fact something quite a lot different. For he wasn't just tossing in the half-pound or so of meal that constituted the average day's ration. He was measuring it out. Now of course that wasn't surprising. Lots of them did that. If you wanted a reasonable meal next Thursday, supposing Friday was ration day, you would be just plain sensible to be sure you got seven reasonably equal divisions of the weekly supply. Yes, of course he was just prudent to measure it out.

But he wasn't doing that. At least he wasn't just doing that. 'Hey, Joe. Come and have a look again. Ezekiel's not as simple as he looks. You come and watch him. He's only just up and he'll be starting in a moment.'

'Well! What do you know! Dan, old man, I reckon you are right again. Fancy measuring the food out on scales like that. I just take four fist-fulls and it's always come out pretty even over the week. But watch him! Weighing it out to the absolute grain! You'd think the stuff was as precious as gold dust!'

'Yes, but keep watching. Look at the water.'

'Why, Dan, that's just plain crazy. That's an ordinary half-pint measure, and he's handling it as if it's the only water he's ever going to see! Now. Did you see that? He even waited for the drop that ran down the side to fall into the meal. Listen, Dan. He's just plain psycho, and I don't think it really means anything at all. Just nuts, I'd say.'

'I don't know, Joe. I don't think you are quite right. Sure, he's nutty, but I reckon there's some real sense in it. I think he's acting a famine and drought. Look! See that? He does that every day. He puts the rest of the water back in his humpy and that's all he drinks for the whole of the day. He must be as dry as can be at times, like the rest of us, but I haven't seen him drink any water except that bit in the measure.'

'H'mm. Perhaps you *are* right, Dan. You might be quite right.'

'Yes. But that's not all, Joe. I don't like to say this, and especially about a priest, but this is really terrible. Yesterday I was watching him, and I saw him light his fire, and do you know what he was using for fuel? Dung! Now what did I tell you! That makes you think, doesn't it? A fellow like Ezekiel, all prayer and religious like he used to be before he went dumb. But I'll swear that was dung. And if you could have seen his face as he handled it you could see it just about killed him. I thought he'd burst out crying, he looked so absolutely miserable. He must have hated it like nothing on earth.'

Yes. It was dung. And now the camp began to buzz and twitter and the story began to fly around the whole encampment. Ezekiel, the priest, cooking his damper on a dung-fed fire! This was scandalous. This was horrifying. And, what is more disturbing still, Ezekiel himself was shocked and scandalized by it more than any of them, and yet he kept on doing it. Day after day, week after week, month after month.

And now the drama began to take real form, and a form that no-one could mistake and no-one could escape. It was a bleak, a grim drama if ever there was one. Famine, thirst, utter deprivation and need, in every poignant feature of it. As he lay there each day, always on his left side, hand outstretched, face set towards the brick model of the city, eating the damper that had been cooked on that disgusting heap of dung, they knew now what he was saying. He was preaching a sermon they could never fail to understand. Nor could they ever forget it. And the months rolled on and the year itself ran out.

Now unless we have in Australia some very unrepresentative descendants of that little group, then I am certain that someone among them was running a book on it all. And the odds against it lasting the year got shorter and shorter – and the bookies lost! It went the whole year!

Yes, the year had come and the year had gone, but the same sermon still went on. Until I am sure the last little bit of excitement had been drained out of it.

F

For it's six years now since Jehoiakin was deported. Going on for seven. Sure, Ezekiel's made his point, but take no notice of him now. He's just run out of ideas. Three hundred and seventy days, this makes it. Just how monotonous can a man get. . . . Three hundred and eighty days. . . . Three hundred and ninety days. Why, it's just too dull! If he'd stopped at the exact year, that might have been rather striking. If he'd stopped at a feast day, or something like that, then it might have amounted to something. But not just this.

Look, this is the three hundred and ninety-first day he's been doing it, and it seems his brain has gone curdled or goodness knows what. But there he is, just the same as always, over by his precious brick, lying on his left side and . . . Say! Am I seeing things? Hey, fellers. Come and see! Look at Ezekiel! He's moved! After three hundred and ninety days. Look, he's on his right side!

Well! What a commotion. There's just no doubt about Ezekiel. If life gets too dull, then go and find an Ezekiel. You just never can tell, can you? I'd never have believed it. I thought he'd got stuck like that till doomsday.

'Yes. And we'd all just about give him up completely. And he nearly got away without anyone seeing him do it. Abe, it's just as well you've got sharp eyes. I'm not the observant type. I just get so used to seeing him lying there I'd never have noticed him turn over. I wonder how long this will go on. I hope to goodness it's not another three hundred and ninety days. I just can't stick this place another year. And certainly not with Ezekiel eating his famine ration in front of us all the time like that. And I don't reckon he'd last as long as that himself, either. He's taken a terrific punishment, all this time, water so carefully rationed as he makes out it is. His health wouldn't stand it.'

But there is no need to worry. Ezekiel's friends need not be over-anxious for his health, because he is the watchman, and God doesn't appoint a watchman and then just kill him off with the job half done. Oh no. God may well end a man's life, perhaps making the ending itself the alarum to the beleaguered people. Did not Latimer and Cranmer do just that for England, as the flames engulfed them?

Oh yes. God is love, and He is not subject to the emotional limitations which so characterize the behaviour of men. But never forget, too, that love is always concerned for those same emotional limitations of men. God is not 'unable to sympathize with our weaknesses', as one New Testament writer says so simply. Oh no! Because of His likeness to us, He has been tested in every way Himself. He knows full well the limitation of Ezekiel, as of every one of His followers. And Ezekiel was now lying on his right side, every day, day after day. But not month after month. No. It was for forty days, and forty only.

The sermon was over. The watchman had proclaimed a message that has certainly never been paralleled in human history. Four hundred and thirty days, it lasted. Three hundred and ninety of them on his left side, lying there as if bound to the spot. And forty more, on his right side, as if bound again in this new position.

'Say, Dan. You seem to have a bit of an idea about some parts of this act. What do you think it means? I guess some of it is clear enough. I know he reckons Jerusalem is going to be besieged and famine rates and rationing will come. But what is this awful cow-dung he uses for fuel? What does that mean?'

'Oh, I think that's pretty clear, Joe. I think he's saying that our people will have to eat their food unclean – and so far as we are concerned here, he's only too right : none of our food is real Kosher, not here in this stinking spot at any rate. We have no hope of carrying out the proper hand-washing ritual and preparation of food that our Law requires. He's certainly very right in regard to us. We might as well all cook it on dung, we're already so far from the requirements of our religion that something else wrong wouldn't really matter. Sure, I reckon he's made a very telling point there. But I think he's trying to tell us it will happen to the whole of Jerusalem. And that sure burns me up inside. I don't like that idea one tiny bit. I want to get out of here and back to my little home. This is all going on much too long for my liking.

'But I wish I could understand those three hundred and ninety days on one side and forty days on the other. That just has me beat. Have you any ideas, Abe? Remember, it was you who saw him turn over. Can you make anything of it?'

'I don't know, Dan. I've been puzzling about it for days. I

think I have a sort of clue about the three hundred and ninety, but not about the forty.'

'Well, that's a start. What do you reckon about the three hundred and ninety then?'

'Oh, it's pretty vague really. But you know how it is when you are out there digging and digging all day. You get to thinking. And I often start counting. I used to do that as a kid. I used to count the doorways on the way to the Temple every morning. I used to count my heart-beats during the lesson – it helped the time to pass if the priests were too long-winded. I count the shovels-full to a bucket now, count the buckets too! And I started to count back in our history. And I think that's what the three hundred and ninety might stand for. I wish I knew more of what I used to hear in the Temple, but from when King David first set up his kingdom in Jerusalem to the arrival of these so-and-so Babylonians is pretty close to three hundred and ninety years. And Ezekiel could easily have worked it out at that, give and take a few years. I reckon the three hundred and ninety days just represent those three hundred and ninety years. But I wish I knew what the forty meant.'

And this time it was Joe who spoke. And there was a very subdued look on his face. Very subdued indeed.

'I think I know what he means. I think I know what it all means now, and I feel sick. You remember how he used to lie there? Dan, you remember when you said to me how he lay there just as if he were tied to the spot? I think you were right. He was telling us that he was tied there like a sort of sacrifice bound on an altar. And I think that's exactly what he meant. I reckon he was symbolizing a sort of punishment scene, a sort of sacrificial substitute, each day standing for a year of our history. And this really gets me, because I think when he turned over he is saying God is going to tip the whole city upside down and for forty years we will have to take our own medicine.'

It was evening, and the cool desert air was beginning to chase away the heat of the day. But Joe stopped and mopped his brow, and even in the dim starlight his friends could see the glint of the reflection in the sweat-drops on his forehead, as he continued. 'And, listen, I reckon he may really be pretty right, and this is what really worries me. Because we've had some incredible luck over all the years. Ours is the only single city in all this part of the world to have stood right through. And say what you like, we can't really say we deserved it. We tied in on so many deals with other nations and mixed ourselves up in dozens of other religions and the like, and always we got away with it. Damascus went, Samaria went. Even Nineveh has gone. But there little old Jerusalem still stands. And I have a nasty feeling Ezekiel is right, and God is going to make us see it His way. And if that is true, then this is a forty-year sentence at least, and that means I'm here for the rest of my whole life and you bet I don't like that idea. And I'm absolutely sure Ezekiel doesn't like it either, but that doesn't stop him saying it's true.'

Yes. The message got there. The sermon that took fourteen long months to preach began to sink home. The watchman was clear of the blood of the people.

And the long months still kept slowly rolling by, and those long months became even longer years, years of mud and digging and slavery. The Get-Out-of-Here Campaign was beginning to drag heavily now, and even the priests and the elders of the slave community were letting the corners of their mouths hang down. The cheer-up attitude was wearing a very forced smile indeed.

Nebuchadrezzar was himself in his late twenties and going on from triumph to triumph. No doubt some of the men in the camp remembered rather wistfully that it was only eight or nine years since Nebuchadrezzar had taken quite a drubbing by the Egyptians. But that seemed long past. The young Babylonian king had gone back home to build up his great war-machine until he was strong enough and tough enough to sweep away every last trace of Egyptian power east of Suez. Egypt was a very broken reed indeed.

For that was just where they had themselves come in. It was on his return from that campaign that Nebuchadrezzar had gathered up those very men, along with their king, Jehoiakin. And while it was true that whispers on the grapevine hinted that Zedekiah was still keeping one ear to the ground for any possible rumble of Egyptian stirring, it all sounded very indefinite and years and years ahead.

Yes. It all looked very grim. Very bleak. Yet hope dies hard. Have I not already insisted that in any medical practice that is worthy of the art there is no such thing as a hopeless case? That there is never a depth of the despair of fear into which some gleam of the hope of help and support cannot penetrate? Of course there is not! To admit that is to abandon medicine as a vocation and reduce it to a mere technological science.

And if I say that so strongly and so feelingly of my own clinical world, think how persistently that same answer kept returning time and time again in the slave encampment. For hope dies very hard indeed, even in Babylonian bondage.

And Ezekiel knew that his message was still but little known. Little known in the one way the truth of God may properly be said to be known. For doctrine is always like that. As Dorothy Sayers says so simply, 'doctrine must be experienced to be understood.' The truth of God is not like the binomial theorem or the use of the subjunctive tense. It is not a mere proposition which the clever student can simply learn well enough to gain an A-plus, a High Distinction, a First, a University Medal. Indeed, it is a proposition, but it is a proposition in the living of a man, where even a miserable tax-gatherer may experience great truth as he 'beats upon his breast, saying, "O God, have mercy on me, sinner that I am."' It is a proposition in the living of a man where even a highly cultured theological scholar may experience no truth at all.

And this was what Ezekiel now realized. He realized that the people knew his message only like this. It was a grim piece of information to be added in with all the other grim things in their unhappy lot. But it was no more than that. It was accepted as information; it was altogether disregarded as a way of life.

Indeed, I rather think that Ezekiel could sense almost that his long and powerful sermon had somewhat strengthened their hope. He had made the truth so clear that the only answer the men had, the only alternative open to them, was to take cover in hope. To find their own human answer to God's pronouncement of doom. Ezekiel had never heard of a cross; but he was called to preach the cross. He was to proclaim this concept: the concept of the death of a man's own self-programme as the only single doorway to the God-programme of life. As Jesus Himself put it so graphically, it is the concept of the death of the grain of wheat as the only known way to produce the rich, waving, golden, full-grained ear.

And this was the truth that was still missing. This was the desperate situation where the sensitive, imaginative intensity of Ezekiel told him that he was still not really free of his responsibility as the watchman. The message had been sent out. The message had been received. But still, no action.

So that I think I am very likely to be right in thinking that Ezekiel was ever so careful in preparing his next sermon. This was to be a sermon which he could not repeat. It was a once-only sermon and I feel sure that Ezekiel waited for just that very right moment, that unique day, that occasion which was chosen in the deep intensity of critical analysis which always belongs to real prayer.

For this was a sermon altogether different. Those tiring, endless, four hundred and thirty days just lying on the ground were over. And this sermon was to be of so different a pattern that I am sure he gave nearly as much careful thought to its occasion as he did to its content.

And that is why I like to think it was the king's birthday holiday. Now you who are experts, please don't just laugh at me. I'm only a hard-toiling doctor and can't possibly find time to look up the minutiae of Babylonian lore, even if I had the required amount of brains to be capable of so doing. Of course I don't know whether or not Nebuchadrezzar gave a holiday to his slaves on the occasion of his birthday. But I think Nebuchadrezzar was the sort of king who was very fussy about what people thought of him. He was Big! In fact he was Biggest; and he liked everyone to know that he was Biggest. And he liked everyone to *say* he was Biggest. And the best way to be sure of all that was to get everyone to *think* he was Biggest. He may have been thousands of years before Freud (and Adler and Jung and the rest), but that doesn't make his applied psychology less astute.

No. The king who was so concerned about being The Biggest King, so concerned as to have set up a huge eighty-foot gold image for all — repeat *all* — his subjects to worship when the band played, was just the sort of king, I am sure, who would follow it up with a public holiday and perhaps even with drinks on the house.

Now I may be completely wide of the mark, but that

doesn't matter much in following the rest of the sermon, for it was a sermon of such seriousness and intensity, a sermon of such poignancy and drama, that even the Hollywood cartoons could scarcely rival it.

And so it is for this reason that I think Ezekiel waited for just such a public holiday to turn up. Waited for just that day when he could find seats for priests and elders and public in plenty. That day when the sharp call 'Back to work' will not distract and destroy the insistence of the message.

And make no mistake. The crowd was there all right. And the priests were there and the elders too. Let the loneliest disciple take great heart from this. If your Lord calls you to be the watchman, just as he called Ezekiel two thousand, five hundred years before you, He will have listening to you just the audience of His choice.

And so it is, in all the sympathy and understanding of which I am capable, that my imagination takes me back those two and a half thousand years to the Kebar river bank.

For the crowd is already there. Ezekiel has been preparing, as every wise preacher must prepare; and the preparations are certainly unusual.

It is still in the same old pulpit that he is to preach – that hard-dried brick model of Jerusalem round which all his sermons have been formed. But all sorts of preparations are under way. A large clean cloth is there spread on the ground. A little fire is laid in the very centre of the city model. The scales – those scales with which he so carefully weighed out his food each of those long four hundred and thirty days – they are there too. And perhaps most curious of all, there is a sword. Yes, a sword.

Now I am guessing again, and don't pretend that this is anything but a guess; but I guess that was a Babylonian sword. For I can't for the life of me understand how it could be anything else, not in a slave group. The slaves had shovels, for sure, splendid big, strong shovels to scoop up fine diggings of clay and mud. Iron platters to bake their damper on. Little mud-brick humpies to sleep in. Oh yes, they can have these, they must have these. But not swords. It's the Babylonians who have the swords! Why, from Dartmoor to Alcatraz it's the universal practice to equip warders with the batons and the tommy-guns, not the prisoners. No, *not* the prisoners.

But Ezekiel had a sword. And no sissy ceremonial trinket that wouldn't really cut butter. No, this was the genuine article, just the thing to knock out the vitals of anyone in the place, and literally sharp enough to shave your head with! You may be quite sure that if the sermon became dull no-one would be dozing off. Not with the naked sword there in front of them, so deadly and so sinister, and so razor-edge to boot.

And I may be engaging in mere wishful thinking, but I most warmly maintain that Ezekiel, dumb and peculiar and all that he was, was still the only man in that whole camp to whom the Babylonian guard would have entrusted that sword. Remember, when the earthquake shakes the prison doors open, it is the madcaps Paul and Silas, with all their praying and psalm singing, who see to it that the gaoler keeps his job and his life. And I am sure that the Babylonian gaoler of Ezekiel's time had lent him that sword because he could sense that Ezekiel was the one man he could trust with it.

And the tension in the crowd was at breaking-point as at last Ezekiel came to preach. He had to pick his way ever so slowly through the dense little crowd that gathered, coming at last to the clear place in the centre, beside the brick city-model.

There is no need to drop your voice or stop chattering, because Ezekiel doesn't say anything. He is dumb – remember. He just acts. And he doesn't even have the captions which the old silent movies found necessary so often.

But the men weren't chattering. There was in fact a tense hush, words coming only in monosyllables, and whispered at that, as every eye was turned on the prophet. And the sermon began.

I was standing on a few bricks I had managed to stack, and I had quite a close grandstand view of the whole affair. There had been quite a bit of speculation and discussion as the preparations had been going on, but I noticed that while some of it was deliberately light-hearted, not a single word of it had been flippant. It was rather like the casual shrug-of-the-shoulder attitude, in which a brave man may discuss his malignancy. But cancer is never a trifle.

And the speculations and discussions had ranged widely and freely, as you may imagine – but no-one had even remotely guessed how the sermon would begin. For Ezekiel

G

picked up the sword ever so seriously, carefully ran the edge of the blade between his fingers just as many a surgeon has done with many a fine blade since – and began to shave! Yes! Bending until his head was over the centre of the clean cloth that he had spread on the ground, he slowly and methodically proceeded to shave off every hair on his head. His long black locks, reaching almost to his shoulders; his beard, long enough now to be properly presentable, but as yet with nothing of the coveted length of the beard of the venerable elders; his whiskers, his side-levers, everything. There it all lay, the whole crop, in a thoroughly impressive heap in the middle of the cloth.

And then he set up his balances, and slowly – for it is a slow enough business, if you have ever tried using them – he proceeded to weigh out his hair into three equal parts. His cleanly shaven head, as he bent over the balances, looked quite unreal. Not that a bald pate was unknown at all – a man would occasionally have his head shaved because of some skin disease, or even for a religious vow. But this was a new thing in Ezekiel, and only his intent and altogether serious attitude prevented this new appearance from being an entire distraction.

But at last the task was completed. The final few hairs and whiskers had been placed in their allotted bundles, the balances were placed well to one side, and Ezekiel stood up and turned to the brick model of Jerusalem, where the fire had been laid right in the middle of it.

And he then set light to the little fire he had laid. And as the flames leaped up he took one of the three heaps of hair and tossed it into the fire! There was just a sudden blaze of crackling glow as the hair was swept up in the flames. And an odoriferous whiff with the pungency of burning organic matter came to me, drifting down-wind on the hot desert breeze.

For Ezekiel was now all action. The quiet, careful, very deliberate manner was gone altogether.

As the flames were still licking up that fist-full of hair, Ezekiel snatched up the second heap and danced madly around the brick 'city'. And with every step he would drop a little bundle of the hair and then slash savagely at it with the sword which was again in his hand. As every lock of hair fell he would lunge at it fiercely, and then chop away at it as it lay on the ground. And so piece by piece, thrusting and cutting, right round the little city he went, beginning to breathe heavily now as the intense exertion began to tell.

And no sooner was this done than he picked up the third bundle of hair, and now proceeded to toss it high into the air, to be caught away, wisp by wisp, in the drift of the morning breeze. And even this would not do. For as it blew away out flashed his sword again, almost in a frenzy of destruction, lashing out at the disappearing strands.

And then he changed again, altogether as suddenly as he had changed just a minute or so earlier. For even as he hacked away in the air, he would stop for a moment, gather up some of the hair as it fell, moving quickly still, but with an urgent gentleness that was in dramatic contrast to the sheer savagery of the moment before. We could almost feel the tenderness with which he hastily picked up a few strands here, a few there. And as he gathered them he slipped them into a little pocket he had made in the skirt of his robe as it folded over his leather girdle.

It was all so lightning fast, so terribly intense, and yet so crystal clear in its imagery, that the whole group was gripped in an utter spell of breathless attention. The rapid padding of Ezekiel's feet and the panting of his sharp-drawn breath were the only sounds to be heard. I even noticed, in that suddenly incongruous way that belongs to such moments of great emotion, the droning of a bee a good four or five yards off. But the whole crowd was as motionless as if carved out of lifeless rock.

I have known the same still concentration in an operating theatre, where the click of the artery forceps and the sharp clink of instrument on instrument was the only break in the utter silence. I have shared the same rapt stillness with over two thousand others in an audience, as contralto and orchestra under the baton of Klemperer brought Mahler's 'Song of the Earth' to its whispered climax.

And as the last tuft of hair was thrown to the wind, as the lunging sword made its last thrust, as the precious last strand was hastily retrieved, I could hardly bear to look longer. The men weren't breathing, their unblinking eyes were staring out of their heads, their jaws were sagging slightly, it seemed almost as though life had gone altogether. But now there came that sudden release, that return to physiological normality, as breath and movement broke in on the scene. And I saw, too, that with many of the men the breath seemed almost to choke them, the blinking was in fact a chase of tears, the licking of the lips was really a part of swallowing a great lump in the throat!

Oh no. There was no mistaking the meaning this time. This was a bitterly clear and tragically simple drama if ever there was one. A tale of a people consumed in the devouring flames of pestilence and famine. A people ravaged by the utterly implacable and ruthless ferocity of total war. And a people of scattered remnants tossed into the dispersing winds of heaven.

Yet all eyes were still fixed on that tiny handful of hair that Ezekiel now held in his tightly clenched right fist : those few wisps that had been recovered from the scattering breeze and the chasing sword. As the silent priest had withdrawn this tiny collection from the fold in the skirt of his robe, they knew all too well that this was truly themselves he was symbolizing. And himself, too, never forget. That great intensity of mood was not an affectation he had simply assumed for their benefit. His was nothing of the role of the actor playing a part to entertain or to impress a packed house. Far far from it. This was much more than that. This was the clear declaration of the man of God in which he was proclaiming that the purpose of God was true, in his own experience, just as much as it was true for the rest of the camp.

And yet the crowd stood still. And Ezekiel quite deliberately held his ground. There was a look on his face such as is rarely seen among men, and if ever a man was at sheer breaking-point it was true of Ezekiel then. For obviously the sermon wasn't over. And if the matter had so far been sad and tragic and foreboding, I could sense all too easily that the final bitterness was still to be told.

He opened his right hand, slowly, almost reluctantly, felt. There were the few strands of hair which represented this very group on the bank of the Kebar. His left hand stole across and turned the hairs over in his right palm, as solemnly his gaze began to move around the crowd.

This was really the first time he had clearly acknowledged their presence, even, and this made it all the more significant. For as he stood there, looking at them so intently, he seemed to be studying every single man there individually, personally. It must have taken a full five minutes, and I have never known minutes so unbearably long. I remember, in my days as a House Surgeon, holding on to a bleeding arteriole in a lacerated gum beside a tooth socket, for five minutes by the clock – and I felt my thumb and index finger would drop off at the roots! But that was a light-hearted gesture in comparison with this. For Ezekiel slowly turned right around, full circle. Every single man in the group came under his gaze, priest and elder and all alike. For he was now openly acknowledging to them, as to himself, that this was for him all the nation he would ever hope to claim as his own. This was to be for him the only kinship earth would ever contain.

And as at long last the circle was completed, I could see his lips trembling and his hands shaking with the emotional distress into which his next move was to hurl him. For as he looked now into his open palm, he was no longer seeing a few tangled strands of hair – he was seeing the men themselves, the men who were his friends, his kith and kin, his flesh and blood. And with a sudden movement it was done. With a great sob of uncontrollable grief, he finished the sermon. He simply picked up some of the hair in his right hand and threw it into the fire – and fled sobbing from the scene, the few remaining hairs now clutched to his breast in both fists.

There is something in the sound of grown men crying aloud that is quite shocking to our Anglo-Saxon mind. A sudden cry, of anger or agony or even of anguish, we understand. But men breaking down and sobbing and sobbing out loud, and not just in ones or twos, but many, is horrible.

And I have no possible question in my mind that as Ezekiel left that circle two thousand, five hundred-odd years ago, there were dozens of men doing just that. And let me say this now, for I will never ever find a place more suitable for saying it. That if you can find in your Bible the story of a single man of faith who has not first come under the clear understanding of the awful judgment of God, and who is not in fact broken-hearted and altogether distraught, then you and I have been reading different Bibles. The ways of God are truly like that. And the ways of man as he comes under the enormous pressure of the love of God are most truly like that also. For God is Love. And our human loves are so much smaller, they are so deeply tied to our emotional structuring, that God in *His* love comes into the conduct of a human life with just that tremendous impact.

No. I'm not surprised to think that there were grown men with tears streaming down their cheeks and great sobs seemingly breaking them to pieces inside. No. I'm not surprised. And let me say this with great conviction and in a sense of very deep humility – that I know nothing on earth quite so moving as the occasional discovery of this even in the restrained Anglo-Saxon himself. That man whose face conveys no hint of the anguish within, that man who appears so unconcerned as he attends the ordinary routine duties of life when everything within him wants to quit in utter despair. For this is surely the unique privilege of medical practice. That privilege which entrusts the doctor with a glimpse into the very spirit of his patient, in terms of grievous pain and heartache. And how constantly it keeps recurring in the day-to-day experience of life. Theism which is not as simply down-to-earth existentialist as that is a tragically sub-Christian philosophy. And an existentialism which is not as heaven-sized as that is the bleakest philosophical error which ever blew upon the human scene.

Oh yes, I am very sure that there were aching hearts and bitter cries that day on the banks of the Kebar. And even if you may think my imagination has re-lived the scene in a way quite foreign to your own thought, then I don't mind at all. For you must at least agree that the watchman was now finally free of his nation's blood. He had proclaimed his awful warning, and if they disregarded that warning then the guilt was not his.

And so the years rolled on and on and on. And Nebuchadrezzar grew stronger and stronger and stronger. Until at last it seems that even the priests and the elders had to admit that they were wrong. The terrible warning of Ezekiel began to be accepted as being the simple truth. For the hopes and longings of nearly nine long years in slavery were at last admitted to be merely human hopes and longings. The sheer undisputable fact of their condition had simply proved them wrong.

And now they began to come to Ezekiel. Dumb though he might still be he was being sought out, his advice respected, his counsels heeded. His visions were just as insistent in their drama, his concern and care entirely undiminished. Read, if you so desire, of his exciting attempts to tell them of these visions; of his insight into God's judgment, as he says, 'I sat in my house, with the elders of Judah sitting before me.' Watch with warmest admiration his earnest and most strenuous attempts to reduce to the symbolism of drama the advice and instructions his extraordinary visions continued to contain. As he came out of his little mud house with all his bags packed as for exile; as he dug through the walls of his hut in dead of night to symbolize his escape; as he expressed the trembling of uncontrollable terror by dribbling the food out of his very mouth; as symbolically the violent shaking of sheer panic slopped the water out of the cup he was drinking from. Yes, you read that, if you care. And read, too, if you care further, his devastating insight into the real motives in so very much of his nation's history.

Yes, read it all. And when you have done that you have in fact read only half the message!

For this is the real wonder of the ways of God. The wonder that this is still only half of the story. For to learn the truth about God is most certainly to learn of His judgment, of His righteousness, of His unrelenting authority.

But that is only half. That is the only half that the rebel that is a man may ever know. The other half is the truth that only the man of God may know. It is the half that exults: 'Hard-pressed on every side, we are never hemmed in; bewildered, we are never at our wits' end; hunted, we are never abandoned to our fate; struck down, we are not left to die.'

And now the other half is to come. And Ezekiel will take us nearer to it than any other Old Testament writer.

And he's still dumb. And he's still a slave. And he's still the watchman. But he does know the truth, and it is for the prophet to show forth the truth.

There are perhaps three days in the previous history of the Jewish people which have especially outstanding significance. The first would be that unique day when Abram and Sarah collected up their goods and retainers ('and Lot went with him') and set out from Haran in Old Babylonia for God's unknown.

The second would certainly be that day some six hundred years later when Moses led the Hebrew slave people out from the clutches of Egypt under the outstretched arm of God.

I think that the third date of comparable significance was that memorable day when King David himself led the ballet in the great ceremonial procession in which the Ark of the Covenant was carried into Jerusalem.

And now the fourth such historic date is most certainly the tenth day of the tenth month of the ninth year of Jehoiakin's captivity.

For that was the day Ezekiel had to begin to tell the people at Kebar the other half of the wonder of the ways of God.

And as I try to tell you of this I confess to that feeling of littleness, that humbling thing that comes to me in any working day in my life, when I see the sheer courage and fortitude of weak men in the strong hand of God.

For that was the day that Nebuchadrezzar finally threw his great Babylonian pincer-grip round little Jerusalem, that grip which was not going to relax until it had squeezed every single drop of life-blood out of the city. This was in fact the date of fulfilment of all those warnings and entreaties of all the prophets in Judah's history. The longsuffering and mercy of God in sparing the city would now save the city by destroying it! Everything Jeremiah had been saying and writing in the city itself was now to come into being. Everything Ezekiel had been dramatizing in Kebar was at last to come to pass.

It was the tenth day of the tenth month of their ninth year in exile.

And that was the night Ezekiel's wife died.

You see what I mean? You see how strange the ways of God who is love appear to men who are so largely just emotion? Of all the cruel hurts to a man already so cruelly hurt this would surely seem to be beyond all limits. For Ezekiel was dumb. And as the man responsible for dashing all their human hopes of escape, he was surely the most lonely figure in all the camp. But in the warm intimacy of Ezekiel's own home, in the understanding that can enable two people to live as one, the language of love will still speak when the tongue is dumb. And the companionship of marriage is all the company true lovers really need.

And she died.

Ezekiel speaks of her in only a single phrase, but what a lovely phrase it is. He simply refers to her as 'the delight of his eyes'. Surely, if in marriage a man sees less than that in his wife, he may well be pitied. But Ezekiel was rich in marriage, married to 'the delight of his eyes'.

And she died. Died 'at a stroke', he says. Indeed, it may very well have been with a stroke. Or a coronary. Or from plague. Or from anything you care to name.

For to the tragically, bitterly bereaved Ezekiel, the exact diagnosis is not one tiny bit of use. He is alone, he is deserted, he is in the absolute ashes of despair.

And yet God is God. It is God who controls human destinies. It is God who makes us alive, it is He who keeps us living, it is at His hand life is taken away. Ezekiel knew this. He knew it well. Had he not taught it, year after year now, since that fateful thirtieth birthday? Had he not been telling his people just this very truth? That God who had built and preserved them as a nation would end their national life in His own precise time?

And now he saw the truth of it. As he stooped over his wife's dead body he realized just what was the real meaning of her death. Jerusalem was dying! Yes. That was what God was telling him. His wife, 'the delight of his eyes' that she was, was suddenly snatched out of his arms. And his intensely sensitive, God-attuned mind recognized instantly that this was God's way of telling him that Jerusalem was herself cut off for ever from his people.

For there was no radio network, no co-axial land-line tele-communication system to flash the information around the world at the speed of light. No fast aerial courier mail service. Nothing like that at all. And for a slave people rotting to their miserable death over in inland Babylonia there would only ever be the news that trickled in by the grape-vine of rumour, perhaps by the arrival of an occasional batch of slave replacements for those who had failed to survive.

But the truth must be told. The purpose of God must be made clear. And as his beloved wife, the delight of his eyes, died in his arms, Ezekiel knew just what God was saying. This event of most tragic personal loss was in fact God's way of telling him that their national loss was just this too – Jerusalem was besieged, and her doom declared. This was the day when they lost 'their stronghold, their joy and glory, the delight of their eyes and their heart's desire'. Jerusalem was in her death throes.

I don't think you need to have a Ph.D. in sociology, you don't even need to hold a simple bachelor's degree in psychology, to realize how the news was felt in the camp. As the gossip flew from door to door, as the hearts of the people felt that sudden little clutch that the story of death always brings in human experience, I am quite certain that the response was kind and sympathetic and most genuinely warm. Even the most disagreeing of the priests dropped all thought of their disagreement in the wave of emotion they felt for the bereaved Ezekiel.

And so it was with that wave of real warmth of feeling that I joined the group that came early the following morning to give that simple grip of the hand, that rather inarticulate sentence, which tries so hard (but fails so miserably) to express the sympathy and encouragement that we feel so deeply. I was with a few men who had been over on the opposite bank of the Kebar when the word came through. We came over at a half-run, eager to express our regard, reluctant to meet the tragedy we knew we would find in the experience of the tragically forlorn prophet.

It was barely dawn when we arrived at Ezekiel's hut, but even then there was quite a crowd assembled. Yet even before we got close to his place, we could recognize something strange. The people were in mourning, as well they ought to be – we could see that at quite a distance, even in the half-light. Their heads were uncovered, their feet unshod, a few had even managed to find a piece of sackcloth with which to gird themselves – these things we could see well enough.

But it was different. I could sense that it wasn't an ordinary occasion of mourning. But what it was that was just different I couldn't quite see, peer as I may in the dawn-break. And then I recognized just what it was that was unusual. It was the silence. We had been half-running, talking a little as we jogged along, and the few words and the padding of feet on the hard desert ground had tended to fill my ears, to distract my hearing.

But that was it! The crowd was silent. Painfully, awkwardly silent. The loud lament, the uninhibited cry of anguish, the free-flowing tears which belonged so normally to such a group in their culture – all that was missing. My companions sensed it too. It was their world, of course, and they were even more alert to the oddness of it all.

Which explains why we were really sprinting as we covered the last couple of hundred yards. And now it was even more remarkable. For we could see that there were no hands held over the mouth, as was their custom; there was no ceremonial mourning bread being passed around. In fact the little crowd looked almost nonplussed, rather self-consciously foolish.

A sudden hope leaped into my mind – perhaps she is not dead. Perhaps the rumour of her death was not true. But the thought died out as suddenly as it had arisen. For there was sorrow on every face, but a sorrow that was mixed with sheer perplexity and embarrassment.

Until at last I could see. With a little bit of undignified but good Australian shoving, and using the few extra inches of height, I could see what was disturbing them.

It was Ezekiel. It was the chief mourner, the lonely, bereft, forlorn and isolated husband who had lost the delight of his eyes.

For he was not in mourning at all. There he was in fact, all spruced up like nobody's business, turban neatly tied on his head, sandals nicely cleaned and laced up, face washed and altogether in his Sunday-go-to-meeting best, the picture of the carefree husband and man-about-town. And not a sob, not even a slight sigh, as he sat there on a low brick stool by his doorway, nonchalantly tucking into the most ordinary breakfast in the whole camp.

My thoughts flew back to that day he had first made that little clay-brick model of Jerusalem, and the impression that sermon had made on the camp. I remembered again all those long days lying on first this side, then that side, his dung-fired meal always in his hands and mouth, and the heart-searching that four hundred and thirty day's sermon had provoked. I thought further of that later day when he had shaved off all the hair which was even yet not recovered in its length, and of the great spiritual impact that event had made on this people.

Those occasions had been exciting. They were tantalizing. They were provocative and stimulating and altogether arresting. But this – this was almost shocking.

There was indeed a stunned look on every face except that of Ezekiel himself. Yet there could be no possible doubt. This wasn't a piece of imaginative make believe on the boards of the local playhouse. Oh dear no. This was stark tragedy. This was sudden death and loneliness and personal misery. There, in the shadows inside the little hut, I could see past Ezekiel himself to the sombre, motionless bundle that was the body of his little wife, already wrapped up ready for burying. There is no play-acting about that, for sure.

And I looked again. Looked closely, carefully, this time. It was the experience of so many years as a doctor that made me look properly now! And I saw what I was looking for. Oh, sure enough, I saw Ezekiel sitting there munching his regular morning ration of damper. Saw him wash it down with a swig from the water-jug beside him. Saw all these little commonplace enough details that belong to any cheery commonplace enough day in their lives.

For the roll of his jaw was too jaunty, the toss of his head was too light-hearted, the smack of his lips was too noisy, the arc of the path of the water-jug was too expansive as he lofted it for a draught. In fact it was all overdone. It was flamboyant, exaggerated. If this had in fact been the bill of fare at the local playhouse then the crowd would be pelting the actor with rotten eggs and overripe tomatoes. For it was amateurish, overacted, strained. And – yes. I could see it now. There was this time no mistake at all. That set smile was in fact just a set smile. It was the mask behind which the real Ezekiel was holding in such tragic grief. That blinking was not caused by the glare of the slanting sunlight of the early dawn – it was to hide the tears that were so fiercely burning in his eyes.

And I saw something else still. For I saw that the crowd had seen this too. And now there was a whisper and a murmuring and a movement in the crowd. For Ezekiel was preaching his last of all such sermons – and this time he was preaching the other half of the story of the wonder of God's way with man.

I could never imagine that there has been a single day in man's experience that may equal that day. The sheer strength of the controlling power of faith that can take a man to such limits of self-discipline is very hard to credit. And yet there it was, there it happened, away back on the bank of the Kebar on the tenth day of the tenth month of the ninth year of captivity.

And if I saw this heart-wrenching obedience in Ezekiel, think what reactions it evoked in the crowd, as they saw it too. For they were better skilled now in interpreting his message, and this one was bitterly simple. They knew what Ezekiel was saying now. As he sat there with that sunny smile pressed on his face, as every taut nerve in his body was compelled to relax, they knew all right. If Ezekiel, the man of God, could calmly and happily declare in the death of his wife the peace and serenity of being in the will of God, then they, the people of God, were to expect just this same certainty of tranquil security in the destruction of Jerusalem.

For on some of the faces around Ezekiel that morning the truth came home with the impact that God's love must always have upon men who are to be safe. Some of them were too broken, too altogether broken, for tears. As the word flashed around – 'Ezekiel says Jerusalem is besieged!', 'Ezekiel says Jerusalem is lost!' – as the truth at last became part of their experience of life, some repented. The broken-hearted insight that comes to the few men of God came to some that day by the Kebar.

And there I saw sheer black hate, too. The bitter rebellion of men who know, know clearly now, the strength and dominion of God as He controls the very details of human destiny – I saw that too.

For any clear statement of God's way is always like that. To one man it is an entreaty to forsake the littleness of human feeling and human goals, and to seek comfort and hope in the strong hand of Almighty God. To the other it is the challenge to cling even more desperately than ever to the tiny freedom that is a mere man, to retreat if need be into the deadly futility of the obscurity of the outer darkness.

Yes, Ezekiel began to proclaim the other half of the wonder of that plan of God. On that historic day, that tenth day of that tenth month of that ninth year of Jehoiakin's captivity, the great truth began to appear.

I don't know just when the first runner came through, the first bearer of eye-witness news. I don't even know whether he was perhaps another slave, another captive from the beleaguered little city in this her last hour of doom. As he told with starting eyes and trembling voice of the vast task force that had at last rolled up and encircled Jerusalem. Told of the enormous earthworks, the myriad troops with the mighty assault weapons. As he told, and told with particular insistence, of his own good fortune in even being alive at all.

Indeed, for all I know, the news might have been broken by one of the Babylonian guards. Perhaps even told in that cocky way that belongs so unworthily to the man of little gift who still wields great power. 'Hey! Listen, creeps. Got some good news for you! What do you think of this? The Big Boss is on the job now. King Nebuchadrezzar himself has taken over, and it's curtains for Jerusalem. I've just been chatting with a half-colonel from the Seventh Division, and he's just back on leave from Jerusalem. He says the king is there in person and has slapped the siege right on your little old home. Wipe-out this time, boys! Aren't you lucky you're out here digging nice big canals for us? Better than sitting shivering to death in Jerusalem, eh, wondering just which bit of the wall is going to tumble in first! Boy, I've seen that happen. I was at Ashkelon nearly fifteen years ago, and did those walls come tumbling down! I'd just hate to be in your little town now, with Nebuchadrezzar holding the big whip! Back to your digging, scum. Dig up big and hearty, that's all you can hope for now.'

No. I don't know. Whether from slave or from overseer doesn't much matter. But what does matter is that the news in fact came through. And when it was pieced together, when dates were compared, times arrived at, the full significance appeared.

For it was, in very truth, on the tenth day of the tenth month of the ninth year of their captivity that the siege was laid. The very day Ezekiel's wife died. The very day that the prophet of God began to smile and rejoice and express in a

setting of such poignant personal conflict the exultant truth
of the purpose of God.

And now I have no possible question that Ezekiel became
a compelling focal point for those few who had accepted in
this great personal tragedy of their lives and hopes the even
greater wonder of lives now at peace with God. And dumb
though he still was, Ezekiel was for them the one with whom
they could most warmly share their concerns and their hopes.

And still the news began to come in day after day. And
every day told a tale of even greater destruction and of assault
pressed harder and harder still. As month succeeded month,
as the first full year of siege gave way to the second, the news
was altogether of the same pattern of malignancy. The Millo
was crumbling; the outer walls were down; the earthworks
were mounting and ever mounting against every part of the
city defence line; the air was black with arrows – such was
the grim monotony of the tale of relentless destruction of
doom.

There were dreadful rumours of the ghastly ravages of
famine and pestilence and death and fire. And as if the pitiful
condition within the city did not wring your heart enough,
the story from the Babylonian camp was even worse. For the
guards would now regularly regale the toiling slaves with
taunting tales of Nebuchadrezzar and his fierce determination
to rid his empire of this rebellious outpost, to end for ever the
story of perfidy that was Zedekiah, and his lying treachery.
For Nebuchadrezzar had left the comforts and duties of royal
Babylon to take up again the soldier's life, all these long
eighteen months assembling and deploying every single piece
of mighty assault equipment he could muster, as he himself
supervised and directed the battle.

And at last the end came. Stumbling in out of the desert,
more dead than alive, no-one could mistake this new arrival.
This was a fugitive from the city itself. This poor, dishevelled
wretch must for sure be one of those pitiful final defenders
who had survived the famine and the pestilence and the fire.
He had indeed seen the troops of Babylon come pouring in
over the walls, he had seen the mighty conquering hosts come
flooding in through the broken-down gates. His eyes had seen
the swath of carnage and death carved out by the pitiless
sword of Babylon. He had actually been hiding behind a

fallen curtain as he saw Zedekiah, the king, seized and led off to blindness and death. All this he could tell, for he had been there.

Yes. For he had escaped the death that was now Jerusalem, satisfied enough to share the life that was slavery in Kebar.

And as the tale poured from his parched throat and sun-cracked lips, why, whom is he talking to but Ezekiel! Yes. It is Ezekiel. And Ezekiel asking the questions, Ezekiel discussing it so carefully, chatting away so sympathetically.

For the dumb prophet is no longer dumb! Those long years of silence are over. The words that could be thought, that could be felt, that could be intended, those words that had so long been merely dramatized and acted, those words could now at last be spoken!

And what words! There are no words like them in all the Old Testment records. For now the prophet is free to finish the story. Now he can tell his people all the truth. Out pours the most imaginative, exotic and altogether unrestrained symbolism and imagery in all the apocalyptic text in the Old Testament. Imagery which stretches to every limit as the prophet seeks to explain the vastness and the wonder of the purposes of God.

For the tongue that had been silent for over five years is now free to speak. And remember, if you please, how all those five long years were spent trying to understand and interpret the purpose of God for His people. And remember too, if you still please, that this was not the detached thinking of an academic producing an esoteric facet of philosophical abstraction. Oh dear me no! This was the desperate struggle in the very soul of a man who was watching the whole world of his nation and his religion being ground to dust and ashes as he battled for his very life in the abject poverty of slavery. And if you don't catch any other single glimpse of the truth as Ezekiel came to see it, you must at least realize that he was seeking truth of this size. It must be truth that is big enough, and real enough, to include this problem of war and destruction and all the human misery and wickedness that goes with it.

And may I say this, before I ask you to come and watch the excitement and wonder of Ezekiel as the truth can now be told: that if you have a philosophy which is not big enough, and not real enough, to include the tubercle bacillus and the malignant carcinoma, as well as the hydrogen bomb and the crooked business take-over, then you have missed the truth as it is seen in Christ. If you think of the cross as a historic symbol, then you may be wise to straighten up your thinking. For the cross was a gibbet, it was a rough wooden pole on which you left your wretched victim to die in the slow torture of dislocated joints and agonized exhaustion. And the wretched Victim on this cross was none other than God. The true Christian faith is as bitterly down-to-earth as that.

And, what is far more important still, in your analysis of truth you must include the fact that that sordid killing on that Passover Friday morning was 'by the deliberate will and plan of God'.

Truth, as God teaches truth, is as big as all that.

So come, then, and listen now to Ezekiel as his tongue is loosed. The truth is now told.

I begin to turn the pages, reading eagerly now to pick up the exciting strands that must surely be unfolded. Yes, I am reminding myself, if this second part of the truth is so great that it can persuade a man to celebrate the death of his lovely wife with a smiling composure that utterly embarrassed his mourning friends, then this truth must be absolutely heaven-sized. This is going to be a feast of sheer exaltation and delight that will surely set my heart ringing and my whole life dancing with gaiety and pleasure.

And even as I say it, I find I am wrong. It's not that at all. In fact it's nothing in the least bit like that at all. It's an absolute out-blast against Ammon! A whole solid chapter, full of fuming vitriol!

I turn the page quickly, puzzled a bit. But let us press on. I'll come back and have another look at that chapter later – perhaps it's an editorial mistake and should really be better understood or located in some other context. Surely, the great answer of God to the tragically bleak cry of His people in slavery in Kebar has nothing to do with the utter devastation of the Ammonites. Quick, see what comes next.

And this is worse! For this time it's Tyre. It's the great trading port of Tyre that comes in for it. And not just the one chapter that told of the devastation of Ammon. It's three chapters, three frightening chapters, this time, ending with the almost unbelievable words:

> 'I turned you to ashes upon the earth
>   in the sight of all who saw you.
> All who know you among the peoples
>   are appalled at you;
> You have come to a dreadful end
>   and shall be no more for ever.'

But, dear oh dear! It's getting worse and worse! For now it's Egypt. Egypt, likened to a glorious cedar growing on the rich Lebanon forest slopes. But the forest giant is uprooted and fragmented to splintered shreds, a disgusting blot on the mountain side, a disgraceful and unhealthy contaminant of the limpid stream. Yes. Egypt and her mighty pharaohs, four chapters this time, chapters of lament and distaste and doom.

Say, listen, Ezekiel, I burst out now. Can't you tell us anything better than that? Surely this can't be the answer. I want to know the breath-taking answer God gave you that night your wife died. That night you held her limp little body in your arms, snatched from you 'at a stroke'. That night you lost both 'the delight of your eyes' and your city and home. That's what I came all these thousands of years back in history to discover.

Ezekiel – and now I'm speaking fast, and I mop my brow because I am feeling a tight little flustering inside me – please, Ezekiel, there must be something else altogether. I'm not sticking up for the Ammonites. Not that I know much about them, but there's a lot of Ammonite wickedness here and there in Sydney and we could certainly get along better without it. And I'll grant you that there may have been some pretty crooked dealing down on the coast at Tyre. And I admit that even a postcard picture of an Egyptian pyramid almost makes my back ache as I think of all the slave life burnt out in those greedy monuments of human pride. But have you nothing better to offer? Is the wonder of God's plan for His people simply a smack in the eye to their enemies?

And I turn the page, hesitantly, fearfully.

And it's just as if Ezekiel had known, two thousand, six hundred years ago, what was in my twentieth-century mind.

For there, staring at me as I stare at it, is the sombre, stern, solemn statement about the watchman. That very same warning statement which had left Ezekiel overwhelmed for seven days among the exiles in Kebar.

And I bow my head, awed by the seriousness of it, abashed by the urgency of it. Ezekiel, I half whisper, I'm sorry. I should have known better. I'll read to listen, now. To learn. I'll try and hear what God Himself says His purpose is. Never mind what I think it just ought to be. Enough of this human arrogance which says 'I don't think God is like that.' The human pride which declares, 'That's not my idea of God at all.' No. Ezekiel, I'll just read on and stop trying to make God in my image. I'll try and find out what He Himself says He is like.

So that it is with heavy hand and leaden heart that yet again I turn the page. That chapter about the watchman is so horribly sombre, don't you think? In a culture where all the driving voices of society urge us to press on, to make good, to advance, to keep out in front: then the role of watchman is the most altogether static, unprogressive appointment you could conceive.

But I am willing now to wait for God to tell me Himself just what He is planning. To wait, if need be, all my life. . . .

You know the way a fluorescent tube lights up? There is an instant deep glow in the starter; than a sharp flash as perhaps one end of the tube arcs across – and it's off again, pitch dark. And a vivid flicker as the arc strikes again. Darkness. Perhaps another burst. And then the flood of light !

I can think of no finer imagery with which to describe what Ezekiel now begins to say.

For I leave the heavy warning of the watchman, and out shines the warmest glowing beam of pure comfort your heart could ever wish. Listen : 'I, I myself, will search for my sheep, and will seek them out. . . . I will rescue them from all places where they have been scattered. . . . I will save my flock, they shall no longer be a prey.'

What wonderful, what simple imagery. In the endless conflict of scattering that really makes up the story of life : the physical decay, the moral struggle, the spiritual encounter. Hurrah ! I shout. God has it in hand. He is still watching. He is always out to help. He, He Himself, will save !

Then darkness. Thick, black, darkness! The horrible enveloping evil of Seir, of Edom. But I don't mind. In fact, I can nearly rejoice. For if the Shepherd God will seek, will rescue, will save His flock, then of course Seir and Edom and all those other evil blots must go — the little flock will only ever be hunted and scattered and devoured by them while ever they last. Hurrah, again!

For now the whole high tension glows! The great arc of truth strikes and I blink my eyes in the sudden dazzling beam. It is just a single flash, but what a fantastic scene it lights up.

It is a valley. And a valley filled with dead bones which suddenly come to life! There it is, one moment a ghastly place with myriad human skeletons, every trace of flesh picked clean away by the vultures and the maggots, the bones bleached white by the merciless glare of the sun. And that next single moment the bones rattle, they move, they begin to join together, to be knit by tendons, to be clothed by flesh, to . . . Yes, to breathe and live again!

Ezekiel, I burst out, that is fantastic. Unless you had been there that first Easter morning, unless you had met the Risen Lord Himself, you couldn't possibly have known more!

Ezekiel, just across the north-east corner of the Mediterranean Sea some great Greek philosophers are beginning to ponder this mystery, but their answers will be quite wrong. To reach their answers they will need to rely on good brains and the principles of logic. Sure, that is the right and best equipment to use to solve the problems of time and space, to which they belong. But intellect cannot probe heaven. Reason cannot discover God. Man is creature, and man is equipped only to handle the creaturely. If we are to know anything of the Creator Himself, then He must show it to us.

Ezekiel, I don't want to stop and discuss the dualism of Plato. I want to exult with you in victory over death! But I must say it here, because I must at least remember it always. So let me tell you, Ezekiel, that the purpose of God for His people is not just to bring them back to life, as it were by some high-power system of cardiac massage or mouth-to-mouth resuscitation, wonderful though that would be. But in fact His plan is vastly greater than that. His purpose is to re-create His people, altogether. 'As we have worn the likeness of the man made of dust, so we shall wear the likeness of the heavenly man.' Ezekiel, doesn't that stagger you? Doesn't that almost shock you? To think that man, the creature, could have life restored to him after death is surely wonder beyond wonders. But to claim that man, the creature, may in fact find a place in the very life of God Himself would be blasphemy beyond blasphemy if it were not in fact true.

What a wonderful glimpse of God's goal for man was that glimpse given to Ezekiel in his valley of bones !

And I don't mind at all that it's black again. In fact I'm glad it's black, because it's Gog and I don't know anything about Gog except that Gog and Magog are altogether against God and out they must go. These enemies from the far corners of the world are banished to the outer darkness where they can no longer destroy and disrupt and despoil.

And even as the darkness closes over them for ever, we are altogether enveloped in the brilliant final light of truth.

For now it's the Temple. Yes, that Temple which Ezekiel remembered so vividly still, missed so deeply after more than twenty-five years of exile. In actual life, in time and space, he is fifty years of age, a slave in Kebar. But in his exultant understanding of God and His purpose he is back in the city, back as a priest in the Temple. The new Temple, of course. The Temple of God's own building, of course. The Temple that no enemy will ever again break down, of course. . . .

Have you ever had the rich pleasure of watching children at play, listening to the chattering of the wonderful world of make-believe of youth? Have you seen the little fellow as he works and hammers away with Dad's big tools, just murdering a few bits of timber with ragged saw-cuts and bent-over nails, making that hideous piece of junk that he calls his space-ship? Have you ever looked critically at that positively grotesque piece of stuffed rag the little girl is nursing in her arms?

It's his space-ship, he says. He circles the moon. He's been to Venus, he's fought the Martians, he's chased little Pluto, as he grrrrs and zooooms and tat-tat-tat-tats his path in orbit.

It's her baby, she says, and her name is Penelope and she's a very good baby but sometimes she's naughty and I don't

spank her *very* hard 'cos she might get sick and then I'd nurse
her all night and take her temperature and give her pills and
not the needles the cruel doctor gives children and when she's
big she'll go to school and . . .

Have you known anything like that? I hope you have; and
I'm more than glad that I have.

But if you find this puzzling in children, if it baffles you at
all, then I strongly advise you to keep away from Ezekiel and
the new Temple.

For as you go round with him as he describes it, measures
it, calculates it, lays it all out in reeds and cubits and spans,
you just can't help seeing that it is surely the corniest little
shack in all the modern world! You could poke it into St.
Peter's in Rome and it might well be six months before anyone would even notice it. And in the vastness of a modern
automobile factory or steel rolling-mill it would be one of the
minor outhouses.

For Ezekiel never saw it like that or intended it like that.
Ezekiel is just not like that. He has the intuitive fancy and
the spiritual imagination to see it as something else altogether.
For we have just finished measuring up all the courts and
chambers and (would you believe it?) the kitchens even, when
in the very next sentence he describes a stream of water
coming out of the Temple. And we start to wade across this
stream, to find that after five hundred yards it is ankle-deep.
And we tramp on, another five hundred yards, and it's knee-
deep. And on again, another five hundred and it's up to our
loins and by two thousand yards we are starting to swim.

Just think what churlish folly it would be to say to Ezekiel,
'Hey, wait a moment. That little Temple is only about as big
as my tennis court. And the whole thing, inner court and
outer court and kitchens and all, is only the size of a decent
cricket field. How do you get that small Amazon coming out
of the Temple threshold like that? That's ridiculous! And
how is that river going to flood the whole Jordan valley and
fill the Dead Sea and water the Arabian desert and still leave
the salt flats there for salt?'

No. You don't talk to Ezekiel like that, any more than you
tell the boy that his wonderful space-ship is just a few beaten-
up bits of timber; or the girl that her cuddly baby is a dirty
old bit of rag. No. You just don't do that, please.

For if you think like that and see Ezekiel like that you are in danger of seeing God like that. And lots of men have seen God like that and His kingdom like that. Last century it was all too tragically popular indeed to think like that. A bit more education and a bit more food and a bit more manners and a bit more democracy and a bit more Union Jack (especially a bit more Union Jack) and the kingdom is on earth!

Oh dear! That's not what any prophet of God is saying. That's certainly not what Ezekiel is saying! That's not what his ten-foot-high wall around his seventy-five-foot Temple is saying.

'For of course,' he insists, 'you measure life in reeds, cubits and spans. Measure it in pounds and ounces, months and years, dollars and cents, measure it in any and all of the scales of human experience. And then blink your eyes and stand in open-mouthed awe as you see what God is making of it.'

'But that doesn't fit Jerusalem,' you reply. 'That merely ignores the simple geography of Palestine. That makes mockery of the limits of time and space, that defies the science of mass, length and time.'

And I see Ezekiel's face light up as his eyes simply sparkle with delight as he flashes back, 'Then you've nearly got it! You're really learning it at last! For the Temple of God is now teaching you what all those years in exile and slavery taught me and some of my people.

'For that is the truth about God at last. The Temple is not there to make mockery of time and space, but to make heaven of it. The Temple doesn't ignore the geography of Palestine, it re-structures it altogether. It doesn't defy the limits of mass, length and time, it delimits them with the freedom of the throne of God Himself.'

And I see a great seriousness now, as he speaks more slowly, more softly. 'For the Temple is filled with the glory of God, and filled with the glory of God alone! Not a single trace of any other. Not a tiny speck of any other, man-made glory. No remaining hint of Ammon, not a glimpse of Tyre, no merest speck of Egypt, not a breath of Seir or Edom or Gog or Magog or any of those rebel peoples who dared pit their vaunted human weakness against the goodness and long-suffering of the God who is Love.

'And there is not even the softest whisper of an opposing

voice in the priestly worshippers themselves, for God has given them a new heart altogether – the old rebellious heart has been rooted out of them utterly, for ever – a new heart, the heart bearing the Law of God engraved in its very substance, is now within them.'

Ezekiel – and I find it very, very hard indeed to reply – you have told me things I think I should already know. But you have told me of them out of an experience so deeply moving and in words and imagery so captivating that they seem to be almost new entirely.

For I came back into your life in the mud and death of Kebar the better to try and understand my own so different world. And what I have learned is not just the amount that fills a book : in the love and the grace of God it may prove enough to fill a life.

For before I met you I met Isaiah. And as Assyria, mighty Assyria, bellowed her deadly threats, Isaiah quietly sat down, and without even glancing around, wrote : '*God* is our refuge and strength.' Ezekiel, I trust that during no single day in my life may I forget the impact of that scene. For I saw right into the very soul of Assyria, and what I saw terrified me every bit as much as it terrified Hezekiah. For I saw it in my own world, in my own nation, in my government and my business houses and my profession and even (most terrifying of all, this was !) in myself. And I saw how truly I and so many others have made the mistake Hezekiah made – we built new walls of precept and strengthened the Millo of self-help and threw up towers of good advice as we armed ourselves to the hilt with every man-made weapon of comfort and technology and therapy that the inventiveness of man can supply.

Ezekiel, I think I came away with at least a trace of the humility which will see all that for what it really is; and I will pray with bowed head and humble heart : God is my refuge and strength.

And, sir, Jeremiah taught me this again and taught me much more beside. For he let me see the dishonest complacency that is really the endless selfishness of man. As he showed me the greedy heart of Jehoiakim and the cowardly opportunism of Zedekiah, I assure you, sir, I saw something

that was so like my own world and my own humanity that it
nearly broke my heart. And when I then saw that mighty
saint of God serenely and happily squander his seventeen
precious pieces of silver on that useless bit of land over in
Anathoth, why, sir, I could almost hear the thunderous
applause in the very courts of heaven. For that is where the
real accounting is done, that is where all the genuine title-
deeds are held. Sir, I pray again with all my heart that I, too,
may be as eager to exchange every earthly bauble for the title-
deed to the heavenly home-site God has prepared.

But, sir. . . . And again I falter, not because I am shy about
saying it to Ezekiel, but because I must say it to myself.

But, sir, I begin again, I have heard something from you
that only you could tell me. For I saw in you the personal
poverty and the spiritual wealth that marks out the duty of
the watchman. I saw that as perhaps it has never been shown
more clearly in this world except by the Lord Himself.

And I learned so clearly from you, as you yourself learned
it so clearly from God, that the whole of the glory is of God.
There's not a whit that ever came from men's hands. Egypt
didn't contribute a hint even, pyramids and pharaohs and
three thousand years of culture notwithstanding. The merchants of Tyre and the militarists of Assyria have no finger in
it at all. And, sir, how sternly you heard God say of the East
Gate : 'This Gate shall remain shut; it shall not be opened,
and no one shall enter by it.' I'm sure I understand you
correctly, sir. No Babylon in that Temple, not in God's
Temple. Babylon was fulfilling your destiny, surely enough,
but God doesn't need any help from Babylon to strengthen
His hands.

And – I stop a moment, because I can feel the embarrassment of what I must now say – and I think you have made
rather terribly clear a truth I know I have always known, but
a truth I find most difficult to live with. For the Glory of God
filled *all* that Temple. And that means there was no glory
belonging to the nation of priests who worshipped there. Even
you, sir, contributed nothing. All those long years of service
as watchman down in Kebar were not the occasion for you
to do your bit to help God : it was the occasion for God to do
His part in re-shaping you.

And now I see it so clearly in my own world. For there is

no glory of the British Empire there. No Union Jack hanging over the altar. There is not a hint of Stars and Stripes. God hasn't had to call on Science to help, still less the Medical Associations. The Conservative Party is as altogether absent as the Democrat and the Republican and the Labour Parties. And you must see just how difficult it is for us to realize that Anglicanism and Methodism and Presbyterianism are as totally absent as Roman Catholicism and Lutheranism. That seems almost shocking to us men, at our first reaction. And even the big get-together affairs that we label Union or United, Ecumenical and Interdenominational, God sees for their essential man-size, and He has no need of a single one. He is Himself the Unity, because He is Himself the All.

Ezekiel, there is certainly no mid-grey in your world. There is the blackness of Gog and Magog, the down-to-the-Pit horror that is Elam and Meshech and Tubal : and there is the Glory of God. Surely you made that most disturbingly and excitingly clear.

And now, sir, I am leaving you, as I left Jeremiah before you and Isaiah before him. I am going back to my workaday life of medical technology and medical practice. I shall leave you in your desert mud and blistering heat of two and a half thousand years ago, to take up my own twentieth-century life in air-conditioned operating-theatres and centrally-heated consulting-rooms.

And so it is Sydney again, the tiring but never tiresome medical life in the throbbing pulse centre of our great Australia.

Yet all those centuries of time and all those endless miles of distance have merely changed the scene, changed the setting. The people are the same; their needs are the same; and the God who meets those needs is altogether the same.

Yet I am curiously unhappy. In this journey into God's recorded history I have seen the wonder of men, mere men, in the great hand of God! I have stood almost aghast as I have seen whole armies crash in disaster and death as men of faith lived on. And I have seen something triumphant in death even, death in all its ugliness, as again men of faith exulted in the hope that comes from knowing God Himself.

And yet I am curiously unhappy. For I should like one more answer, one clear and certain answer, if only it may be had. The answer to the simple lives of the simple ordinary people with whom I live and work so personally, so closely. Never mind about the British Commonwealth; forget all about Australia; don't even give a thought to Medical Science. It is the one answer that each individual man and woman is seeking. For it is the answer to the future. It is the great heart-torn cry of all human history—Whither?

For this is the answer which Isaiah, Jeremiah and Ezekiel could never give. There was no need even to ask Isaiah. Of 'the things prepared by God for those who love him' he says simply that there are 'things beyond our seeing, things beyond our hearing, things beyond our imagining'. Thank you Isaiah. You were seven hundred years too early to know that answer, and we thank you for your honesty in saying that.

But Jeremiah had seen a little more. He had lived to see the downfall of Jerusalem itself. As he saw the boots of Babylon trample the whole city of God into the dust, he still knew that God held the title-deeds in His hands, and that somehow God defends His city through life *and* through death.

And Ezekiel knew with utter certainty that even though Solomon's Temple had been reduced to rubble and match-wood, God's Temple still stands, and stands filled altogether with His divine Glory. Yet Ezekiel was also too early. Nearly six hundred years too early.

And so I roll the calendar forward those six centuries, and take ship for a tiny little Greek island near the south-west coast of Asia Minor. On our reckoning the date would be nearly AD 100; and there, on that little island of Patmos, I sought the last remaining one of those original twelve disciples of Christ.

Yes, it was none other than John, the white-haired old disciple of such warm fatherliness and such mellowed sympathy, that I was to speak with in this last, brief journey.

Sir, I said, if there is one man in this whole world who can give me this answer, it must be you. It is the answer to the beyond, the answer to death. Sir, if you lived in my time you would understand, perhaps, how important this really is. You had Gnostics in your time, we know. But, sir, if you could meet the Gnostics we have today, occupying all too often key

Chairs in Theology and Divinity, Principals, Deans, Wardens and Staff, it would nearly break your heart. As they try to make it quite clear that they are not in fact atheists, as they insist that they are not really pantheists – why, sir, this is right inside the institution that is called the Christian Church! And meet then the declared atheists and the woolly flock of Monists and the like, who are at least honest enough to affirm that they are outside the Church, and you will most certainly understand my purpose in coming to you.

For in astonishing truth you say you saw God. You say you talked to Him as He talked to you. You even held His arm, you actually rubbed shoulders with God, you say. But that is not all. You say you saw God die. Think of that, sir. That is surely the most unthinkable thing in all human experience. To say you saw Him at all is beyond sense. But not to die! But you do say that. You have told us how you were there that black Friday afternoon as His life left Him. All the others had fled from Calvary and its three ghastly crosses. But you were still there when that Roman soldier nonchalantly tossed a spear through His dead body. No wonder you lost heart. I'm sure I should have lost heart before He even got to Annas and Caiaphas. Yes, Christ died.

And then one by one you have seen all your other fellow disciples die. Your own brother James was the first to go. Herod got him. Now they've all gone except you. Peter was crucified, we know. And it is you who told us that his Lord had actually warned him about this. We think Paul, your later companion, died in Rome too, under Nero. We have a tradition that Thomas got as far as India with the gospel. And now you are the only one alive. But tell me this, please. What of them now?

And while the lined old face of the fisherman lit with the most gracious of all possible smiles, I could see that flash in his eyes that seventy or more years before had had him nick-named Son of Thunder.

'Yes,' he said simply, 'I have seen them since. I saw them all. A vast throng, from every nationality and tribe and people and language in all history. I couldn't possibly count them. I can't tell you how wonderful they looked. I can only say that they were robed in white – I'm just lost for words to describe them, I couldn't recognize them, they were so dazzling, so resplendent. One of the heavenly elders said to me, "Who are these men in the white robes? Do you know where they came from?"

'And I couldn't possibly answer him. How could I? I have only ever lived on earth. I've only ever seen men like myself. "My lord," I said, "you know, not I."

'And he said to me, "These are the men who have passed through the great ordeal; they have washed their robes and made them white in the blood of the Lamb." And I remembered Simon. He was crucified upside down, the rumour came back to us. At least one was burned at the stake and I think some might have been thrown to the lions. How could I possibly recognize these maimed and withered comrades? Have you ever seen what gets dragged out of a fire? Did you ever see a body that has been hacked down from a cross? But you are a doctor. Perhaps you know what I am thinking, as I saw these radiant beings in such dazzling splendour.'

Sir, I burst in, Isaiah was sawn in half, we think. Jeremiah ended his life of endless years of torture and trouble down in Egypt, most probably. Ezekiel just rotted away in Kebar under the yoke of Babylon. Did you see them? Were they there, too, all glorious like the rest?

No need for him to answer that one. I knew that answer.

But what did they do? I asked. A man's job is very important to him. To do something useful, something purposeful, something worthy. Why, sir, that is important indeed.

The old patriarch looked at me with a spark of fire in his eyes. 'I have been a fisherman, and that is a worthy job for a man,' he said, 'but do you know what the heavenly elder told me they did? Listen : "They stand before the throne of God and minister to him day and night in his temple; and he who sits on the throne will dwell with them." '

Just think, I said, speaking now to myself. Some of them used to work for the government. Some worked for industry, for science, for their own little business affairs, for their families. Some were just company directors, some simply clergymen, some merely doctors. And now they are actually working with God, ministering to Him.

Sir, I burst out again. But what about their illnesses, their troubles and sorrows and all the things that make life so difficult? Ezekiel's wife died 'at a stroke'. I think she was lucky. I've seen people just die of old age, and spend an eternity doing it. And I've treated lepers, even. Ugh! What a living death! How are these people of God now? What risks are there now from degenerative disease and malignancy and even the H-bomb?

St. John was himself a very old man indeed, and I half expected a stern rebuke for my near-rudeness in speaking to him like that. But his eyes, old and heavy-lidded though they were, were simply dancing with sparkling life as he said, ever so softly, ' "He who sits on the throne will dwell with them." ' I felt my cheeks beginning to redden as he repeated this so-wonderful statement. But before I could think of some word in reply, some face-saving trifle to cover my embarrassment in not at first recognizing the real wonder of this truth, he went on, still quietly, serenely, ' "They shall never again feel hunger or thirst, the sun shall not beat on them nor any scorching heat, because the Lamb who is at the heart of the throne will be their shepherd and will guide them to the springs of the water of life; and God will wipe all tears from their eyes." '

My head was spinning, as well it might be. For the tale of death, which to the doctor is the final limitation to all that he knows in medicine and therapeutics, is to God the doorway to total and endless health and delight!

I was turning away, more than half convinced, yet half perplexed, when a sudden all-disturbing thought flashed into my mind. And I spun round and almost shouted as a torrent of words poured out.

Sir! That is wonderful! In fact it is altogether too wonderful to grasp in a few seconds. But listen. I'm a doctor and I live in a world of investigation. We are not Greek philosophers who sit back and ask questions of nature in an armchair. We go out and probe nature. We pull her apart. We use our eyes and our hands and our hearing, and if we can't get the answers that way then we use all the fantastic equipment that our huge research laboratories can supply.

Sure, sir, that was a wonderful idea. But you got that in a vision. How do I know you didn't just dream that up? Could it not have been due to some rare hallucination? I'm not saying it was in any sense wrong, but have you any other evidence? Isaiah and Jeremiah had visions. And as for

Ezekiel, I often thought he found it pretty hard to keep his feet on the ground at all. Are the things you have been talking about just the same as those others?

The old disciple didn't answer me at once. He started to rummage around in a pocket in his long cloak, and at last pulled out some papyrus scrolls covered in writing. He thumbed through them before he found the one he was seeking. Then he spread it out and started to speak. 'Yours is not a new question. I have been asked to answer it before. And I once even wrote a little answer – you might call it a letter, but you might call it a tract or pamphlet. I'll read you a few words from the opening paragraph.'

I could see his eyes scanning the writing, as he said, ' ". . . we have heard it; we have seen it with our own eyes; we looked upon it, and felt it with our own hands; and it is of this we tell." ' He stopped reading for a moment and looked up at me. 'Of course we didn't have X-ray plants and electron microscopes and all your modern gear, but I don't think that would have made any real difference.' There was quite a twinkle in his eyes as he said this; but he read on. ' "Our theme is the word of life. This life was made visible; we have seen it and bear our testimony." '

And his old bearded jaw snapped to an attitude of unshakable strength and his gnarled old knuckles shone white as he grasped the papyrus in his fingers.

I had my answer all right! You try asking the physicist to forget that huge galvanometer deflection he has just recorded! Tell the geneticist that those larvae might have got into his experimental specimens by mistake! Suggest to the radiologist that he should report the lung fields clear when he is in fact staring at the tell-tale shadows in the films!

I wasn't blushing, but I felt I should be, as the old apostle relaxed and began to smile. 'Thomas was like that, too. He was actually invited to put his hands in the huge gaping wound in our Master's side, and yet there Jesus was, altogether as well as can be. Ask your colleague, Luke. He was a Greek doctor. He wrote to a friend about it, I know. He pointed out how Jesus had walked miles and miles on feet that had had nails wrenched out of them only thirty-six hours before. Ask your orthopaedic colleagues about that! You will need more than X-rays to explain the Risen Lord. Your physicists will be out of their depth trying to explain Him! That's what we saw.' (And those sharp seafaring eyes don't miss overmuch, I thought to myself!) 'That's our answer. Don't you see that that is the only final answer God has ever given to man concerning the final destiny He is planning for His people? That risen body of our Master is what you in your world would call the prototype. He is what your production engineers call "the first one off". Just think of this: He, who is the only begotten Son, is bringing many sons into glory. And that vision He gave me that day, here in this very island, was surely to help me try and understand and to say something of that. That's how true it is!'

And now I do turn away. I have no more questions to ask. I have no more information to seek.

But far, far more important still, and this is what now terrifies me, is the realization that there is simply nothing I can do to get it. For how can a mere 180 lbs. of chemicals, even though fashioned into the being of a man, hope to attain a glory like that? The wildest science fiction on record has no thought of a wonder like that. All the combined achievements of medical science in all the world can't begin to match that.

And if ever I felt my poverty, my nakedness, it is now. In the lush riches of this most lavish era of history, in what must surely be the wealthiest of all the lands in the world, I have precisely nothing to buy that with. I have exactly no skill which may achieve it.

And as if my very thoughts are being read, I hear a voice speaking ever so clearly, ever so kindly, ever so close to me. And this is the voice that will for ever divide life in two. To many, alas, it is the cheekiest, rudest, most unwelcome voice in life. To the others, the few, this is the one and only voice in life. It is His voice. Listen: 'I know all your ways. . . . You say, "How rich I am! And how well I have done! I have everything I want in the world." In fact, though you do not know it, you are the most pitiful wretch, poor, blind and naked. So I advise you to buy from me gold refined in the fire, to make you truly rich, and white clothes to put on to hide the shame of your nakedness, and ointment for your eyes so that you may see. . . . Here I stand knocking at the door; if anyone hears my voice and opens the door, I will come in and sit down to supper with him and he with me.'